From the
White House
to the
Amish

ISBN: 978-1-950791-55-2
Cover and text layout design: Kristi Yoder

Published by:
TGS International
P.O. Box 355
Berlin, Ohio 44610 USA
Phone: 330.893.4828
Fax: 330.893.2305
www.tgsinternational.com

From the
White House
to the
Amish

A story inspired by the life of Thomas E. Kirkman

KATRINA HOOVER LEE

White House Layout

FAMILY DINING ROOM

USHER'S OFFICE

STATE DINING ROOM

RED ROOM

BLUE ROOM

CROSS

GREEN

← TO WEST WING

WEST COLONNADE

SOUTH PORTICO

DOCTOR'S OFFICE

MAP ROOM

CEN

CHINA

DIPLOMATIC RECEPTION ROOM

Adapted from National Parks map

SECOND and THIRD FLOORS

ENTRANCE HALL

CROSS HALL

GREEN ROOM

FIRST FLOOR

EAST ROOM

LIBRARY

CENTER HALL

CHINA ROOM

SOCIAL ROOM

VISITORS' FOYER

EAST COLONNADE

TO EAST WING →

GROUND FLOOR

Table of Contents

Preface

My husband and I met Brad Kirkman for the first time in the library of a southern Indiana Bible school. We exchanged pleasantries and seated ourselves at a round table.

As we began to chat, we asked Brad if we could record our conversation.

"Just because we are recording doesn't mean you are committing to this book project," my husband Marnell explained to Brad.

"Oh, I'm committed—as of fifteen minutes ago. I put out my fleece, and God answered," Brad said, referring to Gideon's sign from God in the Bible story.

He never told us what the fleece was, and we didn't ask. It was enough to know that our key witness to the life of Thomas Ellsworth Kirkman supported the project because he felt confirmation from God.

Brad spoke with us for over an hour, sharing memories of his father and pointing us to documents and photos he had copied.

He finally told us he needed to preach the next day, and that he really must go.

"But I have one more story," he said.

Each time he finished his story and nearly left, our conversation led him to another story. Finally, after another half hour had passed, he stood and we saw he was really leaving.

"It's your story now," he said. With a smile and a wave, he disappeared through the door.

Prologue

Tom and Sharon left Washington, D.C., on a warm spring morning when the cherry trees were in full bloom. The birds and the buses woke up together, chirping and honking, each in their own language. Tom opened the back door of the pale green Renault and threw in their luggage. The little Renault was a good car for getting around the city; he hoped it had the stamina to make it all the way back to Indiana. Sharon and Jeff soon fell asleep, and Tom was left with his thoughts.

Did I really work beside President Eisenhower? he asked himself. If someone had told him that he would someday do sketches for President Eisenhower in a small room of the White House, he would not have believed it for a minute. If he had been told that the President would at times burst into the room and talk to him as he painted, it would have seemed an idle tale, like a strange dream. But now, Tom's life seemed more like a nightmare, and working in the White House was a reality that had passed.

Tom turned onto the Route 1 bridge. He could not see the White House, but he knew it was there to the north of the Washington Monument. The White House calligraphy team would be designing nametags, menus, and invitations—without him. Although President Eisenhower was feeling much better after his illness, he and Mamie still avoided stacking the calendar too full of social events. Now that Eisenhower's second inauguration was over, the calligraphy department was slow.

Once across the Potomac River, Tom did not look back. He pulled onto Route 50 and headed for the topsy-turvy West Virginia hills. At least this trip was better than the last trip he had taken from Washington, D.C., to Indiana.

Tom's mental state was calmer than it had been on that other trip. Gone was the adrenaline and the shock. Gone was the desperate tension of hoping his mother would recover. He no longer hoped, no longer prayed, no longer made bargains with God. The bargains were over and done. God had not heard, had not cared, had not moved on the behalf of Tom Kirkman. And now God could not expect Tom to move on His behalf either. Perhaps there was a God who had created the world. Tom wasn't sure. But was there a God who did great things?

No.

Part one

chapter one

The Chicken House

Tommy Kirkman entered the world in 1934, at a time when the country exhaled misery and gloom. The shops and streets in southern Indiana echoed not with coins falling into cash registers, but with dark gossip. Several years later, as Tommy toddled after his father into the local hardware store in Bedford, he could hear the anxiety in the voices of the adults. But their words meant little to him.

"Have you seen that hotel in Vincennes, Doc?" the hardware store owner asked Tommy's dad. "Great big building, six or eight stories high. Started building it before the crash, and then . . ."

The man slapped his hand onto the counter of the hardware store, making the screws in Dad's purchase bounce and roll. Dad's real name was Roscoe, but his friends called him Doc. Dad was a powerful skyscraper of a man with a deep, firm voice. His dark wavy hair was piled on top of his head like a dome of black wire. When he smiled, which was not often, he liked to keep his mouth closed to hide two crooked teeth.

"Yes, I drove past a few months ago," Dad said. "It's a shame. Think of all the money that went into those steel beams. It's all just going to waste."

"Whole country is crumbling," the hardware store owner mumbled. "Everything okay with you, Doc?"

"Yes, we are fine. Don't have a lot, but we are fine," Dad said.

Tommy didn't care about Wall Street or foreclosures or President Hoover or President Roosevelt. He didn't care about the depressing black and white photos in the newspaper or the bleak headlines. He felt no distress about the lines of grown men standing outside soup kitchens. The mysterious word *Depression* did not trouble him.

Tommy was fine because every morning he awoke to his mother's soprano voice singing, "Praise the Lord, Praise the Lord!" or some other cheerful melody. He smelled cooking oatmeal or sizzling pancakes and heard the clatter of bowls and spoons. Coffee always brewed in the kitchen. It was the Kirkman curse, according to Dad, who drank it in large quantities.

Tommy was fine because Grandpa and Grandma Franklin had given them a dog recently. Tony was a black and white shepherd pup with soft fur and, surprisingly, one brown eye and one blue eye. Tony and Tommy understood each other and were best friends, even though one of them was not allowed to live inside the house.

Tommy was fine because he could draw pictures. Sometimes he drew on scrap paper. Sometimes he drew in the sandy soil outside the house—as long as his little one-year-old brother Joe stayed out of the way. Sometimes his older sisters Patsy or Carol let him use their Crayolas to draw on a piece of notebook paper.

Tommy was fine because on Sundays the Kirkmans attended Avoca Baptist Church. They listened to God's Word and sang. While some churchgoers barely mouthed the words of the Gospel songs, the Kirkmans sang without inhibition. On the rare occasions they were absent, the church's singing suffered. On Sunday afternoons, the family played games, read books, drew pictures, and sang. Often Tommy's older brothers Bob and Bill turned on the cabinet radio, and together they listened to music and voices from far-away places like Chicago or Washington, D.C.

Tommy was fine because in the evenings, when the cow had been milked and the light grew dim, the family sat peacefully around the living room. He loved to watch his mother crocheting in her rocking chair, her silver hook flashing like electricity in and out of the bright strands of yarn. Above the yarn, her bright, intelligent eyes darted from her needle to the family sprawled around the room. Her quick smile revealed perfectly straight teeth. He loved watching his father, uneducated but intelligent, reading the newspaper. Sometimes Dad whittled away at wood projects or mended a broken household tool. Every now and then when a song came over the radio, Dad got to his feet and held out his hand to Mom. Laughing, she put her hand in Dad's and they twirled around the room until the song was finished.

Every night ended the same way—with the whole family singing together. Then, before Tommy fell asleep, he would hear his father say "good night" and see his mother's beautiful smile.

But then in 1938, suddenly Mom stopped singing, and Tommy was not fine.

It happened when Dad came in with the announcement that he had lost his construction job. He then tried to get odd jobs, but no one had enough money to hire him. With no income, the family fell behind on the mortgage, and the bank foreclosed on their house. Tommy's parents were $500 short. But with no money to spare, it might as well have been a million dollars.

One evening when a sloppy spring rain was turning everything to mud, Dad came in the front door. He took off his muddy boots and went to the kitchen where Mom was making supper. Tommy, four years old, trailed after him, arriving just in time to see Mom's hand frozen in mid-air, holding a spoon.

"A chicken house?" he heard Mom ask, her face as pale as milk in a bucket. "To live in?"

"Not for long, Bernice," Dad said. "Just until we find something better."

Tommy could not see his father's face, but his voice sounded tired and gray. Tommy knew his dad and mom did everything together. They sang together. They prayed together. They planned together. They loved, taught, and disciplined their children together. Now, they suffered together.

That night, Mom didn't sing.

"Thank God it is almost summertime," she kept saying over and over again as the family sat down together. "If you think that's best, Roscoe, that's where we will go for now. Do you think it's dry?"

"If it isn't, we will make it dry," Dad said. Everyone felt better instantly. Since Dad could fix anything, it would be the easiest thing in the world for him to fix a leaky roof.

The next day they all walked down the road to look at their new home.

The neighbors' chicken house was a wooden rectangular building. On one side of the house, the wooden shingle roof was so high that a person couldn't touch it even by reaching up, while the other side was low enough for adults to bump their heads on it.

Near the corner on the high side of the chicken house was a door. It was made of planks, held together with a Z-shaped brace. Two windows let light in beside the door. They were covered with oiled paper, so you couldn't see through them.

Tommy thought it was going to be a great adventure to live in a chicken house. He scraped old chicken droppings off the floor and spread clean straw for a bed for himself and baby Joe. Dad tied a string from wall to wall and hung up an old sheet to divide the chicken house into two rooms, one for sleeping and one for eating.

"Oh, dear Lord," Tommy heard Mom say as she swept the floor. "If only we had a new broom!"

Tommy had never noticed his mother's broom, but he looked at it now. It was worn down to the wire that held the broom bristles together. Here on the rough chicken house floor, the broom was almost useless.

Tommy was still staring at the broom when Mom looked up and caught his eye. She smiled a tired smile.

"It's okay, Tommy," she said. "A broom is just a little thing. But still, we can pray about little things. God hears big prayers and little prayers."

A few hours later, as the family continued setting up house, Jimmy, the Fuller Brush salesman, arrived in his peddler's truck. Fuller Brush was a company that sold all kinds of brooms and brushes. They offered brushes for horses and hairbrushes for humans and cleaning supplies of every kind. On the outside of the truck, bright new brooms waved their bristles toward the sky.

Jimmy knew everyone in the area—and he also knew how the Great Depression was affecting each one. He knew that Doc Kirkman had no money to buy his brushes or cleaning supplies. Still, he stopped to check on them. Everyone liked to talk to him as a way of staying in touch with the community. Today, Jimmy didn't have much to say when he heard that the family was moving into a small chicken house.

"Can we get a broom?" Tommy whispered to his mother.

"Shhhh," Mom said. "We don't have money for a new broom. That's why I prayed about it. If God wants us to have a new broom, He will provide one."

Jimmy chatted with Doc Kirkman for a few minutes, wished everyone the best, and drove away with all his lovely brooms and bristles waving back at Tommy from his truck.

After the chicken house had been cleaned as well as possible, Tommy's older brothers Bob and Bill brought in the kitchen table and the chairs, as well as Mom's rocking chair and the cabinet radio. They also carried in the family's two bed frames and mattresses. Tommy's older sisters Patsy and Carol made the beds. For the boys, they laid blankets on the straw on the floor. Tony, the black and white puppy, raced around, darting between

Tommy, right, with his brother Joe.

everyone's feet and making everyone both frustrated and more cheerful all at once.

When the kitchen table had been set up in the middle of the front partition of the chicken house, Mom set a white doily on it. "Carol, run to the woods and pick an armful of trilliums," she said. "Just because we live in a chicken house doesn't mean we aren't going to decorate."

Mom cleaned the straw and dirt out of some chicken nest boxes that were nailed to the wall. Each big wooden box was divided into four rows of smaller boxes with holes about a foot square. Mom said the chickens went into the little boxes and laid their eggs there.

For now, Mom used the cleaned boxes to store her dishes. The dinner plates went into one nest box and the tin cups into another. She then carefully put her glass pitcher into another one, and the crock of coffee and the coffee pot went into still another.

A few days later, Tommy awakened early. Unwrapping himself from his blankets, he heard Carol go outside to get water from the pump. She had barely left the chicken house, however, when she burst back in.

"Mom! Mom!"

"Carol!" Mom said. "Not so loud! You'll wake up all the others. The sun is barely up."

Tommy scrambled out of his bed on the floor and peeked around the curtain to see what was going on.

"But Mom," Carol went on, "there's a broom lying outside!"

There was a moment of silence as Mom looked up from the eggs she was cracking. She eyed Carol over the top of her glasses.

Then, without a word, she set down the bowl of eggs and followed Carol outside. There, lying in the grass close to the road, was a brand-new broom.

"Well," was all Mom said.

Tommy and Joe had followed Mom out of the house. Even Dad, who had been washing at the pump, came over to see the broom.

"Perhaps God sent this broom for us," Mom said. "But it could be that it fell from Jimmy's truck. Remember how he sets them into slots on the sides of his wagon?"

"But Mom!" Carol said. "Can't we use it?"

"No." Mom's voice was firm. "We will not use this broom until we check with the peddler. But let's take it inside so Tony won't get it."

"When will Jimmy come again?" Tommy wondered.

"Probably in a few days," Mom said. "If it his broom, we will give it back."

What a beautiful broom! How majestic, how straight, how golden! The handle stretched smooth and long from the crisp, honey-colored bristles to the rounded top. The bottom of the broom was smooth and even to catch all the dirt.

A few days later, the clattering noise of the Model T announced the arrival of Jimmy the Fuller Brush peddler. Every member of the family raced out to meet the truck. Mom carried the broom in one hand like the flag of an advancing army.

Tommy fell in step at his mother's right hand, in the very shadow of that exquisite, honey-colored broom. Tony followed close at Tommy's heels.

Tommy had always wondered if God really heard prayers. Now he was seconds away from finding out.

chapter two

The Perfect Life

Jimmy lifted his straw hat in astonishment at the sight of the family spill-ing from the house. Usually, eagerness meant that people had money to spend, but he knew that could not be the case with the Kirkmans.

Mom held out the broom.

"Could you have lost a broom?" she asked. She told Jimmy where they had found it.

"Why, I certainly have not, ma'am," he said. "Nothing's been missing from my truck for weeks. If that broom was left beside the road, it's yours! Can you use it?"

That night, when supper was over and the dishes were washed, the family gathered in the flattened grass outside the front door of the chicken house.

Inside, Carol swept the floor thoroughly for the first time since they had moved in.

Mom took a deep breath. "Let's sing," she said. Bill brought Dad's guitar from inside. As the golden sun disappeared behind the treetops, everyone joined in singing Mom's favorite song. The words swelled to the sky.

"To God be the glory, great things He has done!
So loved He the world, that He gave us His son,
Who yielded His life an atonement for sin,
And opened the life gate that all may go in!"

Tears streamed down Mom's face as she sang the words. It made Tommy feel like crying too. He wondered if Mom was crying because she was thinking of the blind lady who wrote the song or because they had to live in a chicken house. Or was she crying because God had sent them a broom?

It seemed as if God heard two prayers in a row, because a few days after that, a neighbor came to talk to Dad.

"I'll make some coffee," Mom said, hurriedly dipping water from the water pail.

"Oh, don't worry," the man said.

"It will just take a moment," Mom said. "Kirkmans always have coffee."

"Good for you," the man said. "A whole lot of people are drinking stronger stuff these days. If they can get their hands on it."

"Not me," Dad said. "Never. I watched my father kill himself with alcohol. I've never touched the stuff, and I never will."

By the time Dad had been eleven years old, his mother had died in childbirth. That's when his father, dark with despair at the loss of his young wife, took up drinking. He soon found himself ill with his addiction, finally dying from a bout of pneumonia that most young men would have survived.

The man nodded sympathetically and then got down to the point of his visit.

"Doc," the man said, "there's forty acres for sale up the road here for $500."

Dad said nothing. If he had $500 to spare, the family would not be living in the chicken house.

"There's a poplar grove on one side," the man said. With his finger, he drew a square on the kitchen table and divided it into two lots.

"I have a suggestion, Doc. I'll loan you the money, then you can build a house there. You know how to build."

Roscoe did know how to build. He had an engineer's mind, even though he had only been to school for a few grades. When Dad and his siblings had found themselves orphans, Dad had dropped out of school to make money. While the younger children were sent to live at their grandma's house in another town about forty miles away, Dad had stayed in Avoca to make money by chopping wood. As he swung his ax, he transformed his teenage muscles into bands of steel.

Yes, Tommy's dad certainly knew how to use an ax. Tommy had heard the story of his aunt Irene, Dad's little sister. Dad told it whenever Tommy got in his way and was in danger of getting hurt.

Since her brother Roscoe was her main connection to life before their parents had died, little Irene wanted to be near him. One day she climbed onto the train

Tom's parents, Roscoe and Bernice Kirkman

close to Grandma's house and got off in Avoca, where she found Roscoe at his job chopping wood. Roscoe sent his little sister back to Grandma with instructions to stay, but she kept coming back.

Every time it happened, Dad sent word to Grandma to let her know what had happened to Irene. Finally they gave up. If Irene would disappear, they would all just assume she had run away to be with her brother.

The problem with Irene, Dad told Tommy, was that she hindered his wood chopping. She would dart in from behind and put her hand on the woodpile just as Dad was about to swing his ax. His heart would jump up almost to his throat. Finally he took a double spring trap and had Irene sit on it. It was folded open, and every time Irene started to get off, the trap would pinch her. Now Dad could finish his wood chopping, and Irene could watch without getting injured.

This wood chopping and babysitting was the beginning of a life filled with both construction and children. Dad's reputation for woodwork had made its way around the community, and the neighbor with the forty acres was confident in him.

"Build yourself a log house with those trees on this side of the lot," the neighbor continued. "Sell off the other twenty acres to pay me back, and then pay the rest as you are able. If it takes twenty years, it takes twenty years."

Mom was still fussing with the coffeepot and two stoneware mugs, but Tommy could see one side of her face. A tear rolled down her cheek and she pinched her lips together as if she were trying to gain composure. As she picked the coffee percolator off the small burner and began to pour the coffee into the mugs, her hand trembled.

She took the mugs of coffee to the men and then sat down beside Dad with her own mug.

Dad held his mug in his hands and let the steam rise into his face. "You don't need to do this," he said.

"Doc, don't mention it," the neighbor said. "You would do the same for me."

The site for the new cabin was just up the road from the chicken house. That evening Dad and the boys decided to go take a look at it. Rabbits and squirrels darted away into the thick woods as they walked. When they crested the next hill, they could see the cabin site not far ahead. It sat at the corner where Trogdon Road turned off toward the town of Needmore, where Tommy's older brothers and sisters went to school.

The next day Dad, Bob, and Bill began to chop down trees for the new log cabin. When permitted, Tommy, Joe, and Tony joined them. Tommy liked to play with the wood shavings and the log cutoffs that were not used. He listened to the whirr of Dad's whetstone as he sharpened his knives and axes. As the sides of the log house began to rise, Tommy and Joe played with sticks and small limbs and built miniature log houses of their own. Best of all, Tommy and Tony ran through the grass and stumps around the new cabin. Sometimes they would fall into the scratchy grass and roll around and around. Tony licked Tommy with his scratchy red tongue, his mouth wide open and laughing.

Neighbors traveling up North Pike Road stopped to check on the progress of the Kirkman cabin. Whenever Grandpa Franklin visited, he asked Tommy if it wasn't about time Tony moved back in with him. Tommy was pretty sure Grandpa was joking, but all the same it made him nervous. He couldn't imagine being separated from Tony.

Some days, cousin Opal helped the men build. Opal was Bob's age, and he had a real football made of leather. During break time, or in the evening when the work was done, Bob and Opal practiced spiraling the football in a high arc in the clearing beside the rising cabin. Tommy and Tony watched them. When the ball escaped and careened into the brush, boy and dog tore after it.

Tommy was glad Mom prayed so much. They had gotten the broom because she prayed, and now they were getting a new house too.

The worst was over, surely. Tommy supposed that once they moved into the new cabin, there would never again be sad days.

They finally moved into the cabin and, just as Tommy expected, they were happy. Mom sang and sang, and the whole family joined her in song every evening.

Tommy was seven now and Joe was four. Life was perfect. They lived in a real log house instead of a chicken house. They also had a new baby sister Joan, the cutest person the world had ever known. It was 1941 now and the Depression was officially over. True, the newspapers were filled with stories of war in far-off Europe. But Tommy didn't know why everybody talked about it so much. After all, they didn't live in Europe; they lived in America. Tommy was now in second grade, and he was pretty sure he knew almost everything.

It was Sunday afternoon—December 7, 1941. Tommy and Joe lay on the floor by the wood stove. Tommy loved to draw, and Joe tried to do whatever Tommy did. Mostly, Tommy drew solar systems. He drew Jupiter, decorated with many moons; Saturn, with its rings; and Earth, with the continents in blue oceans. On this particular day, Tommy was making a sketch of the tall glass vase from Grandma Franklin.

"This vase was made by a glass blower," Mom had told Tommy when she carried the vase over on the day they had moved to the chicken house. "Someday we might get a chance to see a glassblower in action."

Tommy had stared at the vase, trying to imagine someone blowing hot glass. How could someone create glass that looked as if it had grown in the woods?

Tommy studied the vase, trying to sketch it just right. The vase was narrow at the bottom and wide at the top. The top edge of the vase dipped and rose like a road on the side of a hill. When Patsy or Carol cleaned the dust off the vase, their rag went up and down over the edges.

Tommy looked down at his paper, then up at the bookshelf and the tall glass vase. He made the top of the vase wider than the bottom. Carefully he drew in the glass rings that made the vase look like the trunk of a palm tree. The ruffled top almost stumped him. There were not only the ruffles on the near side of the vase, but also those on the far side. Those pieces of ruffle had to be drawn too, or it wouldn't look right. Tommy sketched and then erased over and over.

Bob and Bill, eighteen and fifteen years old, played a game of checkers on the floor in front of the couch. Thirteen-year-old Patsy sat on the couch above them, playing with baby Joan, and ten-year-old Carol was curled up on the other end of the couch, reading a book. Mom was in her rocking chair, rocking gently to the rhythm of violin music coming from the radio. Dad dozed in his armchair, close to Mom, on the other side of the radio. His feet rested on the brown upholstered footstool Mom had made. Mom didn't mend clothes or crochet on Sunday, and there was no newspaper. Instead, they listened to fine orchestras from distant places like Chicago or New York.

"We interrupt this broadcast to bring you a special bulletin from NBC," a voice broke into the music program.

Mom's eyebrows shot up at the sudden stop of the music and the hurried voice of the announcer.

Tommy didn't know what it meant to interrupt a broadcast. But he didn't like the look on Mom's face. Something was wrong.

chapter three

Prayers and More Prayers

D ad rose up from his nap like a giant steel man coming to life. He quickly turned up the volume on the radio. Bob paused with a checker between his thumb and finger. Tommy sat up, partly because the floorboards were pressing against his ribs, and partly because everyone else had changed positions. And because Tommy sat up, little Joe sat up too.

"From the NBC newsroom in New York: President Roosevelt said in a statement today that the Japanese have attacked Pearl Harbor, Hawaii, from the air. I'll repeat that . . . This bulletin came to you from the NBC newsroom in New York."[1]

Tommy knew President Roosevelt was a courageous man who suffered from the terrible disease called polio. He knew President Roosevelt had tried to cheer up people during the Great Depression when the Kirkman family had to live in the chicken house. Tommy's teachers at school spoke about the Fireside Chats President Roosevelt held to connect with the country. But Tommy did not know what Pearl Harbor was, or why his father's face grew so pale, or why tears began to form in his mother's beautiful eyes. He didn't know why Bob bit his lip and stared at the wooden walls of the cabinet radio as if there might be a person sitting inside the cabinet who could explain more.

Tommy went to the rocking chair and touched his mother's knee.

"What's Pearl Harbor, Mom?"

His father answered. "It's a naval base in Hawaii," he said, his lips set in a grim line. "Leave Mom alone for a minute, Tommy."

Mom reached for a handkerchief in her pocket and wiped her eyes.

"It's okay, Tommy," Mom said faintly. "We will trust God."

The checkers game forgotten, Bob and Bill moved to the floor on either side of the radio. Joe sidled over and climbed onto Mom's lap. Baby Joan cried. Sensing Mom's need for silence, Patsy took the baby to the kitchen. The family listened as updates on the tragedy trickled in. President Roosevelt had met with the Japanese ambassadors in Washington, D.C., that afternoon—on a Sunday. And everyone knew that meant it was serious. The President then called for a special meeting of his advisors at 8:30 that evening.

There was going to be war.

That night before the family retired, they sang together as they always did. Everyone helped—even Mom—while Dad played the guitar.

The next day the United States declared war on Japan. Bob was soon drafted and joined the Navy. A few months later, he left to join the submarines and ships fighting against the Japanese in the Pacific Ocean. Cousin Opal reported for duty as well. He joined the Air Force and trained to fight in an airplane.

Now the war did matter to Tommy—it had taken away Bob. Every night, when the family gathered around the radio, Tommy heard new announcements about the Japanese Navy in the Pacific Ocean. The Japanese had many warships to fight against the American ships. So far, the Japanese were winning most of the battles. Tommy heard President Roosevelt's voice occasionally, speaking from the White House, updating the American people.

One morning Grandpa and Grandma Franklin came over. It was springtime, and Tommy and Joe had been playing outside with Tony.

Tony was now a full-grown dog. His hair was a lovable mess of a random patchwork of black and white, which Tommy tried to comb out at least once a week. Tommy loved Tony more than ever, and Tony loved Tommy more than anyone else. On this day, Tommy and Tony raced around and around outside the cabin, slipping in the spring mud. Tommy stopped on the porch to hear what Grandpa and Grandma were saying, because Mom was looking at them intently. Even Tony seemed to sense the solemn spirit. He sat quietly on the porch, his two white front paws close beside each other in an attentive manner.

"Grandpa had a dream last night," Grandma Franklin was saying. "He woke me up to tell me about it. 'Bob is in trouble,' he said. 'We need to pray for him.' "

Mom's face turned white. Dad was gone on a construction job, and she missed the support of his powerful frame.

"What happened then?"

"We prayed for him," Grandpa said. "My dream was so real. It was as if I was standing on the deck of the Navy ship and could hear the enemy guns blasting. The sky was black with smoke."

Everyone was as still as if watching a storm approach. Then Grandpa spoke again.

"Did you hear if Bob was going into battle?"

"No," Mom said. "We haven't heard anything."

That night as the family sat around the radio, they heard reports of a huge battle between the American Navy and the Japanese Navy in the Pacific Ocean near an island called Midway.

The next day the newspapers told more of the story. The Americans had intercepted and decoded Japanese messages, so they knew the Japanese were planning to attack somewhere in the Pacific. They weren't sure where because the Japanese used the code name "AF." The Americans were fairly certain the

Japanese were also eavesdropping on their radio messages, so they sent out a new message.

"Midway Island is short on fresh water," the Americans radioed.

Sure enough, a Japanese message soon followed to their own people, which was intercepted by the Americans: "AF is short on fresh water."

When the Americans heard that, they knew AF was a code name for Midway, and that Midway Island was the place the Japanese were planning to attack.

Unsuspecting, the Japanese followed through with their raid to destroy the American fleet at Midway. After bombing the island, the Japanese planes returned to their aircraft carriers. It was then that the Americans struck, catching the Japanese by surprise. For four days the battle raged. The American fleet lost one ship and more than 300 men, while the Japanese lost four ships and 3,000 men. It was a moment of victory for the Americans, because up to this time the Japanese Navy had been invincible.

Was Bob one of the 300 men who had been killed?

"If he would be injured or missing, wouldn't they have told us by now?" Mom asked Dad.

"I think so, Bernice," Dad said, running a hand through his wiry black hair. He sounded as if he were trying to convince himself. "I think so."

But neither of them smiled or sang that day. Instead of singing, they prayed.

Several weeks later, the Kirkmans received a short letter from Bob.

"Mom, Dad," they read. *"You probably heard about the big battle here in the Pacific. I want you to know that I was in the thick of the battle, but I am not hurt. Let me know where Opal is fighting if you find out. Love, Bob."*

Tears slid down Mom's face. This time Tommy knew why she was crying. It was because Bob was okay. Tommy was so glad Mom was happy. He could not stand life when Mom was sad.

"Let's sing," Mom said that night, and Dad picked up his guitar.

That night Tommy realized how much the war really mattered. War didn't always just take people away for a time—sometimes it was forever. And it wasn't just Bob and Opal to be concerned about. If the war kept going, Bill would be called too when he turned eighteen.

But there was something mysterious about Bill. As Tommy lay in bed that night, staring up at the ceiling, he thought about it again.

Every morning Bill went to the barn with his bucket to milk the cow. For a few weeks now, Tommy had noticed that a short while after he entered the barn, he would reappear behind the barn. There was a back door in the barn, and Bill would leave through that back door and walk toward the woods. He would then vanish behind the trees and shrubbery. After a while he would come back, pick up the milk bucket, and come back to the house. Sometimes a piece of underbrush stuck to his shirt from his tramp in the woods.

This happened every morning, and Tommy wanted to know where his older brother was going. As soon as Bill came back to the house with the milk pail the next morning, Tommy stepped out. He was determined to follow his brother's tracks. Tony raced across the grass to meet him, running ecstatic circles around Tommy.

It was a stunning morning in early May. The sun had risen over Avoca, and its rays shot the world full of splendor. The grasses behind the barn waved in a light breeze, some of them trampled where Bill had walked.

With an eye to the path, Tommy inched through the grasses. He walked between two trees, and past a stand of nettles. Here the forest floor was thick with last year's fallen leaves, and less undergrowth grew. Tommy worried that he would lose Bill's trail. But no, there it was; a small stand of nettles crushed by a foot and a muddy path where feet had broken through the dryness of the leaves.

Tommy came to a beech tree and frowned. It was strange. The path seemed to lead to the tree. He looked on the other side of the tree, but the floor of the woods was unbroken by human evidence. The dry leaves lay crisp and natural between patches of grass and white trilliums.

Then Tommy realized the truth. The beech tree itself was Bill's destination. The tree was inside the woods just far enough so it could not be seen from outside the woods.

Could Bill be meeting someone here every morning? Tommy wondered.

He looked at the tree and the ground more closely. On the bark of the tree, at the level of Tommy's stomach, Tommy noticed a shiny patch. Had Bill leaned against the trunk? No, Bill was much taller than Tommy. This was not the right height for Bill's shoulders or arms.

Tommy looked at the ground at the base of the tree, and suddenly he understood. In the leaves, two indentations showed the places where Bill's knees had been. If Bill knelt there, his head would rest against the shiny place. Or perhaps his hands would rest there to protect his forehead from the hardness of the bark. But all the same, Tommy understood. Bill did come into the woods to meet someone every morning. He came to meet God.

Tommy felt better instantly. He remembered the broom God had sent them. If God could hear Mom's prayers for something as simple as a broom, then God could keep Bob and Opal and Bill alive, even in a war. Deep in thought, Tommy retraced his steps to the house.

One morning Tommy and Joe built a fort in the shade behind the barn. Tommy decided to lay out the solar system with pieces of wood, bark, and leaves. The fort was the sun and the planets stretched along the path to the house. Tommy couldn't quite remember the chart at school to know how far apart the planets were, but he thought his scale was pretty accurate.

"I'm hungry," Joe said.

"Me too," Tommy said. "Let's go in and see if lunch is almost ready."

Dusty and green from their morning in the dirt and grass, the boys burst in the front door. Tony, banned from the house, curled up in a patch of shade outside.

"Something is burning," Tommy said.

He ran to the kitchen to see what Mom was doing. But she was not there. On the stove, smoke wafted up out of a metal pot and hung in the air. Tommy ran and looked into the pot. It was full of green beans from the garden, but they were turning black and smelled awful.

Fear squeezed Tommy's heart like a giant hand of steel. Mom never left food to burn on the stove.

Where was she?

chapter four

The Sickness with No Cure

Tommy and Joe ran to the living room to make sure they had not missed Mom when they came in. No, she was not there. Tommy ran back outside to check the clothesline on the north side of the house. Maybe she was doing laundry and had simply forgotten the beans. But no, she was not there either. Tony ran around, delighted to see his hero so soon again, but Tommy ignored him and ran back inside.

"Tommy," a quiet voice called.

Tommy stopped. Where was Mom's voice coming from? It must be the bedroom. He ran to his parents' bedroom. With relief, he saw that his mom was there. She was lying on the bed. But why would she be in bed in the middle of the day? Behind her, in the crib, Joan napped peacefully.

"Tommy, I'm all right," Mom said. "I just have a really bad headache."

"I was looking for you," Tommy said, confused. "The beans are burning."

Mom sighed. Her face drew together tightly, but she did not jump up to get the beans.

"Tommy, I want you to very, very carefully lift the beans off the stove and turn it off. Joe, can you bring Mom a drink of water so I can swallow an aspirin?"

From that day, Tommy became Tom.

It wasn't that everyone instantly switched to calling him Tom. They didn't. In fact, Mom and Patsy called Tom "Tommy" for the rest of his life.

As Tom lifted the kettle of burning beans into the sink, a terrible fear lodged in his throat. Even when Mom felt a little better and came out to make sandwiches for the two boys, Tom could hardly eat. What terribly evil kind of headache did Mother have? As soon as Dad got home from work, he said he would take Mom to the doctor the next day.

The doctor said he did not see anything wrong with Mom, except that her blood pressure was high. He suggested she see a cardiologist if the headaches came back. A cardiologist, Dad explained, was a doctor who specialized in treating the heart.

Mom felt fine through the summer of 1942 and through the fall. Around Christmastime she had another bad headache, and Dad told her to schedule an appointment with the cardiologist. On the day of Mom's appointment, Dad was busy with a construction job that he could not leave. The appointment was in the late afternoon after school. Patsy had to stay home to make supper, and Carol did the laundry. Joe had a friend from school over to work on a science project. Since Tom's homework was finished, he got to go along with Mom to keep her company. Patsy and Carol would keep an eye on Joe and his friend Jim and take care of little Joan.

"Comb your hair, Tom," Carol said before they left. "Here, let me do it. It's all messed up."

With a comb, Carol carefully combed Tom's unruly hair until it was flat and neat.

At the doctor's office the nurse came into the room. She sat on a wooden

From the WHITE HOUSE *to the* AMISH

stool with a leather seat and four legs that swooped gracefully to the wooden floor of the exam room. She took a fabric cuff and wrapped it around Mom's arm. Mom had explained this invention to Tom. The cuff had compartments that could be filled with air. The nurse pumped air into the cuff, and at the same time listened to the blood pumping through Mom's arm. When the pressure of the air in the cuff was higher than the pressure of the blood in Mom's artery, the heartbeats went away. Then, as the nurse released the air in the cuff, she watched the pressure dial. She recorded the pressure number when she once more heard the beat of blood in the artery. Mom said the cuff pinched as it got tighter and tighter.

Behind the nurse, Tom saw glass jars filled with cotton balls and cotton swabs. He saw a small paper box labeled *Thin Oval Bunion Plaster*. He saw the label *Johnson & Johnson* on paper wrappers with rolls of fluffy white bandages inside. The nurse frowned when she took Mom's blood pressure.

"Mrs. Kirkman, let me try again on your other arm. I think I must have made a mistake." The nurse went around to the other side of Mom's chair and tried again.

"Hmmm. Maybe I'll let Dr. Elliot take your measurement himself," she said.

The doctor was a lanky, gaunt man who ran his hands through his curly red hair as he talked. He was dressed almost entirely in brown: brown pants, a brown shirt, and a brown jacket with green buttons. The jacket was thrown open, and Tom could see wrinkles marching along the button line of the doctor's shirt.

He also took Mom's blood pressure.

"Mrs. Kirkman, this is the highest blood pressure I've seen in a while," he said.

"Really?" Mom asked. "I didn't think I was sick."

"That's the strange thing," the doctor said, running a long-fingered hand through his red hair. "It's little ladies like you who sometimes have these high numbers."

"So at least I'm not the only one!" Mom responded.

"Here, step over to my office," Dr. Elliot said.

Tom looked around the doctor's room. On the wall hung portraits of

Theodore Roosevelt and Abraham Lincoln. In a bookcase covered with a glass front, Tom saw books about World War I and the Civil War as well as one about Lewis and Clark.

"No, you aren't the only one," the doctor said, when he had dropped his long body into the office chair behind his desk. "You are quite young to experience this, however. You are only my age. I just wish we could find a cure for this disease, especially for young people like yourself."

Mom had gotten married when she was only fifteen years old. So now, even though Bob was twenty, Mom was only thirty-six. Behind the doctor's head, Tom saw certificates and diplomas hanging on the wall. *Indiana University School of Medicine. Certificate of Excellence in Cardiology. How could he have studied so much but still not know how to cure this disease?*

"Some doctors will do bloodletting," the doctor said. "It's controversial, and we don't do it here. But there are reports that it is effective with some people."

Mom sighed. "I don't know if I'd want to have blood taken out of my veins," she said.

"I know," the doctor said. "I just wish someone would come up with a medication that would treat high blood pressure. Some are being investigated, but so far nothing has been safe for humans."

The doctor told Mom that he usually advised people to lose weight. But Mom had no extra weight to lose. Cutting back on salt helped too, he said.

"What happens if it doesn't get better?" Mom asked.

Tom caught Mom glancing his way, almost as if she wished she had asked her young son to stay outside the room. But Tom wanted to know. He had to know.

"High blood pressure is hard on all organs of the body," the young doctor said gravely, running his left hand through his hair. "Sometimes kidneys fail or people go blind after many years. Of course we worry the most about the heart and the brain. Heart attacks in the heart and strokes in the brain can be caused by high blood pressure."

Tom looked at Dr. Elliot with horror. He did not know exactly what those words meant. But they sounded serious. He looked away from the doctor. He wanted to run out of this place and never come back.

"How does high blood pressure cause a stroke?" Mom asked.

"Well, ma'am, if the pressure is too great, the walls of the blood vessels can weaken over time and become thin. Eventually they can burst and bleed. We call it a cerebral hemorrhage."

As they drove away, Tom tried not to think about all the awful things the doctor had said. But he already knew one result of high blood pressure: Mom did not sing as much anymore.

Tom focused on the great gray limestone structures outside the window of the car. Dad had told him how famous Bedford was because of the limestone that came from nearby fields. Many buildings in Bedford were made from it. Once, in the public library, Tom had seen a photo from the 1920s. On the photo, a string of train cars lined the track that went through downtown Bedford at the bottom of the courthouse hill. In each car, a giant limestone pillar rested, heading for a special building in Pennsylvania. A few years before Tom was born, a large tower called the Empire State Building had been built in New York City with Bedford stone.

Everyone in Bedford was proud that such a wonderful tower had been built with stone from their town. Many of the people used this stone when they built their own buildings. Bedford had a lot of limestone churches, public buildings, and houses.

"Mom, look!" Tom exclaimed. "They painted it red and green!" He pointed to a small eating place built on a triangle of land bordered by three roads.

The front of the restaurant, the skinny part that squeezed between two streets, was painted green. The fatter end of the restaurant was painted red. A brand-new sign with block letters said "GRECCO'S" in red letters and "PIZZA" in green letters. New metal awnings protected the windows from the sun. There was no space for shade trees on the tiny triangle of land.

"It must have new owners," Mom said with interest. "See, the name is new too! It's called Grecco's now! Shall we stop and get a soda, Tom? We can get a bottle of Coke for Joe and Jim to share at home too. It's nice to have special treats when we have guests over."

"Oh, yes!" was all Tom could say.

They parked beside "O" Street because the little triangle of land was too small for a parking lot. Tom liked how the streets in Bedford were named in order of the letters of the alphabet. It made it so easy to know which one came next. If you knew the alphabet, you could find your way around town.

As they walked into Grecco's, they smelled the new paint on the outside and new paneling on the inside. The paneling was brown and looked like wood. Black lines, spaced irregularly, ran down the paneling from ceiling to floor. The chairs and tables looked new. At the end of the dining room, a counter covered with the same paneling held the cash register. Several stools sat in front of the counter, inviting guests to eat there if they wished. A wood stove stood off to the left in front of a brick section of wall. On the right, a radio chattered, giving guests the benefit of hearing the latest news while they ate. Tom thought it was a great idea.

"Look at the paintings!" Mom said.

Above the windows, Tom saw framed art. There was a basket of apples, spilling out. There was a picture of a lighted candle surrounded by clusters of grapes and other fruits.

"Two Coca-Colas, please," Mom said. "And do you have bottled Coke as well? I will take one bottle."

Tom broke out of his reverie. He looked at the young man behind the counter taking Mom's money. Then a boy a little older than Tom came from the back of Grecco's. His head was almost hidden under a large cowboy hat. He slipped a plastic yellow horse into his pocket as he approached.

"Disshhes," he said to the man behind the counter. "Disshhes." He made the *sh* sound last for a very long time, and said no other words.

The man behind the counter turned to the boy. "Not yet, Billy," he said. "Don't get the dishes until they are done eating."

"We're finished," a construction worker said. Billy clomped across the floor, obviously showing off his cowboy boots. He focused on the task of carefully picking up the two men's plates and stacking them together. After a fierce battle with a piece of uneaten crust, Billy let the crust fall to the floor.

"Th-hank you," he said to the men and clomped away.

Mom looked at Tom. "Would you like to sit on the stools to drink our Cokes?" she asked.

After the frightening doctor's appointment, sitting at the counter with Mom drinking Cokes was the most wonderful experience Tom could have imagined.

Billy clomped past in his cowboy boots and carried the dishes to the back. The young man behind the counter whispered, "Billy is my nephew. He's slow, but he does okay with the dishes, so I got the owner to give him a little job."

It didn't matter to Tom that Billy was slow. He envied him, getting to work in this wonderful place. *I'm going to work here some day!* he told himself.

But on the way home, Tom remembered what the cardiologist had said. He prayed as the snow-covered fields flashed by his window.

Tom didn't remember much from science class about the function of kidneys, so he didn't pray about them. Kidneys seemed to be the least important of all the things the doctor had said. He didn't exactly know what a heart attack or a stroke was either. He certainly didn't understand what a cerebral hemorrhage was. But he knew they were bad things. And he did understand what it meant to go blind.

God hears our prayers, Tom reminded himself. *If He can wake Grandpa in the night to pray for Bob, He can heal my mother.*

When Tom and Mom returned from the cardiologist, Tom burst into the cabin with the Coke. The whole house smelled like cookies. Patsy grinned at them from behind a large platter of sugar cookies. She held a knife in one hand and a bowl of green frosting in the other. A trail of scattered crumbs traced a path from the kitchen table to the fireplace where the two boys were sitting.

"Why, Patsy already has made you a treat!" Mom exclaimed with a smile. "Maybe the boys don't need a Coke, Tommy!"

"Oh, yes, Coke! We still want Coke!" both boys cried. Their lips and tongues were stained green from Patsy's cookies.

Tom poured the Coke into two cups for the boys, who had been quizzing each other about their upcoming science test. The science chapter was on planets, Tom's favorite subject, so he offered to help them.

"What is the third planet from the sun?" he asked.

"Mars!" Joe shouted.

"No, Venus!" Jim said.

Tom sighed. These boys really needed help.

"Let me make you a little drawing to help you remember," Tom said. "This is Earth."

"I thought Earth doesn't count," Joe said.

"Yes, it does," Jim said. "Remember the saying? 'My Very Efficient Mother Just Saved Us Nine Pennies.' "

Tom taped together several pieces of Mom's writing paper and drew the nine planets for the boys. Joe was not surprised, of course, but Jim watched in awe.

"You forgot the moon!" Joe said. So Tom added a tiny moon beside Earth.

"How do you know when the moon is broke?" he asked in parting.

The boys frowned up at him.

"When it's down to its last quarter!" Tom said as he got up to leave.

chapter five

Bob, Bill, and Opal

In the early spring of 1944, Bill turned eighteen. He was old enough to go to war.

Tom knew a lot about war by now. It had been three years since Bob had joined the Navy. Tom knew the names of the two sides of the big war. The United States, England, France, and the Soviet Union were called the Allies. The Germans, Italians, and Japanese were called the Axis Powers. The Germans were also called Nazis, because that was the party of their leader, Adolf Hitler. Tom knew that Adolf Hitler was a very bad man, though he didn't exactly know why.

All the children knew these facts because everyone worried about the war. Tom heard about the war on the radio and at school. The Axis Powers had taken control of France, as well as other countries in Europe. To keep the

Allies from recapturing France, Adolf Hitler ordered his men to build fortresses along the coast of France. He built so many barricades along the coast that it was called the Atlantic Wall. Even if all the Allied countries worked together, they would have a hard time breaking through the Atlantic Wall.

Tom knew that President Roosevelt had chosen General Eisenhower to lead the charge through the Atlantic Wall. But no one knew when General Eisenhower would tell the Allies to attack. And no one knew if they would succeed when they did attack. Perhaps the Germans and Italians would fight back so hard that the attack would fail. Perhaps many soldiers would die and nothing good would come of it.

No one knew, but everyone hoped the attack would succeed. They hoped the war would be over soon.

Bill reported to the local draft officer. Later that night, he told his parents what had happened. Mom rocked in her chair, her crochet needle flashing. She was making a set of glass holders out of yarn. The glass holders would be fuzzy sleeves for the bottom of water glasses. They would protect the glass and soak up drops of water. Mom had already made a purple one with light green trim. Now she was making a dark green one with orange trim.

Bill had begun speaking, and Dad put down his newspaper to listen.

"I told them I am a conscientious objector," Bill said.

Mom and Dad looked at Bill and then at each other. "The Baptist church doesn't take that approach," Dad said. "Even our pastors support fighting during war."

"I know," Bill said quietly. He was sitting on the living room couch. He leaned forward, his elbows resting on his knees. His eyes seemed to study the cracks between the wooden floor planks. Bill had always been a quiet, thoughtful boy. He had always taken his relationship with God seriously.

It wasn't just his prayer meeting under the beech tree in the woods. Lately Tom had seen him reading his Bible as if it were a textbook he was trying to study. He knew Bill still prayed a lot, and he had heard Bill at church discussing verses with people much older than he was. Tom was not surprised that Bill was having a serious discussion with Mom and Dad. But what did it mean to be a conscientious objector?

"Why do you think you should be a conscientious objector?" Mom asked.

"It's just that I've been reading the Bible, especially the words of Jesus," Bill said slowly, cautiously, as if he didn't want to disrespect his parents or his Baptist faith. "I just don't feel that I can be involved in taking someone's life."

"So what did the officer say?" Mom asked.

"He asked if I had experience in construction and I said yes, I helped build our family's home."

"Indeed you did," Dad said. "And a good hand you are with tools too."

"So the officer placed me in the Seabees," Bill concluded.

"Oh," said Mom.

Tom was sitting on the floor listening. He was ten years old now. Joe sat beside him, staring at Bill with big eyes. Would Bill leave like Bob had done? Joe could only faintly remember when Bob had lived at home.

Outside, spring peepers filled the dusky evening with music. Inside, the electric bulbs threw a warm yellow blanket of light over the rooms. Tom looked up at his mother, and he could tell that she wished the officer had told Bill that he would not have to join the Army at all.

"What's the Seabees, Bill?" Tom asked.

"It's the construction branch of the Navy," Bill said. "The Seabees build things. Barracks, bridges, roads, whatever."

"Is it . . ." Tom wanted to ask if people were shot at when they worked in the Seabees. He wanted to know if the Seabees ever went on boats that were sunk by enemy ships. But he couldn't bring himself to ask a question that could have a horrible answer. Bill, with his thin face and warm, thoughtful eyes, would just have to be okay. So he changed the ending of his question.

"Is it interesting to work on the Seabees? Do you go to other countries?"

Bill smiled a slow, kind smile as if he guessed what Tom had really meant to ask.

"I suppose it will be interesting," he said. "But we don't know yet where we will be sent."

"Just don't pick up whiskey," Mom sighed.

Bob now drank whiskey frequently at his Navy post in the Panama Canal. He had said so himself in a letter to Mom and Dad.

"I keep having dreams," Bob had written. *"I step out of the hatch and see all those bodies floating in the water after the Battle of Midway. I tried to figure out whose hands this blood is on, but I can't. I drink to make the images leave my mind. I don't think there's any point in hiding the truth from you. Whiskey is what is keeping me from going insane."*

Tom considered Bob's words and Bill's devotion to God. He admired the way Bill thought about following Jesus and thought perhaps he would serve God too when he was older.

But Tom wasn't sure. It also sounded exciting to join the Air Force as Opal had, or perhaps the Navy as Bob had. Doing construction work seemed so normal. That was what Dad did at home all the time. Maybe it would be more exciting to fight like Bob and Opal.

Tom looked up at his mom. She had started a third glass holder. This one was yellow.

"What color are you going to use around the edge of that one?" Tom asked.

"What color do you think goes well with yellow?" Mom's smile faltered tonight, but she knew how much Tom loved to design and draw.

"Green," Tom suggested.

"Green and yellow, just like spring," Mom replied. "All right, it will be green!"

His mother rarely complained, but Tom could tell when she was having her headaches. He could see from her expression that one was starting now.

Tom knew his father noticed her headaches too. They had been coming more and more often, and Dad often took her to the doctor in Bedford. But the doctor did not seem to be able to help her very much.

Lots of people gave Mom advice. She ate chicken fried in garlic. She drank hibiscus tea every day. She took warm baths. Sometimes these treatments helped her feel better for a short time. But nothing worked for long.

From the WHITE HOUSE *to the* AMISH

"Well, it's time to go to bed," Dad said.

A swath of light lit up the yard outside the cabin. A car engine approached and then fell silent with a final rumble. Dad rose to his impressive height and went to the front door. It was Grandpa and Grandma Franklin.

"Come in," Dad said. "Is everything okay?"

Tom remembered how Grandpa and Grandma had come before to tell how Grandpa had awakened to pray for Bob. Perhaps this had happened again.

"It's Opal," Grandpa said quietly.

Tony slipped inside between Grandpa's legs. No one chased him back, so he sidled over to Tom and lay down.

"Not Opal," Mom whispered. "Come in. Sit down."

Tom threw his arms around Tony's shaggy black and white neck as Grandpa and Grandma sat down. Tom thought about Opal.

He knew Opal was a tail gunner. The Air Force planes had guns mounted in the back so they could shoot at enemies following them. Opal operated the tail guns, trying to shoot down enemy planes before they could shoot at him.

Three years had passed since Bob had joined the Navy and Opal had joined the Air Force. Bob was fighting in the Pacific, while Opal was fighting in Europe or North Africa, somewhere on the other side of the world from Bob. Tom thought of the football games in the old days before Bob and Opal had gone to war. He could just see the football, spiraling high through the blue of a summer sky.

Tony got up and licked Tom's face as Grandpa began to talk. It was almost as if Tony knew something was wrong.

"Sit, Tony," Tom whispered, pushing the dog to the floor. Tony obeyed, although the wild black and white strands of his tail swished back and forth, swatting Tom's pant leg.

Mom sat still in her rocker. Beside her chair in a basket was her crochet hook, stuck motionless in the yellow and green glass holder.

Grandpa did not have much to say. "Opal is missing in action," he finally told them. "Somewhere over Italy his plane has been shot down."

Mom lowered her head and broke into sobs. "I just can't tell Bob that his favorite cousin is gone!"

No one spoke. For many minutes, there was only the sound of sobbing and nose-blowing.

"And Bill is ready to go too now," Mom went on. "If only General Eisenhower would break into Europe and end the war!"

But the war did not end, and Bill had to leave. Even though he would be doing construction work, he was still joining the Navy. Anything could happen.

chapter six

Interrupted Broadcasts

The coffee was brewing in the kitchen of the Kirkman log cabin on the morning of June 6, 1944. Mom sang softly as she sliced bread to make a sandwich for Dad's lunch. Dad had a construction job in Bedford, and Mom always packed him a lunch. It was early June and school was out, so she had no other lunches to pack.

Dad walked to the kitchen and poured himself a cup of coffee. He walked back to the living room and seated himself in his armchair close to the radio. He liked to read a few verses of Scripture while he sipped his coffee. Then he always turned the radio on for a few minutes. War updates usually dominated the announcements.

Tom went to the kitchen to get the milk bucket from Mom's cabinet. Now that Bill was gone, it was his job to milk the cow. Mom kept the bucket in the new Hoosier cabinet Dad had given her at Christmas.

The new cabinet was a wonderful invention. A rolling door hid a cupboard for bread. On the other side was a flour bin with a sifter built right into the bottom of the bin. A wide stoneware counter provided Mom with a place to keep her mixing bowl. Under the shelf, a big cupboard held the larger items. Here Mom stored the milk bucket.

Tom opened the latch on the cupboard door and slid out the stoneware bucket. He walked across the living room toward the front door just as Dad flipped on the radio.

Beep-Beep-Beep. Beep-Beep-Beep.

Tommy stopped and stared at the radio.

"This is Robert St. John from the NBC newsroom in New York. Ladies and gentlemen, we may be approaching a fateful hour. All night long, bulletins have been pouring in from Berlin claiming that D-Day is here, claiming that the invasion of Western Europe has begun."[1]

Dad sat still, his coffee cup frozen in his hand, halfway to his mouth. Mom came from the kitchen and stared at the radio with shining eyes. Tom looked at the tears forming in her eyes, and he knew from her expression that she had only one thought.

Perhaps the war is almost over!

The announcer continued. Dad turned up the volume.

"Let me read you several of the latest bulletins. This is not yet confirmed by Allied forces, of course, but it says heavy fighting has been taking place between the Germans and the invasion forces on the Normandy Peninsula, about thirty-one miles southwest of Le Havre. Another bulletin, also from Berlin radio and unconfirmed, says that British and American landing operations on the western coast of Europe, from the sea and from the air, are stretching over the entire area from Cherbourg and Le Havre, a distance of about sixty miles . . ."

Patsy and Carol stumbled sleepily into the living room, their hair tousled. They had heard the increased volume of the radio and some of the words of the announcer. Carol settled in Mom's rocker, and Patsy, wrapped in a quilt, sat down beside the cold stove. Mom moved to the couch beside Dad and slipped her hand in his as the announcer went on. In her other hand, resting on her knee, she still held a knife smeared with butter.

"And here's another bulletin just in. DNB, the German agency, says this is unconfirmed but that the most important air droves in the area of the Normandy Peninsula of France have been wiped out. Now I presume that means wiped out by the Allies. As you may have heard on other broadcasts, all free German news agencies have begun broadcasting these stories that the invasion is here. There is no Allied confirmation as yet. The first report came out shortly after midnight, and since then we've been flooded with reports from Berlin. Paris radio, strangely enough, has not confirmed any of these reports. And now we have just been informed that we can expect, in a very few seconds, a very important broadcast from the British capital. And so now we take you to London."

In the silence that followed, everyone exhaled. A couch spring twanged. Then everyone leaned forward again.

"The text of Communiqué Number One will be released to the press and radio of the United Nations in ten seconds. Repeat. Ten seconds from now."

Static poured out of the radio and no voice was heard as the seconds passed. Then the voice resumed:

"Under the command of General Eisenhower, Allied naval forces, supported by strong air forces, began landing Allied armies this morning on the northern coast of France. The communiqué will be repeated . . . This ends the reading of Communiqué Number One."

There was reason to doubt an announcement from Germany's capital, but an announcement from London could not be wrong. The invasion to free Europe from Nazi rule had begun.

Everyone lived in a daze, desperate to hear more details. Bob and Bill were both in the Pacific, so they were not part of this battle. But would this end the war? Would the boys soon be able to come home?

As soon as the newspaper deliveryman came by with the *Bedford Daily Times-Mail*, Tom rushed out to the porch to get the paper.

The *Times-Mail* had just one word across the top of the page: "Invasion." Underneath, a sketch of the coast of France and England showed where the invasion had taken place. Arrows in the English Channel showed the path of the Navy ships across the water. The name *Eisenhower* appeared many times in the columns of print, describing the few things that were known so far about the invasion.

The next day, Dad brought home a copy of the *Indianapolis Star* that his client had passed on to him. "Allies Push Inland," it said. Above a dark photo of soldiers, the headline said, "Full Victory—Nothing Else . . . Eisenhower."

What a great man general Eisenhower must be! Tom thought. He was disappointed that the war would be over before he was old enough to join. He wondered if the Army needed people who liked to draw; someone would have had to draw the maps that appeared in the newspapers. Maybe he would do what Bill had done: join the Army but look for a job that he already knew how to do.

The newspapers also carried warnings from President Roosevelt. He cautioned people that it would still take a long time to finish the war. Yes, the troops had entered Europe, but they had not entered Berlin or Tokyo, the capitals of their enemies. Neither Germany nor Japan had surrendered, and neither country showed any intention of doing so.

When the boys went back to school that fall, the war was still raging. Eager to see their friends again, Tom and Joe were glad to climb back onto the school bus. It swept down, up, down, over the little hills of North Pike Road. When the road got to Avoca, the bus picked up more children for the elementary school.

Tom was in fourth grade now, so he was in the older half of the school. He felt important and no longer worried that he would get lost or miss the bus when it was time to go home. The only thing that bothered him was that he wouldn't get to play with Tony as much.

Tom rushed into the school with the other students and hurried up the wooden stairs to the first floor. He found the fourth grade class easily. He stopped to get a drink from the porcelain bubbler. It was much easier to reach the water now than it had been last year! He wondered if it would also be easier for him to use the toilet seats. He remembered them well—the wooden seats were spring-loaded, so when you climbed off they sprang up, opening a valve that flushed the toilet. It was a great invention, Tom knew, but the sudden rising made him nervous.

Tommy's favorite school task was writing cursive with a metal-tipped pen dipped in ink. Of course, the children felt more modern when they used Crayolas and No. 2 pencils. But in cursive writing class, the teachers taught the students to make flowing letters with real ink. Tom loved this class, not just because it was fun, but because every teacher praised his exceptional work. Sometimes in his free time, Tom wrote extra sentences or doodled in his Goldenrod writing tablet. He did it for the sheer joy of watching the beautiful letters unfold like ribbons from his pen.

He also loved recess. In the winter, the boys would play games of marbles and jacks. Now, since it was still warm, there would be games of baseball and prisoner's base.

A few things changed from year to year. Tom had a new teacher, of course. But mostly, the inside of the gray limestone school was familiar and comforting. Tom loved to read, but he could not understand why he needed to know what adjectives were or why he had to pick them out of a sentence. He didn't mind the multiplication tables, because he learned them quickly. But the long tests were just as tiresome as they had always been.

By late August, about the time school started, the Allies had pushed the Germans out of Paris. Everyone hoped the war would soon be over. But the Germans did not surrender. General Eisenhower directed a long line of Allied troops in a ground war across Europe. Newspapers hinted that not all the generals agreed that this was the best strategy. The weather grew uncomfortably cold, and sometimes the ground where the soldiers walked was muddy. Thanksgiving 1944 passed, and the line of men fought on.

On December 16, when the Kirkman family was thinking of Christmas and planning the best time possible without Bob or Bill, the radios and newspapers had more bad news. In a wintry world of snow and ice, the Germans had attacked the Allied troops again. They chose to attack at a thin place in the long Allied line. The Battle of the Bulge was a disaster, with tens of thousands dying over Christmas, from both the German and Allied armies.

Neither Bob nor Bill made it home for the holidays. They both wrote letters saying they were fine. Bob didn't say anything this time about drinking whiskey, but Tom could tell from the way Mom read his letter that she was still worried about him.

In February, the newspapers reported that the war was going better for the Allies, and it would be only a matter of time before Germany surrendered. The newspapers showed photos of President Roosevelt meeting the leaders of the Soviet Union and England in Europe. The radio told the story of General Eisenhower assuring reporters that the war in Europe would soon be over.

In mid-April, spring came to Avoca. Light green appeared in the lawn as shoots of grass pushed through. Tom dreamed of summer days with Tony and Joe. Maybe Bob and Bill would be home. Maybe if they were home, Mom would quit having headaches.

"Tom and Joe, I want to go to Bedford tomorrow to find a graduation gift," Patsy said after Wednesday night prayer service at the Avoca Baptist Church. "Do you want me to pick you boys up at school and take you along? Maybe we could stop at Grecco's."

"Oh, not Grecco's!" Carol said. "I thought maybe you were going to say Epie's Burgers where the basketball boys go."

"I like Grecco's," Tom said quickly. "I'll go! If Dad lets me," he added with a sidelong glance at his father.

Dad looked over the top of his newspaper and winked. Dad often smiled more freely after the evening prayer service. Mom looked up from the pair of jeans she was mending and also smiled.

"You can take a dollar from us for a treat for the boys," she said.

As she promised, Patsy picked them up after school the next day. "Drop me off at the square," Carol said. "I want to look for some summer shoes while you go to Grecco's."

Patsy, Tom, and Joe ordered Cokes and French fries and seated themselves at a window table with their drinks. Mounted in the corner of the room, the radio clamored for attention as it had done the last time. Billy emerged from the back room.

"Disshhes," he said, in just the same way he had a year before. Joe began staring at the unusual features of the boy, but Tom poked him.

"Hi, Billy!" Tom said.

"Hi!" Billy replied, a rush of air exploding from his mouth along with the word. "Hi!"

A waiter brought the drinks, ice cold, and the fries, sizzling hot.

Tom looked at the ice floating on the dark surface of his Coca-Cola. He took a sip and felt the sizzle of the bubbles popping on his tongue.

"We interrupt this broadcast to bring you a special bulletin from CBS World News."

Everyone froze. All eyes turned toward the radio. By now, Tom knew what interrupting a broadcast meant. Something important had happened.

chapter seven

Deaths and Victories

Everyone waited breathlessly for the announcer to continue. Broadcasts like this were news of either victories or disasters. Which would it be this time?

Germany has surrendered, surely, Tom thought. *The war must be over.*

He took another sip of Coke to try to relax as the voice went on.

"A press association has just announced that President Roosevelt is dead."

"Oh!" cried Patsy. Her hand, which had been around her glass, fell against the table. The waiter kept staring at the radio, as if dumbfounded. An old man sitting across the room swore loudly.

Behind the counter, Billy looked, not at the radio, but at the astonished faces in the room. He reached into his jeans pocket and pulled out the same yellow toy horse he had carried when Tom was there with Mom. Billy rubbed his thumb over and over down the mane.

"Disshhes?" he asked.

The announcer's voice went on.

"The President died of a cerebral hemorrhage. All we know so far is that the President died in Warm Springs, Georgia."[1]

Tom wished he could be like Billy, oblivious to the news he had just heard. So even the most powerful man in America could not keep from having a cerebral hemorrhage—and dying.

That evening the family was unusually quiet. Perhaps, Tom thought, the whole United States was quiet. Everyone had been encouraged during the horrible Depression and the war because President Roosevelt had kept up their spirits with his Fireside Chats. The Americans had elected Roosevelt four times, more often than any other president. Now, just as the end of the war was in sight, he was gone.

"This nation has suffered this day a staggering loss," the voice on the radio said that night. **"President Roosevelt lies with the problems of the nation finally lifted from his shoulders, stricken late this afternoon with cerebral hemorrhage. He passed away this afternoon before his physicians could be of any assistance, if assistance in such a case is possible at all . . . Vice President Harry Truman, who from here on will be President Truman, went immediately to the White House."**[2]

Tom went to sleep that night feeling that the world had changed, and trying to forget what the President had died of. But when he read the newspapers the next day, he saw it again.

For a long time, President Roosevelt had been stricken with high blood pressure, which his doctors could not control. The only medicine they had was phenobarbital, and it was not reliable. An artery in his head had burst, which was called a cerebral hemorrhage.

Cerebral hemorrhage was not just a big term that doctors said to sound intelligent. It was a real enemy. If a cerebral hemorrhage could kill the most important person in the United States, couldn't it also kill Mom?

A few weeks passed. On the last day of April, Germany's Nazi leader, Adolf Hitler, killed himself. One week after that, Germany surrendered to General Eisenhower. Now only the Japanese fought on in the war.

A few months later President Truman approved dropping atomic bombs on Japan. These catastrophic weapons killed thousands of people at once. Just before Tom started fifth grade, Japan surrendered in the Pacific Ocean to General MacArthur. The historic war was now officially over.

On the streets of Bedford, people cheered and horns blared in celebration. Children banged spoons on kettle lids. Everyone was so relieved that the war was over.

First, Mom couldn't stop crying because Bob and Bill would soon be home. Then she couldn't stop smiling. Finally she began making plans.

"Turkey," she said. "That's what we'll have. The boys both love turkey and dressing. And pumpkin pie. We'll have pumpkin pie. It will be just like Thanksgiving! Oh, and I'll save fresh cream to whip with sugar for the top of the pie."

The Kirkman house rang with joy when Bob and Bill returned home. Bill had not been gone long, and he had not changed much. Bob, on the other hand, was a different man. During that first meal with the whole family at home, everyone smiled and laughed and drank coffee. "If only Opal would be home too," Mom said with a sigh after dessert had been served.

With a suddenness that alarmed everyone, Bob put down his coffee mug and got to his feet, the wooden legs of his chair scraping across the floor. He turned and walked out the front door. Mom found him on the front porch, but he would not talk to her about his pain. He only sat on the porch beside the aging Tony, staring straight ahead.

In the Navy, whiskey had sustained Bob's broken spirit. From being carefree, confident, and explosive, Bob had grown silent and morose. Only when he drank did his nagging thoughts dissolve. Only with a bottle in his mouth could he erase the images of the thousands of dead men floating in the water around his submarine. Lifted by alcohol, he felt like the old Bob. He felt like the boy who had spiraled the football to his favorite cousin

Opal or zigzagged around the front yard with little Tom and little Joe on his shoulders. He could keep from thinking as long as he could keep drinking. During Bob's time in the Navy, his crew had gone to the Panama Canal multiple times. But Bob was drunk every time and had not once gotten off the ship to see the famous canal.

Bob tried to settle down. He married Lois, his childhood sweetheart and found a place to live just a short walk from his parents' house. A year later, he and Lois had a daughter. Bob quit drinking for a while when he married Lois. Soon, though, the brooding look came back, and Bob started drinking again. Lois and Mom worried about his habit. Dad told Bob in no uncertain terms that he must stop. He told Bob how his own father had killed himself with his drinking, leaving him and his siblings as orphans. Bob said he would try.

In the summer of 1948, Tom got his dream job working at Grecco's. He was fourteen now, and he felt like an adult. It was good to have some money in his pocket.

One day as he washed dishes, he planned an outing to the courthouse on the square that evening. It was Friday, so there would be a movie being played on the courthouse wall. With his coins, he would buy a Dr. Pepper for himself and maybe for a friend or two. They would pick up popcorn at the sidewalk popcorn cart. Maybe there would be an ice-cream vendor if they were lucky.

He wasn't worried about how he would get home. Surely a friend or neighbor could give him a ride home.

From behind, Billy clomped up and dropped more plates into the water. "Disshhes," he said.

"Thanks, Billy," Tom said. Pieces of pepperoni and half-chewed pizza crust bobbed in the soap bubbles. He tried not to think about the teeth and saliva that had been in contact with those bits of food.

As soon as his dishwashing shift ended, the manager gave Tom his wages.

"Bye, Tom," Billy said, reaching into his pocket for the yellow horse.

Tom was in a great hurry to leave, but he stopped. He had learned that Billy used the plastic horse as a comfort when he was sad or nervous. Apparently he was sad to see Tom go.

"Billy, would you like me to draw you a horse?" Tom asked.

"Horsshhe!" Billy exclaimed jubilantly.

Tom grabbed a paper napkin and a pencil from beside the cash register and quickly sketched a galloping horse. Billy took the napkin with reverence, studying the sketch and tracing it with a finger. Finally he laid it on the counter, put the yellow horse on top of it, and wrapped the horse in the napkin.

"Bye, Billy!" Tom said, pleased. Tom hurried on foot toward the center of town, about six blocks away. In the crowd around the courthouse, he found both school friends and co-workers from Grecco's. With a bottle of Coca Cola in hand, Tom found a seat on the grass as the movie began. He shared puns and wisecracks to complement the film throughout the evening, causing his companions to laugh. Cigarette smoke hovered over the lawn, and drinks passed from hand to hand. After the movie, the sky now black, Tom got up to buy himself another Coca-cola.

"Have a sip, Tom," an older man said. Tom recognized him as Ernest Davis, a neighbor who lived close to the Kirkmans.

Tom knew it was an alcoholic beverage, but he helped himself. The drink burned all the way down his throat, and he made a face.

"Thanks," he said as Ernest laughed. "Could you drop me off at home when you're ready to go?"

Ernest's car had a radio. Margaret Truman, President Truman's daughter, sang "Beneath the Weeping Willow Tree" over the car's speakers. Tom enjoyed her voice because it reminded him of his mother's.

They were nearing the Kirkman cabin when Tom saw a flash of black and white in the ditch.

"Hey, stop!" Tom called. "That's Tony, my dog! Let me call him and give him a lift home."

Tony was an old, arthritic dog now. Tom was shocked to see him out so late, but he knew Tony liked to make his rounds, even if he made them slowly.

Ernest stopped the car and backed down the road. Tom opened the door.

"Tony!" he called as he got out, straining his eyes in the darkness. "Here, boy!"

Tom wanted to wait longer, but he felt bad making his neighbor wait, so he jumped into the car. Ernest stepped on the gas and the car roared off.

Suddenly, black and white fur flashed in the headlights, and Tom felt a thump under the passenger side wheel.

chapter eight

The Test

Ernest swore. "I think that was your dog coming to your call!" he exclaimed.

Blinding pain filled Tom's being as his neighbor stopped the car. Tom jumped out before the wheels had quit rolling and ran back to the lump of fur faintly illuminated in the red taillights.

Tony had collapsed and was panting and whimpering. Tom started to pick him up but felt blood. Sick with despair, Tom ran back to the car. Ernest was backing cautiously toward them.

"Do you have a blanket or anything?" Tom asked desperately.

Ernest fished around in his back seat, but only came up with an old newspaper.

"I'll take it," Tom said. "Can you spread it on the back seat?"

Taking off his shirt, Tom wrapped Tony in it, then picked him up and carried him to the car. Tony looked at Tom with trusting eyes before the eyelids fell shut. Tom knew it was for the last time.

The next morning Tom dug a grave before he went to work at Grecco's. He insisted on doing it himself. He couldn't believe he had called Tony to his death.

"I should have waited," Tom kept saying. "I should have waited a little longer."

After that, he could not listen to Margaret Truman. Every time her voice came over the radio, he had to turn it off or step out of the room.

One evening about a week later, when Tom got home from washing dishes at Grecco's, Bob and Lois had just arrived after walking the mile and a half from their house. Bob was carrying their young daughter Peggy on his shoulders. He and Lois looked troubled and pale. "You won't believe what happened," Bob said, looking straight at Mom.

"What?" Mom asked, looking at Bob and Lois with concern. Even little Peggy seemed to be acting strangely. Normally she babbled and laughed. Today she was oddly still.

"Opal," Peggy said, pointing her pudgy little fist toward the woods through which they had come.

Mom looked at Bob in even greater astonishment. Peggy did not know who Opal was. Opal had died before Peggy was born, even before Bob and Lois had married.

"We saw Opal," Bob said quietly. He lifted Peggy down from his shoulders as if she weighed two hundred pounds and he could no longer endure the strain. He sat heavily on the couch in his parents' living room. Lois sat beside him, quiet. But she was trembling.

Slowly they told their story.

"You know where the trail forks?" Bob asked. "Opal and I used to often meet there."

"Yes," Mom said.

Tom also knew the spot, and he knew that Bob and Lois always passed the fork on their walk over to visit the Kirkman cabin.

When they had approached the fork, Lois, who had grown up in the neighborhood, had looked ahead and gasped, "Isn't that your cousin Opal?"

Bob didn't have time to think or to argue that it could not be Opal, because as he came out from behind the trees, he too saw that it was Opal. Little Peggy pointed at the man and crowed unintelligible words, even though she had never known her father's cousin.

"Opal!" Bob said as they drew closer.

"You're going to have to quit your drinking," Opal said. "You need to give your life to the Lord and serve Him, or you're going to burn."

Then Opal had walked off, disappearing behind a tree.

"Lois and I looked at each other," Bob said. "It wasn't until he left that it really sank in to me that this is a man who is dead. He doesn't live on this earth anymore. I chased after him and looked down the path, but there was no one around."

Everyone stared at the young couple in disbelief.

"Was it a vision, or do you think Opal was real?" Mom asked.

"I don't know," Bob answered. "He looked real, but he disappeared before I could touch him."

Dad and Mom had taught their children about heaven and hell, so Opal was not telling Bob anything new. But this experience changed Bob forever.

"I've got to give my life to the Lord," Bob sobbed from his spot on the couch. "I've been so angry with God for what happened in the war, but that's not God's fault."

"Praise the Lord, Bob. God is seeking you as He does all of us!" Mom said. "I almost can't believe He sent a message to you in that way."

That night, the whole family sang "To God Be the Glory." Tom played the violin, and Bill played the guitar. Tom could see tears shining in Bill's eyes as he sang.

With both of Tom's older brothers now serving God, Tom knew his mother wanted the same for him.

But Tom wasn't sure. Sometimes when Mom felt better for a while, he thought God was answering his prayer. In fact, recently Tom had quit praying about her healing for a while, and had almost forgotten about cerebral hemorrhages and high blood pressure and the search for medication that would cure the disease.

People still bombarded Mom with remedies for her high blood pressure. She still ate garlic and drank hibiscus tea. She also tried to follow the cardiologist's recommendation for exercise and relaxation. Tom had thought these things might be helping her.

But now Mom's headaches were coming back, and her health was on everyone's mind. One evening Dad made an announcement.

"We're moving to Denver," he said, his jaw working like a metal hinge. "I've heard there are good doctors in Denver."

Dad had taken a job as an engineer on the trains, so he and his family could ride for free. That fall, when it was almost time for school to start, the family packed their suitcases and an old trunk from Grandma Franklin.

"We'll be there for the school year," Dad said. "That will give Mom plenty of time to see some doctors. Then we will plan to come home in the summer."

Only Tom, Joe, and Joan would be moving to Denver with their parents. Bill was married now and had a family of his own. Patsy had married in 1947, and Carol was engaged to be married in September. She had a wedding to plan, so she would not be coming along. She would live at Patsy's house until her wedding, at which point the family would come back by train.

Tom was beginning to doubt if God actually answered prayer. Yes, God had sent them a broom and had awakened Grandpa to pray for Bob. But He had let Opal die. And now Mom was sick and not getting better.

God had seemed very real on the night Bob and Lois met Opal. But in Tom's mind the true test was not whether God was real or not. It was whether God would heal his mother.

chapter nine

The Graduate with a Car

1952

"I KE WINS IN LANDSLIDE," Tom read.

After General Eisenhower had returned from the war, the country had given him the affectionate nickname of Ike. No one was surprised when he won the presidential election.

It was suppertime, the day after Election Day, in November of 1952. The Kirkmans were now living in Metropolis, Illinois. Mom was at the stove in their apartment, cooking potatoes for supper. Her face was smooth and clear today, not pinched with pain. She sang as she shook parsley from a glass jar into her hand and tossed it onto the boiled potatoes.

"Keep on the sunny side, always on the sunny side; keep on the sunny side of life!"

Still, the headaches had not disappeared. For a while, the bloodletting in Denver had seemed to help. To do the procedure, the doctors inserted a needle into her vein and removed blood from her circulatory system. Sometimes she got faint because of the loss of blood. Once she had fallen in the kitchen and hit her head on the counter. Another time the needle site had become an angry red, and the doctors had worried that she was getting an infection.

Worst of all, after a week or two, the headaches would come back. So Tom's father moved the family again, looking for different solutions and different opinions.

"Some medications for high blood pressure are being tested," each doctor said. "But nothing is safe yet for you to use."

The town of Metropolis had a doctor who was willing to take Mom as a patient, so they decided to move there. This was at the southern end of Illinois, just a few miles from where the Ohio River ran into the Mississippi.

Tom had gotten used to moving from place to place—to being a stranger in a new high school. Thankfully, he made friends easily, as he liked to talk and loved music and art. Academically, however, he found himself quite disinterested. He especially hated English class. He knew he was intelligent enough to get straight A's, but the constant moving had dimmed his enthusiasm for studying. His love of music and art directed him. He joined the glee club, the band, and shop class.

Every summer the Kirkmans moved home to Indiana when school dismissed, and Tom went back to his job at Grecco's. He had been promoted from dishwashing to pizza making, and he was particularly good at flipping the pizza crusts into the stretchy round discs that made Grecco's pizza the talk of Bedford. Tom could not wait to get back to Bedford again after graduation. He just wanted to do well enough in school to keep from getting kicked out before graduation. But then what?

The Army, maybe. Tom wanted to go to drafting school and learn to draw maps and blueprints. He was sure it would cost a lot of money to pay for the schooling. But if he did it through the Army, they would pay for it. Of course, he would need to train in the Army first.

"Tommy, have you done your English assignment?" Mom asked, setting a spoon on the stove and turning toward him. Joe was stretched out on the carpeted floor, filling out a timeline of the American Revolution while talking about the failed plays of the Metropolis High School quarterback, and what he, Joe, would have done had he been in possession of the ball.

"We didn't have homework today," Tom said shortly. He knew Mom was thinking of the 66% on his report card for the last grading period. She didn't seem to remember that he had gotten A's in band, physical education, the glee club, and shop class—advanced shop class, actually. And the shop class teacher, despite possessing the most unappetizing habit of wiping his dripping nose on his shop apron, was amazed at Tom's designing skill and had recently set him on the hardest project he could offer the seniors.

"Being good at music and art is great," Mom said. "But is that going to get you a good job? Your father didn't have a chance to learn, and here you are, not taking the chance you have. And look, you got a C in math too. Math and English are the most important subjects."

Tom told his mother he would try harder. But inside he felt that he was at an academic disadvantage by being moved from school to school. He could not muster the motivation to work harder, even though he knew he could succeed at English and math if he really tried. After all, his father had made it through life as a carpenter and train conductor with almost no education. Surely he could do the same with twice as much learning.

"Supper's ready," Mom said. She set the steaming bowl of boiled potatoes onto the table with a soft thud.

It was a chilly November night. After supper and a thorough discussion of the election, Joan pulled out the checkers board.

"Joe, will you play checkers with me tonight?" she begged.

"Can't," Joe said. "Homework."

"Tom, will you? Please?"

Tom knew exactly what would happen if he said no. Joan would move up to Mom. Since Mom seemed to be in good spirits, he took the opportunity to decline. But when Mom beat Joan, Tom agreed to play against Mom.

Tom was so glad to see Mom in good health that he didn't even mind when she beat him.

Tom did get a bit of fame that year. The 1952 Metropolis High School yearbook committee wrote an article called "Senior Prophecy." The article predicted life in 1964. In the story, a group of former Metropolis seniors took a spaceship to the moon. When they finally arrived, they were surprised to be greeted by their former classmates. September 5, 1964, was the day they left for the moon, with three years of supplies in their spaceship.

"Much to our surprise, a welcoming committee of our former classmates met us as the ship came to a halt," the article said. *"The committee consisted of the chairman, Robert Ridge; the Mayor of Lunaria, John Hopkins; Patsy Hemphill; Helen Carr; Shirley Bolen; and Tom Kirkman."*

Tom had not helped write the article. He avoided English assignments whenever possible. But he laughed when he read the moon story. Would a human being ever step on the moon? It seemed unlikely. But what a great thing it would be if someone did!

High school graduation photo of Tom

Tom graduated on the first day of June, despite dropping out of English class entirely before the second semester.

Back home in Avoca, Tom bought an old car, a 1940 Plymouth. It had once been a great car, but it was rusting and the alignment was shaky. Still, it cost money to purchase the vehicle, fill it with gasoline, and buy an occasional new tire. Tom took two jobs to help pay for it. He worked at Grecco's as always, but he also picked up a job at Tosti's Standard Service, where he pumped gas and washed car windows.

He took every chance he got to socialize. He spent a lot of time with a girl named Sharon who worked across the street from Grecco's at the Three Pigs Restaurant. Sharon radiated beauty, charm, and good cheer. She was younger than Tom and just ready for her junior year of high school, but that didn't bother Tom. He picked Sharon up every chance he got and took her out for a Coke or to watch the outdoor movie projected on the side of the courthouse. He cringed when his car coughed or stalled, but Sharon just kept on smiling, talking, and laughing. Tom was beginning to think she loved him as much as he loved her.

The only damper on Tom's socializing was his mother. Mom talked to him every time he left the house to go out to town. She didn't like the atmosphere of the crowds of youth around Bedford. Although Tom never smoked or drank alcohol at home, he suspected his mother knew he was doing it with others.

"Drink is what killed your grandfather Kirkman," Mom would say. "Tommy, be sure your sins will find you out. It never pays!"

"I know, Mom," Tom would say. "I won't party much longer. But tonight is a special night because Sharon has friends here, and I promised to take them all in my car."

Or it was her birthday. Or it was the Fourth of July. Or there was a new movie. There was always a reason to drink and carouse, and Tom lived it up.

His mother's words, however, made him so uncomfortable that he resorted to sneaking out whenever possible. He knew it would just make her sadder than before. But at least it got him out of having the conversation right before leaving. He got quite good at sneaking out when she was distracted with Joe or Joan.

One night Mom was sick with a headache. Tom turned the front door knob as quietly as possible. He told himself he was leaving quietly so he would not disturb her. The truth was, he could not endure an admonition from his mother. Not again. Not when she was sick.

He inched the door open. If he moved too fast, it would squeak. If he just made it to the car, he would achieve freedom for the night.

"Tommy!" a voice called from the bedroom.

Tom's heart sank. How could she know he was trying to sneak out when he had not made a sound? He thought of fleeing, pretending he had not heard her. But he could not do that. He sighed and turned back, dread slowing him down. He walked to the bedroom. The light bothered his mother's eyes when she had her fierce headaches, so the bedroom was darkened. "Yes, Mom?"

She was lying on her side, her tiny body swaddled with a sheet, and her eyes squinting with pain. Her voice whispered now, as if the assault of normal volume would be too much for her head to bear. "Are you going somewhere tonight, Tommy?"

For a wild moment, Tom considered lying. He could say he was going to work. Sometimes he worked Friday nights. But she knew his work schedule and would not be fooled. "Just down to the courthouse with Sharon, Mom. We'll get a milkshake or something." He hoped he could convince his mother that there would be no drinking.

"Think about Romans 8," she admonished. "Don't forget Romans 8."

Turmoil boiled inside him as he rushed out the front door, desperate to forget his mother's words. As much as he loved her, he did not want to think of Romans 8. He did not want to walk in the Spirit. Maybe someday.

Another thing that was hard on his mother was Tom's decision to join the Army. As much as he would miss home, Tom was looking forward to boot camp at Camp Chaffee, Arkansas. After boot camp, he planned to apply for drafting school, where he could learn how to draw maps and blueprints.

The only thing that made him want to stay at home was his mother's health. *But if I'm not respectful to my parents while living at home, what right do I have to live here?* he thought despondently.

It was time for him to go out and see the world. He wanted to do something out of the ordinary. He might not go to the moon, but he would find a way to make his mark in the world.

Part two

chapter ten

Making a Mark on the World

August 1954

"What on earth are you doing?"

Tom heard the voice over his shoulder, but he knew better than to turn immediately and ruin the artwork before him. Besides, he could tell from the absence of the "r" sound in *earth* that it was the Boston-reared second lieutenant.

As always, he added his own art whenever he wrote a letter. He wrote *"Dear Mother"* in Old English script that looked as though it had been lifted out of a seventeenth century Bible. He started each paragraph with another giant, ornate letter. Now he finished the tail of the "g" in *August* before he looked up. It was indeed Lieutenant Gray, the officer in charge of the sixteen men in Tom's platoon.

"Writing a letter to my mom," Tom answered.

Tom in the Army

In Arkansas the previous year, Tom had thrown himself into the task of learning to shoot accurately. He knew if he wanted to move on to the Army drafting school, he first needed to be an expert in shooting a rifle. So each time he missed, he had performed a self-evaluation of what he had done that might have caused the error. With the help of the officers in charge, Tom had gotten better and better until he had distinguished himself at Camp Chaffee. Since then he had moved to Fort Belvoir, Virginia, to attend drafting school. He had achieved his goal, passing the basic drafting school course with flying colors. Now he was continuing to take additional classes and had even been promoted to instructor in one of the classes.

"But it looks like . . . like the original Declaration of Independence!" Lieutenant Gray exclaimed as he gazed at Tom's lettering. "Hey, Walters, come look at this!"

Tom had spent a few days at home over the Fourth of July. He had spent time with Sharon and had a picnic with some friends at a local park. He had also had a good talk with his parents, assuring them that he had been staying out of trouble. Mom had been well and happy, but she had begged him to write more often.

"I'll try to do that," he had promised. And he was doing better.

For the sake of elbow room and a large flat surface, Tom often retreated to the lounge to write his letters. Usually no one paid any attention to him, but recently some of the men had started to notice what he was doing. Like today.

It was a sleepy Sunday in early August, sticky and hot. Tom felt a drop of sweat slithering down his back even though only his hand was working. He was aware of a small knot of men gathered around him, but he paid them no attention and continued inking the letters, free-handing the flourishes as he had done since grade school.

"How do you DO that?" one of the men asked.

Tom considered the question, his pen still in mid-air. "I just do," he finally said. "It's just the way I write."

It felt good to be admired, Tom had to admit. But he was still more interested in the contents of his letter than in the admiration of the men. Tom could not believe how much he missed his mother. Somehow, when he had first moved to Camp Chaffee, the excitement of independence had crowded out his homesickness. Now, having found his niche in drafting school, he missed home more. That meant he missed his family more, and most of all his friend, conscience, and confidante—Mom. Long distance phone calls were outside of his budget, so they wrote to each other.

He asked his mother how she was doing and what Joe and Joan were up to. He told her how much he enjoyed attending drafting school in Washington, D.C. He had endured Camp Chaffee in Arkansas as a necessary means to become a draftsman in the Army. But now that he was here in Fort Belvoir, nearly on the outskirts of Washington, D.C., Tom felt two distinct changes. First, as a student and part-time instructor at the Defense Mapping School, he was being trained for the job he loved above all others. Second, living just south of the glittering, bustling city of Washington, D.C., where President Eisenhower lived, he was no longer in hillbilly country.

"Mom," he wrote, *"Fort Belvoir is on a peninsula sticking out into the Potomac River. The Potomac is the same one that goes through Washington, D.C. Did I tell you the meaning of Belvoir? It's a French word meaning "beautiful view." This base used to be called Fort Humphreys, but President Roosevelt changed it to Fort Belvoir. We've been studying the old maps of the place, which were made when Colonel William Fairfax lived here in colonial days and named it 'beautiful view.'"*

Tom almost struck out his words about President Roosevelt. Somehow, every time he thought of him, he could not help thinking of the way he had died.

"Speaking of colonels," Tom wrote hurriedly before he could think of the cerebral hemorrhage that had killed the former president, *"I met Colonel Robert*

Schulz the second day after I arrived. I was admiring a wooden model of the base when he walked by. Well, Colonel Schulz enjoys woodworking immensely, and since I do as well, we had a pleasant chat. You know that Schulz is an aide to President Eisenhower. But Eisenhower is in Denver right now, so Schulz is over here at Fort Belvoir much more often. We also got on the topic of train engines. He was personable despite our differences in rank."

"I see!" Tom heard a voice like a trumpet behind him.

He turned around. It was Colonel Schulz, military aide to President Eisenhower.

A wave of shock ran through Tom as he struggled to rise. He blushed from his neck to his thickly curled head, hoping Colonel Schulz had not looked over his shoulder. Could he have seen his own name in Tom's letter? What on earth was Schulz doing here again?

"I just happened to be passing through when I heard the men remarking about your work. Bring your artwork to my office. I would like to speak to you."

Colonel Schulz settled into his office chair, leaning back comfortably. Tom tried to keep from gaping at the eagle on the edge of his shoulder strap. Lieutenants and majors did not wear eagles. Eagles, symbolic of great heights, were only worn on the lapels of colonels. If a colonel rose even higher to the rank of general, he wore stars.

Tom thought the colonel looked like a fine piece of woodwork himself, as if he had been neatly sanded and varnished. The brass buttons marched up the front of his navy blue coat like so many drawer knobs. The colonel used his hand to sand the sparse mustache on his upper lip as he sat at his desk. It was a small English mustache, parted in the middle and trimmed closely.

He was sparing with his smiles as military men often were, but Tom sensed that he was a pleasant man.

"May I see that letter?" he asked, his voice resonate and deep. "Or is it private?"

Thankfully, the part about Colonel Schulz was on the second page. Tom handed Schulz the first page, which in any case was the best sample of his work.

The colonel held the letter in his left hand, smoothing and sanding his mustache with his right. He glanced over it for about thirty seconds before turning it face down on the desk.

"So winning an award in sharpshooting isn't enough for you?" Colonel Schulz asked, smiling at Tom with his eyes. "You need to have other talents as well?"

Tom blushed but said nothing. Clearly, Colonel Schulz had pulled his file.

"I would like to move you to the White House," the colonel said.

Tom took a deep breath and stared back at Schulz. Had the hot August sun been getting to his head? Had Colonel Schulz just said what he thought he heard? Surely not.

"Sir, did you say the White House? Where President Eisenhower lives?"

As if there were multiple buildings called the White House, Tom thought stupidly.

"Yes. I need assistance in my office in the East Wing in a variety of capacities. Besides, I think there is a shortage of personnel in the calligraphy department. In addition, the White House budget is limited, and military men don't cost the government extra money." The colonel didn't exactly smile, but his lips did curve a bit under the mustache. "What do you say?"

"I would be honored," Tom said. "However, I do immensely enjoy my drafting school classes. Is that something I could continue?"

"I believe that could be arranged," the colonel said. "Though you might not be able to continue at the same pace you could otherwise. I admire your ambition."

Tom kept a calm face.

"Sure," he said. "I'm happy to try it. When do I begin?"

"As you probably know," Colonel Schulz said, "the President is out of town presently. It would be a great time to introduce you to my office staff and the other calligraphers and get you settled. Let me take you over next Monday, before I leave to join the President. You will have to do a polygraph test first, which I will arrange here at Fort Belvoir."

Robert Schulz had made this statement with perfect calm, so Tom received it with perfect calm as well. But inside he was thinking, *Am I really going to the White House?*

"All right then, Kirkman," Colonel Schulz said. "I'll see you then."

Tom slipped out. The August afternoon had merged into evening and it was much cooler. Tom wanted desperately to finish his letter and add a new page to it, but first he had to visit the library on the drafting school campus beside the map room. Thankfully, the library was open and he went directly to the reference section. He pulled a dictionary off the shelf and flipped the pages to the letter "C."

Calligrapher. "A professional copyist or engrosser. One who practices the art of calligraphy."

And below.

Calligraphy. "Artistic, stylized, or elegant handwriting or lettering."

Pleased, Tom closed the dictionary.

It sounded like a good job to have volunteered for.

He sat down, right there in the library, and continued his letter:

"Since I began this letter, I had another conversation with Colonel Schulz. Mom, you won't believe this. I'm going to work at the White House!"

He did not ask her how she was feeling. He did not ask if her headaches had been bad lately. He did not ask if she had found a cure for her high blood pressure.

To those questions, he did not want to hear the answers.

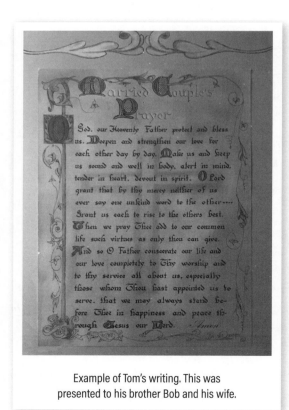

Example of Tom's writing. This was
presented to his brother Bob and his wife.

chapter eleven

The White House

1954

"What is your full name?" the uniformed officer asked Tom.

Tom felt like squirming inside his gear, but he answered calmly, "Thomas Ellsworth Kirkman."

The blood pressure cuff on his arm inflated and deflated. The patches on his chest, connected to wires, rose and fell as he breathed. He felt a sticky probe on his forehead. He couldn't remember if it measured temperature or perspiration or both.

"What is your date of birth?"

"November 23, 1934."

"Have you ever owned a car?"

Tom swallowed, hoping a swallow didn't register as a lie.

"Yes."

"What kind of car did you own?"

"A dilapidated 1940 Plymouth."

The uniformed man permitted himself a faint smile.

"Have you ever cheated on a test?"

"Yes," Tom said. "In junior high school."

"Did you ever have a pet?"

A sick feeling hit Tom's stomach as he thought of the lurch of his neighbor's car as it hit his old friend Tony.

"Yes," he said. "A black and white shepherd dog named Tony."

"Have you ever stolen anything from anyone?"

The uniformed man had explained the polygraph test to Tom. Inconsequential questions would come interspersed with questions about crimes or misdeeds. The basic questions about name and birth gave the tester a baseline for evaluating Tom's responses to all other questions.

"No, I have not," Tom said, after a short reflection. He could remember nothing.

"Have you ever killed anyone?"

"No."

"Have you ever sent a threatening letter to anyone?"

"No."

After about fifteen minutes of questioning and checking boxes, the uniformed man put down his pen.

"I think that is sufficient," he said, loosening Tom's blood pressure cuff. "What went through your mind when I asked you about having a pet?"

Why does he have to bring that up again? "I was in the vehicle that killed my dog," Tom said. "It's a disturbing memory."

The uniformed man nodded. "I'm sorry about that," he said. "Okay, I will get these results to Colonel Schulz. I don't see a problem, but I'm not the final authority. So don't go by my word."

Apparently, Colonel Schulz approved the polygraph results as well. No cancellation came for Tom's White House appointment.

Tom had sold his 1940 Plymouth and had no vehicle at present. He hitchhiked or took public transportation, and in the city that worked fine. He took a bus to the White House on the appointed day.

The glassy surface of the Potomac River blinked at Tom through the roadside trees. Before he realized they had come so far, the bus motored over the Potomac on the Arlington Memorial Bridge and circled around the stately pillars of the Lincoln Memorial. Farther away, Tom saw the Washington Monument, slender and tall, pointing to the sky. Tom knew the great Capitol dome where the lawmaking bodies of the United States met to argue and plan must be just beyond.

As the bus turned east on Constitution Avenue, Tom watched the green lawns outside his window. He noticed a fountain bubbling in the middle of a fenced lawn. Behind the fountain, pillars marked the middle portion of an elegant building.

I'm here! Tom realized. He was looking at the south side of the White House. The bus pulled on around to the north side and came to a stop on Pennsylvania Avenue.

"Lafayette Square and the White House!" a voice announced.

A small crowd of tourists exited the bus. Tom got off with them, feeling immensely important. He was not a tourist.

Tom felt his importance fading as he tried to determine which gate to approach to enter the East Wing. Finally he found the right one. He showed his military ID. The White House Police officer made a notation in his book, as if Tom was listed as an expected visitor. He waved Tom up the steps to the pillared entrance of the East Wing.

Tom felt like a person he didn't know. Could this be real? Was he actually entering the White House, the most famous house in America?

Robert Schulz met him in the lobby of the East Wing and took him to his own office. Typewriters clacked and the room smelled strongly of coffee. Tom took in the colonel's desk and the awards and certificates on the wall behind his desk. Tom couldn't help but notice the similarities between Robert Schulz and his desk. Both were proper and square and neatly attired with the necessary functional accessories and a few military decorations.

There were four other desks in the room, each with a typewriter at the ready. Two of the desks were occupied by secretaries, both of whom looked up and smiled when Tom and the colonel entered. Robert Schulz introduced them as Millie and Barbara. Then he pointed to a chair beside his desk.

Schulz reviewed some of Tom's expected duties. "You and another assistant will always drive to the post office to get the mail from the Boss's personal box first thing in the morning."

"Do you mean the President's personal box?" Tom asked.

"Ah. Pardon my term. Yes. After that comes the most important task of the day." Robert Schulz sanded his mustache. Tom could see that he was expected to ask what this important task might be, so he did.

"Making sure there is coffee made by the time I return from talking to the Boss," Schulz said.

"We will get along well in that regard," Tom smiled. "In my family, coffee is called the Kirkman curse."

Schulz chuckled appreciatively.

"Every day I wait outside the President's door while he eats his breakfast. Usually I read the newspaper while waiting. Then, when he's ready, I walk with him over to the Oval Office. It's at that time that he often tells me about some errand to run, or something he wants me to take care of. Often, if my schedule is already full, I will send someone else after the errand, depending what it is."

Schulz explained the general layout of the White House. The main residence with the tall pillars front and back appeared to be two stories high because of the placement of the windows. It actually contained four—the Ground Floor, the First Floor, the Second Floor, and the Third Floor. There were also two basements. In the main building, state dinners and receptions occurred on the First Floor, also called the State Floor. The President and his family lived on the Second Floor. Guests often stayed on the top floor. The calligraphers carved out a piece of office space in the basement.

"All right, Tom, let's get you down to the calligraphers," Schulz said. "But I did want you to see this room, because I will be requesting your help from time to time. We will check in with the Usher's Office first. Even though technically we are not White House staff, I would like to introduce you.

"When the President is not here, there is much less need for care with our route," Schulz confided as they rushed down a hall. They turned right and headed down a long corridor with large glass windows looking out onto a green lawn. "This hallway is the East Colonnade and connects us to the main residence. As I was saying, if the Boss is here, everyone in the house has to be aware of where he is and where his guests are, so we don't interrupt or disturb him."

"How is that possible?"

"Well, the ushers and Secret Service men have a series of buttons and bells. When the President enters the main residence, the bell rings three times. In the chief usher's room—you'll see it in a moment—there's a panel that lights up the President's location. It's run by buttons throughout the house that any of the staff can press to alert us to where he is. But beyond that, I believe they just develop this sixth sense for where he is at all times. Most presidents, as I understand, have a reliable routine."

"I believe Eisenhower is a man of routine," Tom said, finding that his voice still did work.

"Without a doubt," Schulz continued. "He's up at six. Then he usually has a few strokes of golf. Sergeant Moaney, his right-hand man, goes out with him to recover the golf balls. After that, he has breakfast with the morning paper, unless he has breakfast guests, and then we walk over to the Oval Office. He likes a short break for painting in the afternoon."

"Painting?"

"Oh yes, he loves it. It's a relaxation hobby he picked up a few years ago. Winston Churchill paints too, and they are friends. I'm not an artistic man myself; that's why I brought you on board. But the President doesn't enjoy the sketching part. He loves colors and enjoys mixing them to try to find the perfect shade for his sceneries. But he feels that sketching is a bore. One of my jobs is to find people who will help him with the sketches. Oh, he does sketching himself too, but if he can have someone else do that part, he's happy. And when the President is happy, we're all happy.

"Since the President is not here, I'm going to take you over to the West Wing for a quick tour. We won't go into the Oval Office, but I want you to get a feel for the White House. This is the Visitors' Foyer, since visitors usually come this way."

They had reached the end of the East Colonnade. Tom tried to soak in his surroundings as they rushed across the tiled floor. He saw huge portraits in thick, carved frames. Palmlike plants stood on the edges of the room in pots. They moved through a door into the long Center Hall of the ground floor, with arches that met like a dome above their heads.

"We are walking on the ground floor under the main residence now," Colonel Schulz said.

Tom had seen the long domed hall in photographs. And right now he felt as if he were living in a book too, rather than in reality.

Colonel Schulz did not pause, but pointed out rooms as he walked. "There's the Map Room," he said.

"That's where they had all those huge maps laid out during World War II to keep track of General Eisenhower in Europe. The calligraphers work in the basement, so you'll go down those steps to get there. This room is the office of Dr. Snyder, the President's personal physician. Of course, he travels with the President and is in Denver currently."

A woman dressed in a nurse's uniform stepped from the door of the Doctor's Office. Colonel Schulz exchanged a good morning with her and continued down the hall.

They went through a door into the Palm Room, filled with potted plants, then through another door. Now they were walking down a long open-air colonnade lined with pillars.

"This is the Rose Garden off to the left," Colonel Schulz said quickly, "as you probably know. And the round part of the building ahead is the Boss's Oval Office."

After a quick and confusing walk through the maze of the West Wing, Colonel Schulz and Tom retraced their steps.

Tom felt as though he were riding a train with unfamiliar scenery whipping past him. Beside a room marked "Refrigeration," Schulz turned and ascended a flight of stairs.

"Colonel Schulz," said a voice from inside the heavy wooden door of the Usher's Office.

"Mr. Crim, good morning," the colonel replied. "And Mr. West, meet my new assistant, Thomas Kirkman. He'll be working in the Calligraphy Office with Mr. Tolley and Mr. Fox."

Tom looked at the two men in question. Mr. Crim was a small, balding man with thick, well-trimmed eyebrows arching like rainbows over his wide, all-knowing eyes. Mr. West, a younger man, smiled at Tom. Both men stuck out their hands.

"Pleased to meet you," Mr. West said. "Things are quiet from a social standpoint right now with the President and Mrs. Eisenhower out of town. But we still always have a good deal of activity going on here in the mansion."

Tom took in the panel of buttons and buzzers that recorded the activity of the President. He saw a red hardcover book with gold lettering and striping labeled "Daily Reminders 1954."

"One hundred and thirty-two rooms," Mr. Crim said with solemnity. "It's a small village here."

"These men run the White House," Colonel Schulz explained as they began descending the stairs again. "Mr. Crim is immensely proper. Mr. West is younger and more fun."

"Colonel Schulz!"

They turned to see Mr. West calling from the top of the stairs.

"We've just received a phone call from the President. He wishes to speak to you."

chapter twelve

The Calligraphy Office

Colonel Schulz transformed, his wooden posture evaporating. He took the stairs two at a time, back up to the office. Tom hesitated for a second, then followed.

Mr. West gestured to a spot outside the office where Tom could wait. Mr. West's hair swept off his forehead as if he had just stepped out of a heavy windstorm.

"Got to be careful about appearing to listen in around here," he confided with a wink. "But the colonel would not have brought you here if he didn't trust you. So I'm not a bit worried. Also, allow me to retract what I said about the President's affairs being 'quiet' right now. I should have known better than to use that word."

The colonel reappeared a few minutes later, still in a hurry.

"Well, Tom, I need to take care of a few things," he said. "I'm going to drop you off down in the basement."

"Of course," Tom said. His mind reeled as they headed back down the stairs and then continued down the next flight into the basement. How would he ever grow comfortable here? How could he ever find his way around the 132 rooms of the huge house? How could he remember the appropriate etiquette? He couldn't wait to write home to Mom.

"I appreciate you not asking what the President wanted," the colonel said. "As you might imagine, privacy is of the utmost importance here. It is also critical that one's role not be abused. Not long ago, one of the military aides who helps with state dinners got stopped by a police officer. He was wearing a White House dress uniform and had the audacity to tell the police officer that he worked in the White House and didn't deserve a citation. Unacceptable, Tom. Unacceptable. We've changed procedures here now. The aides wear their uniforms only when they are here."

"I see," Tom said.

"You know something interesting?" continued Schulz. "Mamie Eisenhower actually keeps track of all the birthdays of the White House staff and the President's close assistants like myself. I had forgotten, but I just turned forty-seven last week and she sent me a birthday card from Denver."

"How nice!"

Tom heard himself blurting out two-word clichés. The circuits of his mind were so overwhelmed that he could not keep up with what he was hearing, much less provide intelligent replies. They burst out of the stairway and into the office of the calligraphers.

"Adrian B. Tolley," Colonel Schulz announced. "Mr. Tolley is our expert calligrapher who has been with the office since 1919. What does that make it now, Mr. Tolley, thirty-five years?"

A man with a high forehead and large round glasses was bent over the slanted top of a writing desk. He did not look up immediately, clearly intent on finishing his artwork. Tom felt instant solidarity with this man. With a final flourish, Mr. Tolley slowly put down his wooden penholder and looked around from behind the upright shelving of a wooden desk. From below a head of stately gray hair, steady eyes looked out at Tom. Deliberately, the man rose. His right hand methodically reached out and took Tom's hand.

"I believe it is about thirty-five years now," Mr. Tolley said. He pronounced each word as if he were engraving it on Bedford stone. Tom was reminded of Mr. Crim, the chief usher. "And is this the assistant you spoke of, Colonel?"

"It is," Colonel Schulz said. "Over here, Tom, is Sandford Fox."

"Sandy, if you please," said a much younger man. He leaped up from his seat with a wide smile. He was a short man, but his grip was powerful. He couldn't have been older than his mid-thirties, but Tom saw that his hair was nearly half white already.

"The first thing to note about this office," Mr. Tolley said with perfect gravity, "is that people become gray-haired down here."

Sandy threw back his head and laughed. "Perhaps, Kirkman," he said, "your assistance will relieve our stress."

"Please call me Tom."

"The winter social season approaches," Mr. Tolley said. "Thomas, you may be surprised to know we are working on Christmas."

"I have some business to complete," Colonel Schulz said. "I will leave you here for the rest of the day, Tom."

Sandy Fox pulled a chair forward for Tom.

"Don't mind my pipe," he said. "I never smoke while working on a project, of course. So, since I'm going to be showing you a number of tools, I think I'll have a pull." He reached into a drawer for a tin of tobacco. The tin brought up a shower of miscellaneous business cards and pen nibs.

Around the stem of his pipe, Sandy explained that the Calligraphy Office was a division of the Social Entertainments Office. All invitations, menus, place cards, and certificates emerged from their hands. They worked with the social secretary, with the First Lady herself, and with the butlers, florists, and chefs. As he talked, Sandy pulled samples of work from the wooden slots in the upright back of his desk.

"Have you been a calligrapher long?" Sandy suddenly asked. He pulled the pipe from his mouth and reached for a mahogany-colored wooden case with ornate silver hinges.

Tom considered this question. He decided against telling the story of his library visit last week. It didn't seem necessary to confess that he had only recently learned the meaning of the word.

"Well," he said, "I guess I have no formal training or official tools. I've just always done decorative writing in letters, on school projects, for greeting cards . . . that kind of thing." Tom suddenly felt foolish. How could he be here in the White House Calligraphy Office with such a dismal résumé?

"Never mind, we even take people with no experience at all when we're desperate," Sandy said. He talked just as quickly as Mr. Tolley talked slowly.

"Why do you think I took Sandford on?" Mr. Tolley inserted as he lifted a cream-colored invitation from his drawing board into one of the wooden slots.

Mr. Tolley didn't crack a smile, but Sandy burst out laughing, so Tom concluded it was a joke and joined in the humor.

All afternoon, Sandy talked and smoked and showed Tom around the office. He showed Tom twenty-eight different penholders and brushes and countless metal nibs. Mr. Tolley carved out occasional sarcastic comments, and Sandy laughed. By late afternoon, Tom had so advanced in confidence that he didn't need to wait to see whether Sandy was laughing or not before he joined in.

Then Sandy sent Tom to Adrian Tolley for a writing lesson.

"The different writing styles are called *hands,*" Mr. Tolley said with authority. "NOT fonts or styles or scripts."

He showed Tom how to draw light pencil lines on a blank sheet of paper as a guide. He demonstrated a dozen different hands. Mr. Tolley's pen worked miracles. Letters of all shapes and characters emerged from his hand. Squat Roman or Celtic characters followed flowery cursive letters with ornate tails. Tom noticed that he had filled only half of a broad white sheet of paper.

"Shall I try my hand at it?" Tom asked, pleased at his mild pun.

Mr. Tolley looked up gravely and caught the eye of Sandy Fox. "I fear, Sandford, we have gotten ourselves a pun maker."

"I don't know if we can hand-le it," Sandy said, his bright eyes dancing.

This time, even Adrian Tolley's lips parted, although just a slit.

"In answer to your question, Thomas," Mr. Tolley said, "Yes. Copy what I have done exactly, and let us see how you do."

Sensing a test, Tom sat down nervously at an empty desk. Using the penholders and nibs that Mr. Tolley had used, he did his best to imitate Tolley's work. He held his hand the way Mr. Tolley had told him to hold it. He put his feet flat on the floor. But he could not get it right. Not one of the fonts he tried looked identical to those of Mr. Tolley.

Tom put down the penholder and beheld the sheet with gloom. His eyes moved back and forth from Adrian Tolley's side of the paper to his own side. For all he knew, he had made a list of mistakes that stretched from the East Wing to the West Wing. He sighed and turned around to look for his teacher. To his astonishment, he found both men standing behind him, looking at his work. Tom sighed again and hung his head. He waited for one of them to escort him to the door.

"Well, Sandford," Mr. Tolley intoned into the marble stillness, "Colonel Schulz is right. I do believe we have a natural."

"I concur," Sandy said. "I didn't trust the colonel on this matter, because he's always saying he's a businessman. But I was wrong. Tom, you will be an old hand at it soon."

Tom was so overcome with shock that he failed to hear the pun that Sandy extended from the previous conversation. Tom was looking up at Mr. Tolley's face to see if he could detect sarcasm. But his face was as still and stately as marble. Tom saw a look of genuine appreciation there. Yes, he saw it on both of their faces. Or perhaps it was relief that their training period would be less painful than they had anticipated.

"But . . ." Tom looked again at the paper. "Look at the length of my tail on this G compared to yours. And the thickness of the ink in this font is not at all identical to yours. It's all wrong."

"HAND," Mr. Tolley scolded. "Not font. And, Thomas, you don't need to show me your mistakes. I see them."

"The thing that matters," Sandy offered, "is that you see them too. Easily overcome with a bit of practice, my boy. Easily overcome."

That night, in his barracks at Fort Belvoir, Tom lay on his back and reflected over his eventful day. *I have a job at the White House. Can it really be true?*

Oh, his mother would be so interested and so full of questions. Maybe even the beautiful Sharon would take him more seriously.

"Colonel Schulz," Tom said the next day, "I was planning to visit my home over Labor Day. Is that still possible with my new job?"

"Not a problem," the colonel said. "Just be back by Tuesday morning. It's September slowdown around here anyway. I'll be heading to Denver, and I'll give you the rest of the time until the President returns to learn the trade of calligraphy."

A hopeful thought emerged as Tom contemplated his new job at the White House. *The President has a private physician. Could this man know more than other doctors about the best treatments for high blood pressure?*

Perhaps God had brought him to the White House to save his mother.

chapter thirteen

A Visit Home

Tom hitchhiked to Bedford, arriving in good spirits the Friday evening before Labor Day. He said hello to his mother and took a quick shower at home, then hurried off to the town square. It was a beautiful night. The spirit of a coming long weekend lay over the limestone churches and houses of Bedford like a curtain of light. Laughter sounded over fences. Barbecue smells wafted from backyard grills.

Tom went straight to the Three Pigs Restaurant, where he found Sharon and a group of friends, most of them smoking around a back table. They welcomed him with open arms and passed him a cigarette.

"How is Fort Belvoir, Tom?" Sharon asked.

"It's great!" he said. "I'm signed up for drafting classes in the evening. And I just got asked to help with calligraphy at the White House."

"At the White House?!" everyone exclaimed.

Tom took a pull on his cigarette, trying to appear casual, even though he found the announcement exhilarating.

"What's calligraphy?" someone asked.

Tom shook a bit of ash into the ashtray in the middle of the table and looked at the questioner through the curls of smoke. "Well, you could do what I did and look up the word in the dictionary. After I agreed to take the job!"

The group screamed with laughter.

"It's that fancy writing," a young blond girl said. "You know, like they use to write diplomas."

"Right," Tom acknowledged. "In the White House, it's certificates and invitations and menus and—"

"Do you mean you've been to the White House?" Sharon asked, awe filling her eyes.

"Yes, just a few times so far," Tom said. He decided against giving too much information. He did want to impress Sharon and her friends, but he knew he had to maintain a certain amount of privacy when he worked in such an important place.

He had suspected that his new job might catch the ears and eyes of the girls, and he was right. Sharon gladly agreed to eat pizza with him at Grecco's the next night.

At Grecco's, Tom and Sharon ordered a pizza. Billy brought it to the table himself, because Tom asked him to.

"Pizz-za," Billy said proudly. The waitress helped him slide it onto the wire pizza stand.

Tom and Sharon laughed and talked. They grew serious and discussed their future. Sharon had another year of high school, and Tom was busy with his work. At this point, there was nothing to do but write letters and try to see each other as often as possible.

Before they left, Billy came back to their table. From his jeans pocket he produced a small plastic object, concealing it in his sauce-encrusted hands.

"Horrsse," he said, presenting it to Sharon.

It was a small plastic horse, about half the size of the yellow one.

"Thank you, Billy," Sharon said.

Tom gave Billy a wide smile.

All too soon it was Sunday evening, Tom's last evening in Indiana. It was bitter-sweet. He knew he wouldn't be able to come home again soon. At the same time, he anticipated getting back to Washington and his exciting new life. Tom spent most of Sunday afternoon with Sharon's family. Sharon's mom was a Sunday school teacher, and Tom felt glad that she was just as God-fearing as his own mother. He was beginning to feel sure that he and Sharon were meant for each other.

In the evening, Tom hurried back to his parents' home. What fun it was to lounge on the old couches with Joe and Joan, under the watchful eye of Grandma Franklin's glass vase. How refreshing to see his father in the old familiar spot on his recliner, setting down his newspaper and taking up his guitar. And best of all, Mom sat in her rocking chair, peaceful and pain-free.

"Well, Tommy," Mom said, "I can't believe you need to leave again so soon! We must have a little music. I was hoping Patsy and her family would be over tonight, but apparently they had other plans."

She had barely said this when a knock sounded on the door. Patsy entered, alone.

"I sent the children to bed," she said, "but I couldn't go to bed myself with-out coming to see Tommy before he leaves! Will so nicely said he would stay with them. Are you all about to sing? Oh, this is wonderful! But let me talk to Tommy for a second."

Patsy and Mom were the only two people in the world who still called him Tommy. Patsy seated herself beside Tom on the couch and patted his head as if he were a child.

"Tommy, you have to tell me more about this business of working in the White House. Whatever is that about?"

Patsy listened with interest as Tom told her the details. "And do you eat at the White House too? What does Mamie really look like when you see her up close?"

"There is a staff cafeteria in the basement," Tom said, smiling at all her ques-tions. "And a dining lounge in the West Wing. Mamie has been in Denver with the President, and I haven't seen her yet. I don't know if I'll ever see her."

Patsy could have talked on and on about herself and her children, but she made Tom feel like he was the most important person in the world. She gave him her full attention.

"Well," Mom said from her rocking chair, her voice musical and soft, "are you two going to talk all night, or are we going to sing?"

Dad had been strumming his guitar and now began to play in earnest. Tom jumped up and ran to the piano. "Praise the Lord! Praise the Lord! Let the earth hear His voice!"

The house rang with the song, Tom's heart felt as if it would burst. Sharon loved him. Mom felt well. And he had a job in the White House!

"I say, Tom, I didn't remember you enjoyed the piano that much," Joe said. "You're playing like a professional!"

"He's in love," Joan said smartly from the other side of the piano. "He's just thinking *Sharon, Sharon, Sharon!*"

"And he has a fun new job in the White House," Patsy added. "Our Tommy is finding his place in the world!"

"And he has a beautiful mother with the most beautiful voice in Indiana," said their father, jumping up to his full impressive height and catching Mom up in his arms of steel. Tom struck up a tune, and Mom and Dad swayed and stepped around the room in time to the music. When the music picked up its tempo and they moved faster, the children began to clap. They whirled faster and faster until the song suddenly ended with a crash of Tom's hands on the keys. Dad dropped Mom into her chair, both of them laughing and panting. The four children clapped together and were still clapping when the front door opened again.

"It's Bill!" Tom cried. "Hey, brother, what brings you?"

"Have to see my little brother off, now, don't I?" Bill said with his drawl. "Oh, come on, did I really just miss the music?"

"Oh no, we are going to sing all night!" Mom said cheerfully.

"Well, I'll pour myself a cup of coffee and join you," Bill said. "I was down at the hospital visiting a sick lady from church."

It wasn't hard for Tom to picture Bill visiting the sick. Bill studied Scripture and thought deeply, usually aided by quarts of coffee.

"Oh, there isn't any coffee!" Joan said.

Everyone looked at each other in amazement. How could a houseful of Kirkmans fail to brew a pot of coffee?

"I've got it. I've got it. Don't get up, Joan," Patsy said. She still loved to be in the kitchen. "I'll make some popcorn too, if you wish!"

"I won't take food tonight, thank you," Bill said. Although he didn't say so, his family suspected he was fasting for spiritual reasons as he had often done in the past.

The front door slammed again, and Bob and his wife and daughters burst in. Bob arrived like the firecracker he had always been. The entire family roared with laughter and cheered. Everyone local was now home, not by appointment, but because of their love for Tom. Carol was out of state with her new husband, who was an oil geologist.

It was hard for Tom to imagine Bob as a minister of the Gospel, but he was faithfully doing just that. Ever since that strange, miraculous appearing of Opal, Bob had been a servant of the Lord.

They sang late into the night. Bill slurped his coffee. Joan played with her nieces. Bob sang explosively. Mom's face shone in the lamplight, and tears glinted on her face. As they sang about the blood of Jesus and the hope of heaven, Tom felt the power of the music blending with the power of the words. But Tom wasn't ready to serve God and shook off the nagging feeling of conviction. He was still waiting to see if God would answer his prayer and heal his mother. Tonight, however, Mom was happy. She was radiant—overjoyed at having so many of her children under her roof again.

"Tommy, how are you doing with your social life at the White House?" Mom asked when everyone else had gone to bed or gone home.

"Oh, Mom, I'm just starting. I don't know. But I think I'll be too busy to get into trouble." He knew what she was hinting at. She imagined the city of Washington, D.C., to be a network of bars and brothels, and she wanted to hear that Tom kept a wide margin between himself and those streets. "I'm doing well, Mom. Really, I am. You don't need to worry. I only drink socially every now and then. And I'm going to drafting school classes at night, so I won't be out partying. Really, Mom, I won't."

Mom fingered the soft yarn of the afghan. It was wrapped around her petite body, like a robe. "But Tom, it's not enough to avoid bad things. Are you pursuing good things? Have you found a church to go to?"

Tom kept his mouth closed for a few moments. He knew if he answered lightly and confidently, his mother would know he was just answering to please her.

Instead, he answered slowly, after taking a slow pull at his cup of coffee, now cold.

"There are chapel services at Fort Belvoir on Sundays that people can attend if they desire. I don't make it every time though. But I'll try to do better, Mom, for your sake."

"Tommy, Tommy," Mom said softly. "Not for my sake! Oh, you know I'm so happy to see Bob and Bill serving the Lord as they are. But it's not for me that they serve God! And you don't have to be a minister like Bob to serve God. You need to serve Him for the sake of your own soul, Tommy—not for your mother's sake! Especially if you are thinking of marrying and starting a family." She pressed her lips together, and for a terrible second Tom was worried that his words had upset her and she was getting one of her headaches. But then her face relaxed. She had just been thinking.

But still, Tom had noticed that after her twirl around the room she had winced several times as she sat in her chair, breathing hard. For the rest of the evening, he had watched her closely. Would she suddenly bite her thin lips together and excuse herself from the room? Would she go to the kitchen to hide her pale face so no one would know she was in pain? If she did, the party would be over instantly, and the light would go out of the room.

What would happen if Mom left their circle permanently? If Mom died, the light would go out of Tommy's life. He could not stand to think of working in the White House without being able to write home to Mom and let her know how things were going. He could not imagine marrying Sharon and not having his mother at the wedding. He could not imagine having children and not being able to show them to his mother, to put them in her arms as Bob and Bill and Patsy had all done.

No, Mom must not die. He would put God on hold until he was sure his mother had been healed. Perhaps even now God was working through a scientist to come up with a medication to treat high blood pressure.

chapter fourteen

The Boss Returns

"The prime minister of Pakistan will be here for a luncheon the day after the President gets back from Denver," Adrian Tolley announced to everyone in the Calligraphy Office on the first Monday of October. "We will hit the ground running. Two days after that, on October 18, we have a dinner for the president of Liberia, and a few days later a stag luncheon." Mr. Tolley consulted the file in his hand. "On the twenty-eighth, we host the chancellor of Germany for a luncheon, followed by a dinner for the Queen Mother of England on November 4. The menus have been approved by Mamie, so we can begin working on them. Thomas, I would like you to work on the menu for the prime minister's luncheon. Sandford, please begin on the menu for the dinner for the president of Liberia. I will go check with the social secretary to see if we have a completed guest list yet."

"Assorted olives," Sandy said as he cheerfully arranged the tools of his trade. "Can't get by without our assorted olives, can we, Mrs. Ike? And since the guest of honor is from Liberia, we are serving sweet potatoes."

"So Mamie does all the menus?" Tom asked as he selected a blank page and picked up the menu for the luncheon.

"Oh, well, the chefs come up with them, but she approves them all. Way back in the early days, someone made the mistake of taking a menu to the President for his approval. Later, when Mamie saw it she wasn't very happy and told them that every menu in this house gets approved by her and her alone. Apparently, good old Ike isn't to be trusted with such important matters," Sandy chuckled.

"Have you met President Eisenhower?" Tom asked.

"Oh, yes, a few times at staff events. Great guy. Fantastic smile. They say he yells at people like crazy if they don't perform, but I've never heard that. You might see him a little more often if you are working with Colonel Schulz."

"I'm not sure what I'm doing yet," Tom said, "other than what I'm told to do."

"Hee-hee-hee-hee!" Sandy wheezed. His laugh was contagious, and Tom broke into laughter with him.

"Hee-hee-hee! Relax, brother, that's all any of us do who work in this place," Sandy managed.

"Seriously," Tom said, looking at the menu before him. "What is a demitasse?"

"You don't drink your coffee like that in Indiana?" Sandy asked. "Always thought that was a rather backwards state." He winked at Tom. "It's like a small cup of coffee. Usually with dessert."

"In Indiana we go big or go home," Tom said. "Especially with coffee." He picked up the cup of coffee beside him and took a long drink.

Thankfully, they had just gotten themselves down to business when Adrian Tolley marched back in with a sheaf of seating charts. Mr. Tolley had a sense of humor, but his frugal Italian heritage allowed little time for frivolity. Even the matching wallet-sized picture frames of his grandchildren were arranged on his desk with the precision of rows in a graveyard. Sandy, on the other hand, lived in a profusion of pipe tobacco, picture frames of various sizes, general goodwill, and a clock whose hands were right only twice a day.

Colonel Schulz had flown to Denver on September 2 to be with the President's entourage. The President would not be arriving back in the White House until October 15, about two weeks away. Tom wondered if he would meet the President in the near future. Mamie herself intrigued him. Mom and Patsy and Carol wanted to know everything about Mamie. Did she really sleep until noon every day? Did she always wear pink? Was it true that she could talk to dozens and dozens of guests, one after the other, and still think of cheerful things to say to them?

When the President and First Lady arrived on October 15, the entire character of the White House changed. Tom soon learned to understand the buzzer system, which sounded whenever the President walked into or out of the main part of the White House.

The social calendar burst to life, and Tom began to see how stressful the job of a White House staff member could be.

"Sandford!" Adrian Tolley's voice called one day, minutes before the guests were to arrive at the luncheon for the president of Liberia. "Quick! We need another nameplate for the luncheon. Somehow one of the guests was missed." Still puffing, he sat down in his chair.

"But isn't it starting at . . ." Tom began. Then his voice trailed away as his eyes followed Sandy, who had switched gears in an instant. Tom watched as he snatched up a blank name card and brushed aside his current project. He snatched the name from Mr. Tolley, placed it before him on the board, and with a smooth and steady hand made the card in seconds. He handed it to Mr. Tolley, then glanced at Tom.

"Come along, there are still a few minutes before it begins," Sandy said. "You've got to have a quick peek at the State Dining Room, Tom!"

Adrian Tolley raised one stately eyebrow, but Sandy grabbed Tom by the elbow.

"Hurry, we want to get there before they start!"

They flew up the stairs ahead of Mr. Tolley, all the way up to the Usher's

Office. From the Usher's Office they stepped out into the main entrance of the White House. Military personnel in dress uniform stood in formation among the pillars at the main entrance. The marine band was poised and ready to play. Tom shot a hasty glance at Sandy. Surely this was not allowed!

"I just took you this way so you could see," Sandy hissed at Tom. "We could have gone the back way, but you have to see this Entrance Hall when it's ready for guests."

They rushed from the Entrance Hall and took a right into the Cross Hall, which led into the State Dining Room. The chief butler, smoothing his tie in a hurried manner, appeared to be running through a mental checklist. Mr. Tolley rushed into the room with the nameplate and went confidently to the place setting that still lacked a name. Apparently the place setting itself had just been added, as several butlers were still putting the finishing touches on the arrangement of gold forks and carrying away a silverware box on a silver tray.

"Just a quick peek, and we'll be off," Sandy assured Tom.

What a small feeling to stand in that impressive high-ceilinged room! Taper candlesticks and yellow roses and snapdragons filled the centers of the tables. Long yellow curtains covered the high windows, pulled back by a window sash. Above the heavy fireplace mantle, a large scenery painting hung in a gold frame. A chandelier looked down over the tables, and more candlesticks were mounted on the walls.

All the presidents except George Washington have been here! Tom thought with awe.

"Here, this way," Sandy said. "We'll duck out through the Family Dining Room and then downstairs. Isn't that impressive, Tom?"

"It is," Tom said. "Amazing to see what we are part of."

After returning from Denver, Robert Schulz checked in on Tom. "I could use some dictation help in my office in the East Wing if you don't have enough to do in the Calligraphy Office," he said.

Tom did have enough to do, however. He had begun taking the only night drafting classes that were offered at Fort Belvoir. With a long commute by bus in the mornings and evenings, he often barely made it to his evening classes. He also struggled in making it to the White House by eight o'clock sharp when the Calligraphy Office opened for the day. He always went straight to the Army staff breakroom in the East Wing to get his coffee. Then he arrived, usually breathless, at the Calligraphy Office, a few minutes late.

"Thomas," Adrian Tolley said one morning, lifting his head from his paper and shooting Tom a solemn glance.

Tom had slid into his chair at exactly 8:08 by the wall clock, and he knew exactly what Mr. Tolley was about to say. Unlike Sandy's, Mr. Tolley's clock was in perfect working order at all times.

"Yes, sir?"

"Thomas, you have a job in the White House. If you are unable to make it to work on time, it will be necessary for us to find someone who can." Behind Mr. Tolley, the small white photo frames marched in perfect order across the shelf of his desk. Mr. Tolley's world was not one where anything suffered from lack of precision. Tom knew he would not be in that world much longer if he didn't improve.

"I'll reform my ways, sir," Tom said. He didn't bother making any excuses for himself. He knew that Mr. Tolley wanted military precision and that he, Tom, must improve.

When Mr. Tolley stepped out of the room, Sandy lifted his head and winked at Tom.

"That was me just a few years ago," he said. "You'll get it. But nope, he doesn't tolerate being late. I should have warned you about the mighty hand of the clock."

"I've been looking for an apartment close by," said Tom. "Hopefully I can find one soon."

"Do you know where I worked before I came here?" Sandy Fox asked. "Did I ever tell you?"

Tom studied the bright eyes of his superior, trying to recall. Sandy was such a happy-go-lucky man that Tom could not picture him anywhere else than where he was now, flitting from project to project around the White House.

"I worked for the CIA for six years," Sandy Fox said.

"You did?"

Sandy nodded. "Wasn't quite the job for me, and I wasn't sure what I thought of the judgment calls of Mr. Allen Dulles. But they do an important work all the same. And don't repeat what I said about Dulles just now." Tom had often heard of Allen Dulles, the director of the CIA.

Later that morning, Robert Schulz called for Tom to run a message from the East Wing to the Doctor's Office on the ground floor of the White House. Tom was always glad to take the long walk from wing to wing to break up the monotony of a day in his chair.

In the reception room of the Doctor's Office, a brisk medic took the envelope from Tom. She swallowed a bite of the cookie she was eating, thanked him, and snatched up a memo pad to record the note.

"I apologize," Tom said quietly. "But is Dr. Snyder in? There's something I've been wishing I could ask him. It's entirely of a personal nature."

The medic snapped down the memo pad and stared at Tom as if she were seeing him for the first time.

"You work with Colonel Schulz, correct?"

"Yes."

"Well, Dr. Snyder is out at a physician's luncheon currently," she said. "But I expect him back at three o'clock. He answers questions if he doesn't have any pressing matters. Here, would you like a cookie?" She reached for a plate on the desk beside her and Tom picked one up. It was still warm.

"I begged some out of the kitchen," she said in a confidential whisper.

"I'll stop back at three then," Tom said, relieved that she had not gotten upset.

At three, Tom returned. The medic, still nibbling on cookies, showed him back to Dr. Snyder's desk. She introduced them and then retreated, her heels clicking on the floor. She pulled the door shut behind her.

Dr. Snyder turned from his desk and the many shelves of medical books. He motioned to Tom to sit down. Tom found it difficult to take his eyes off the doctor's hair. It was swept up and back as if he had been in a high-speed chase. He had a long nose, a heavy jaw, and eyes that seemed to be hiding a joke.

"I do apologize," Tom began. "I just thought if you had a moment I would ask you about—uh—high blood pressure."

"Ah." Dr. Snyder glanced up at his bookshelves through the large round glasses propped on his nose. "A very sad problem with not too many good solutions yet. What can I help you with?"

"Well, I guess . . . my mother has suffered with this condition for many years. She gets terrible headaches and often has to stay in bed. That's bad enough, but then I've heard that high blood pressure eventually causes worse things—blindness, strokes, things like that. And I thought if anyone knew of the best treatments in modern medicine, perhaps it would be you."

"Hmmmm . . ." Dr. Snyder got to his feet. He went to the bookshelf and pulled off a book. He flipped through it, sighed, and sat back down. "I am not necessarily on the cutting edge of research," he said. His dark eyes still sparkled, but they had lost the hint of joking. "However, hypertension—high blood pressure—was one of the topics at our luncheon today. There are several medications that are being experimented with in trials. But nothing has proven itself yet. A lot of the therapies that have been tried, such as bloodletting, have almost as many risks as benefits."

"Yes, some doctors in Denver treated my mom with bloodletting," Tom offered.

"Oh, you are from Colorado?"

"No, but my dad worked on the trains, and since he had the opportunity of free travel, he took my mom all over the country searching for answers. It hasn't helped much though."

"I'm sorry, Mr. Kirkman. I wish I could pull a magic secret pill out of my drawer. Tell you what. If I hear of any promising new trial medications, I'll look you up. How old is your mother?"

"Forty-eight."

"Ah, yes. Dear me, that is very young. If I hear of anything, I'll be in touch.

You work with Schulz?"

"Uh, well, yes. I am also helping in the Calligraphy Office currently."

"Yes, yes. I'll be able to find you. Don't worry."

The next morning Tom forced himself out of bed early enough to catch the first bus. He arrived at the White House by 7:45 and made a leisurely trip to the coffee pot.

At 7:56 he walked through the door of the Calligraphy Office.

Adrian Tolley and Sandy were already there.

"Good morning, Thomas," Adrian Tolley said. Tom could not detect even the smallest indication of surprise or affirmation in the marble countenance of his boss.

They all got to work, as if no one had noticed that Tom had reformed his morning habits.

chapter fifteen

On Call

"Tom?" It was Colonel Schulz. "Can you slip over to the lobby in the West Wing this afternoon? I will be over there. You will have to let the calligraphers spare you for a moment. I have a couple of items that need attention and I think you are the person for them."

That afternoon Tom strode over to the West Wing at the appointed time. He walked swiftly past the Cabinet Room, past the office of the President's secretary, and through the corridor that went past the Oval Office. He had not yet met President Eisenhower, and he was eager to do so. But he did not want to appear overly eager. He knew the next door to the left housed a private dining room that President Eisenhower could use for business lunches or as a private study. He hurried on down the hall and turned into the West Wing Lobby.

Across the black and white blocks of tiled floor, Tom saw Colonel Schulz standing beside a lamp talking with a whiskered old man. A crowd of journalists also stood nearby, chatting with each other. Other journalists were rushing in and out of the room. Tom seated himself in an empty leather chair to stay out of the way. A few minutes later, the whiskered man moved on and Schulz turned to Tom.

"Follow me," he said.

They retraced Tom's steps out to the West Colonnade. It was a warm day for November, so they walked out into the Rose Garden. This was the first time Tom got a good view of the South Lawn. Colonel Schulz pointed out the putting green where President Eisenhower practiced his golf every morning with Sergeant Moaney.

"It's beautiful back here," Tom said.

"Even though I am not a gardener," Robert Schulz said, "I would have to agree. Now, Tom, we have a guest coming next week and I need you to help out."

"Ah, the chancellor of Germany?"

"No, I'm referring to the Queen Mother of England."

Tom swallowed. What could he have to do with the Queen Mother?

"Oh," Tom finally replied. "We are also preparing things for the dinner in her honor. We looked high and low, but no one could find the menu from the dinner when she was here in 1939. Finally Lillian, the seamstress, went home and found the menu in her stash of records."[1]

"Interesting!" Colonel Schulz said. "So what are we having? My wife and I don't go to many of the dinners, but we are invited to that one."

"Well, I remember the roast stuffed Long Island duckling," Tom said. "And cream of almond soup and whole-wheat fairy toast. You'll have to wait for the rest. But how does this involve me?"

"Well, it's just this," Colonel Schulz said. "The Queen Mother will be staying here at the White House for a few days, along with her group of staff. They will have the big dinner, and then afterwards President Eisenhower and Mamie will take photos with her. But neither Mamie nor Ike can

From the WHITE HOUSE *to the* AMISH

devote themselves to her attention for the entire time. I'm a man of business myself, and I have to stay at the beck and call of the President. There are a few people who can help entertain her, and of course she has her own personal maids with her. But most of the White House staff have their specific duties, and they can't just drop them and run."

"Right," Tom said.

"So the President mentioned this morning on his walk to the Oval Office that he wants someone to be on call at all times to attend to her in whatever capacity she wishes. Maybe she will need someone to take her and her maids on a walk through the garden while Mamie is busy. Secretary of State John Foster Dulles is planning to meet her at the airport, but maybe she will need some unofficial assistance when she returns to the airport. Things like that. We need someone like you who is young and energetic and can be trusted to protect the privacy of important people. So this is what I need you to do."

"Sure," Tom said. He felt a little like he had when he agreed to be a calligrapher without knowing what the word meant. But he really wasn't afraid of looking after an elderly lady, whether she was the mother of the Queen of England or anyone else. "I mean, as long as Mr. Tolley can spare me."

"I'll talk to him. At any rate, while you are on call for the Queen Mother, I'm going to show you something you can work on close to her quarters." Colonel Schulz turned out of the garden, and they walked briskly up the West Colonnade toward the main White House, through the Palm Room, and to the stairs leading to the Usher's Office. Instead of stopping on the first floor at the Usher's Office, Robert Schulz ran right on up to the second floor. Tom followed him, startled. He didn't think he was allowed to enter the family quarters of the President, but apparently it was okay if the President's right-hand man was taking him.

"Okay, Tom, this is something you'll like," the colonel said. "Right at the top of the stairs here is a small room that the Boss uses as his painting studio. I need you to sketch some scenes on canvas for him."

"Oh!" Tom said. It hadn't occurred to him that the President would have a specific room for this purpose. And never in his wildest dreams had he ever imagined he would be making sketches for the President of the United States.

"He's usually only up here in the afternoons. Generally he doesn't want anyone to be in this room when he is not here. But you can sketch here while you are on call for the Queen Mother and her staff."

"Okay," Tom said. He felt like a dump truck that had just been overloaded, but he tried to absorb the details of the colonel's instructions.

Into the small room they went. On an easel, where light fell in from the window, Tom saw a canvas with a sketch on it and the beginnings of a painting. He could see the rude outline of a barn and several trees.

"Here is where he does his painting," Schulz said, pointing to the easel. "You can see that he started a drawing here."

He went to a cupboard and opened it. "Here," he said, "are some extra canvases. And here, on these greeting cards, are some of the scenes Ike would like to paint next. Here is the artist's projection camera. We'll let the President use a few of your sketches and see how he likes them.

"But let me just say one thing. If you are ever sketching here and the Boss comes in to paint, stand at relaxed attention until he dismisses you or begins painting. Then go on with your work. He doesn't mind having someone to talk to while he works. Just don't talk to him unless he talks to you first. He even has the phone in this room disabled so no one disturbs him."

"Okay," Tom said again. He had once again been reduced to monosyllabic expressions.

"Tom, you have proved yourself to be a trustworthy and private person, or I would never ask you to do either of these tasks. But even with you, I must warn you of the obvious. The President's image must never suffer from any action of his staff. This means that he gets all the credit for everything, no matter who helps him."

"Yes, I understand," Tom said. He saw Robert Schulz taking on his wooden dresser personality.

"I can't begin to tell you how many people help prepare the speeches and dinners that the public sees as Eisenhower's work. For example, he has a television appearance tonight. The people will see only President Eisenhower. They do not see Ann Whitman at her desk, arranging his schedule so he can get to the cameras on time. They do not see the speechwriters that write down the ideas and edit out the Boss's clichés. They do not see the valet who makes sure Ike gets a shirt without wrinkles and a jacket without lint. They do not see the chef who prepares dinner and then has to do it again later because it got cold the first time. In the same way, these paintings are the President's handiwork, not yours."

"I understand completely," Tom said. Then with a smile he added, "I suppose President Eisenhower gets the credit for the beautiful calligraphy on the menus too."

Robert Schulz's lips parted in a rare wooden chuckle.

"If the time were ever right," he said, "it would be a treat to tell him that. He has told me that his penmanship in school didn't even resemble the English language. So I think he would enjoy the irony of being credited for your penmanship."

"Why, Robert, who do we have here?" a pleasant voice came through the doorway.

"Mrs. Eisenhower," Colonel Schulz said, "this is Tom Kirkman, my assistant. He has been working in the Calligraphy Office and picking up little jobs here and there. He's also in drafting school at night."

"A pleasure," Mamie said. "You penmanship people do such wonderful work. Now, are you married, Tom?"

"Uh, no," Tom stammered. He was somewhat tongue-tied at the unusual sensation of meeting a public figure he knew only from newspaper photos and television. He knew Mamie had been a strikingly beautiful and privileged child of a wealthy meatpacking father. Tom didn't think she was exactly beautiful now, but her eyes sparkled beneath her bangs, and her skirts swayed around her as if she were still a capricious teenager.

"Is there a lady in your life at all?"

"Well . . ."

"Oh, come now, what is her name?"

From the corner of his eye, Tom could see that Robert Schulz had allowed his lips to curve into a half smile. He seemed to be watching with enjoyment—although without surprise—the grilling Tom received from the President's wife.

"Well, she—I mean—we aren't engaged or anything, but I do have a friend whom I like to see back home. Her name is Sharon."

"Oh, what a lovely name! And where is home for you, Tom?"

"Bedford, Indiana. It's south of Indianapolis."

"Oh, that's so interesting!" the First Lady gushed. "I was born in Iowa. Even though we moved to Colorado later, I still think the Midwest is one of the nicest places in the world. Do give my love to Sharon when you speak to her again. Robert, do you know if Ike is in his office?"

"Yes, I believe he is. Shall I check with Ann?"

"Oh no, don't bother her. I will just wait and catch him before his speech tonight. So nice to meet you, Tom! And, Tom?"

"Yes, ma'am?"

"I have a particular aversion to footprints on my rugs and carpets. Please do not step on any if you can help it."

"I am good at jumping, ma'am!"

"Tee-hee, Tom, no jumping needed! Just make sure you respect the carpets."

Mamie was off as quickly as she had come.

"She really does take an interest in everyone," Tom said.

"Oh, yes, without doubt," Schulz agreed. "But we must prioritize the preservation of her carpets! At any rate, you now know your assignment. Perhaps the Queen Mother will not need your assistance. But we will have you on call all the same."

Tom squinted at the canvas before him. He didn't mind the sketching; it was actually relaxing. But he was slowed by the fear of doing shoddy work for the President of the United States. Everything took longer than if he had been doing it for himself. As he sketched the light lines, Tom thought about how much time was expended for important people by their assistants. For instance, here Tom stood, on the Army payroll, sketching landscape scenes that would very possibly never strike the President's fancy anyway. Yesterday, he had been closeted here in this room the whole day just to be on call for the Queen Mother of England. She had never called for him, and he didn't expect her to. Why would she need anyone when she had her own personal maids and servants with her?

He had been here, in the room above the North Portico, when the Queen Mother's limousine pulled up. He had caught a glimpse of her in her blue coat and dress and silver fox stole. A bank of cameramen focused on the President and First Lady and Vice President Nixon and his wife as they welcomed the Queen Mother. There had been the dinner in her honor on Thursday evening. Tom heard the Marine Band play "Hail to the Chief" when the Eisenhowers came down the stairs from the second floor with their guest.

Today, he knew, the President was back to his normal schedule. The Queen Mother planned to leave the next day, and Mamie had taken her downtown to the Smithsonian Institution. With any luck, Tom would also be back to his normal schedule soon.

He sighed. It didn't really matter. He was getting paid either way, whether he worked in the Calligraphy Office where they really needed him, or here in a small room above Pennsylvania Avenue, hidden from everyone else and doing nothing worthwhile. But he had to admit—he did enjoy preparing the sketches.

Since he was almost directly above the Usher's Office and close to the stairs that went down to the next floor, he could hear the *buzz-buzz* that sounded when Mamie entered the house and the single buzz when visitors arrived. The buzzes were critical to the entire staff, but especially to the doormen and ushers. The triple buzz was for the President himself. Tom could hear the buzzing beneath him as the important people came and went. He could picture the ushers, Mr. Crim and Mr. West, watching the arrows on their callboard, which showed the exact location of all the important people in the building. He could see them consulting their red appointment book, with its "President" schedule and "Mrs. Eisenhower" schedule. When he had first started working in the White House, Tom had jumped every time the buzzer sounded. He now left the buzzers to the ushers and the people who were concerned with them and focused on his own responsibilities.

"Hey, Tom. I thought I might find you here."

Robert Schulz stood in the doorway of the small room.

"Am I finished?" Tom asked.

"No," the colonel said with a dry smile. "In fact, I am going to ask you to stay late. The Eisenhowers are just planning an informal meal with the Queen Mother tonight. My wife and I are invited, and I would like you to stay as well."

Tom froze. His hand hung in the air, inches from the canvas. A wave of misgivings washed over him. *Eat with the President of the United States? And the Queen Mother of England?*

"I, uh, are you sure? I could just be over here sketching."

Robert Schulz laughed.

"No worries, Tom! It will be just an informal family affair, and I'm sure some of the Queen Mother's attendants will be there too. I want everyone to be familiar with your face in case we need your help with something tomorrow when they leave for the British embassy."

"Well . . ." Tom said. "Okay, if you're sure!"

"It's just the Boss cooking up his beef stew, Tom. You'll be all right. They won't give you three forks! I promise. Oh, and Mamie does not approve of slang, like the word *okay*. So do your best, my friend."

Tom felt relief wash over him. Apparently the colonel could read Tom's mind.

"Okay, where and when? Uh-oh, there I did it again."

Robert Schulz permitted himself an understanding smile.

"It'll be just around the corner in the West Sitting Hall. I'm going to go pick up Dottie, but I think the stew will be ready in about thirty minutes. You'll smell it when Moaney brings it up the stairs."

A few minutes after Schulz left to fetch his wife, the elevator door beside the stairs dinged. Tom smelled the meaty aroma of fresh stew and heard footsteps, but he concentrated on his canvas.

"I believe I should meet this artist myself," a firm voice said from the door. Tom looked up to see the warm smile of President Eisenhower.

chapter sixteen

Dinner with the Boss

For the second time in fifteen minutes, Tom panicked. What does a person do when he meets the President of the United States?

Tom put down his pencil with a shaking hand and stood at relaxed attention as Schulz had instructed him.

"Mr. President," he said quietly.

"And your name?" the President asked, extending a hand. Tom shook it.

"Tom Kirkman."

"Ah, of course. Bob has been telling me about you." The President stepped toward the window so he could see Tom's work. "Excellent, excellent! I enjoy color, but I really do not have time for the sketching part. Or, between you and me, the talent to do it. But come, you must try my stew tonight. We're having a dinner for Her Majesty. Bob will be back shortly with Dottie."

As if in a dream, Tom followed the President. He felt sure his internal organs were shaking and that soon his entire body would begin quaking. He knew he could easily do something thoughtless and embarrass himself before two of the most important people in the world.

Tom had not seen the West Sitting Hall before. He hated to even step on the carpet after Mamie's lecture about carpets the previous week, but he followed the President under the arched doorways anyway. The appearance of the room put Tom somewhat at ease. In the middle of the room, a small round table had been set for the Queen Mother and Mamie. The attendants to the Queen Mother sat against the wall on armchairs. It was Friday night, and the President's son John and his wife Barbara were present, as well as their young children David and Barbara Anne.

A buffet table had been placed in the room. Sergeant Moaney dipped out the fragrant stew and butlers passed the bowls to the small group. Robert Schulz and Dottie soon arrived, and Tom took a seat beside the colonel.

Five-year-old David came to Tom's rescue by asking Tom if he had a dog. David talked about Heidi, the President's dog, and Tom told David about Tony, his childhood dog. He almost told the boy how Tony had met his fate but decided against it. The conversation, however, relaxed him, and when Mamie introduced him to the Queen Mother he felt almost—but not quite—at ease.

Much to Tom's relief, Sergeant Moaney handed him a bowl of soup and a soup spoon. He slid his spoon into the tomato-based stew and came up with a thick chunk of beef and a captivating aroma of thyme and other spices he couldn't identify. The President apologized to the Queen Mother for serving such a simple meal, and the Queen Mother insisted that she had longed to taste it ever since she heard that Ike enjoyed cooking it for guests.

"Tom isn't married yet, so we aren't taking him away from his wife by asking him to stay late," Mamie explained, glancing behind at him. "But he does have a girl back in Indiana," she added. "What was her name, Tom?"

"Sharon, ma'am," Tom said. He had decided that his safest course of action was to be as brief as possible with every comment, to add titles of respect to every word he said, to accept no alcohol, and to leave as soon as he was permitted. He found his plan confirmed by the actions of the Queen Mother's attendants, who sat quietly on the sidelines.

"How old are you, Tom?" the Queen Mother asked. She had the appearance of a person made of china, Tom thought. She was elegant but fragile.

"I'm nineteen years old, Your Majesty." From the moment President Eisenhower had said "Her Majesty" to Tom in the painting room, Tom had known that he would have to use the same expression.

"So young yet, Tom! Well, you have many happy years ahead of you, I'm sure. And how is your mother?"

"She's well, I believe, Your Majesty. She is often ill with high blood pressure, but her last letter said she is doing well."

"Such a terrible disease," said the Queen Mother, and her British accent sounded musical to Tom. "I'm afraid our friend President Roosevelt was afflicted with the same malady along with the ravages of polio. Or perhaps I misspeak, Mr. President?"

"You are correct," President Eisenhower agreed. "It was very unfortunate. But what a great breakthrough that we now have a safe polio vaccine!"

"Yes, I have heard that children are able to receive the vaccine. I treasure the time I had with the President and Mrs. Roosevelt the last time I was here," she said. "George was here too."

George. Who is George? Alarm washed over Tom. He nearly choked on the onion he was swallowing. No, choking would not do. He forced himself to think through the swallow and managed to complete it successfully. But really. Why hadn't he studied up on the Queen Mother's life? He had barely been born when she had last been to the White House, but apparently her husband had still been alive.

What will I do if they ask me if I remember when he passed away? Tom thought wildly. He had no idea how "George" had died, or when. Tom realized with horror that he wasn't even sure if it was George, or the stately woman before him, who had been the reigning monarch. But Mamie saved him by replying directly to the Queen Mother.

"Oh, you must miss him terribly," Mamie said. "I don't know what I'd do without my Ike." The First Lady was known for her sentimental comments.

After the meal, the guests formed little groups. Tom chatted with Sergeant Moaney.

"How about you spend the night, Tom?" Sergeant Moaney asked as he stirred the leftover stew. "Then you will be available bright and early in the morning. There's an extra room on the third floor where Her Majesty's attendants are sleeping."

Sergeant Moaney and Tom talked as Moaney cleaned up his things.

"You go with the President pretty much wherever he goes, don't you, Sergeant?" Tom asked.

"You could say that, sir," Moaney replied. "And everywhere his golf balls go!"

"Ah, yes, I've seen you out running after his practice shots in the morning."

Sergeant Moaney smiled. "It's my morning workout!"

In the morning, Tom reported promptly to the painting room on the second floor to be close by if needed.

Much to Tom's surprise, he was again invited to a light breakfast in the West Sitting Hall. The President was already over at the Oval Office in the West Wing. Tom was amazed at the comfortable nature of the meal and the many things that were discussed. The weather in Washington was compared to that of London. Tom asked the Queen Mother about her voyage by sea. One of the Queen Mother's attendants asked Tom about his career, which led him to confess that he attended drafting school classes in the evenings.

"How interesting," the Queen Mother said. "Have you ever been to the Pentagon?"

"I have not," Tom said.

"I think that would be a wonderful place to visit," the Queen Mother said.

"Would you like to go there?" Mamie asked her.

"Why, I suppose I might if it's not too difficult to arrange," Her Majesty responded.

"Tom," Mamie ordered, "I'm glad you're here. Ring Robert Schulz for me."

Tom hurried to the rotary phone on the buffet behind the breakfast table

From the WHITE HOUSE *to the* AMISH

and dialed Schulz's office in the East Wing.

"Colonel, I have Mrs. Eisenhower here to speak to you."

"Thanks, Tom."

Tom sat down, trying to restrain a smile. He sympathized with Robert Schulz. The Pentagon was not open on Saturdays. What would Bob say to the First Lady?

Sure enough, Mamie soon said, "Oh, is it closed?"

Mamie was silent for a moment, and Tom predicted that Schulz was assuring her that he could find a way to open up the highly secure building.

"Great, Bob, thank you!" Mamie said. "I think we will be ready to go in about ten minutes."

At this, Tom nearly burst out laughing. He wondered if he should run to the East Wing to assist his superior on this impossible mission. But his responsibility was to stay with their honored guest, so he did.

Sure enough, the limousines pulled up beneath the North Portico, and the ladies shortly drove off. Robert Schulz led the way in another car. Tom stayed behind with the Queen Mother's attendants and finished another sketch.

The ladies and President Eisenhower returned at lunch, and the party all ate together again. The butlers served a delicious luncheon of baked smoked ham with pineapple garnish and corn pudding. Tom indulged in the dessert, a jellyroll with maple rum sauce. He decided the stress of the last few days would burn any extra calories.

Robert Schulz looked slightly exhausted, but Tom detected a sense of pride in the way he sanded his mustache. It must have been a great accomplishment to get the Pentagon opened in fifteen minutes.

"She wanted to see the cafeteria and the barber shop!" the colonel hissed to Tom when he passed him privately after lunch. "She asked how many chairs there were in the barber shop and I told her twenty-one, but now I'm not sure I was right. I guess I'd better go do some research."[1]

It was late afternoon when Tom finally drove away from the White House. He had gotten an apartment close by. He drove out the East Gate and around the corner to Connecticut Avenue. He headed northwest past the park benches and fallen autumn leaves and soon arrived at his brick apartment on O Street. He hadn't believed his luck when he first got the apartment address. Washington streets, like those of Bedford, were named with letters! Not only did it assure him that he would be able to find his way, but it made him feel at home.

He went straight to bed for a nap. *After a short nap,* he decided, *I'll write Mother a letter.* There would probably never be another day that he could start a letter quite the same way.

"Dear Mom, Last night I dined with the President and Mrs. Eisenhower and the Queen Mother of England."

chapter seventeen

An Announcement

1954

Christmas dinner was spoiled, and it wasn't just because Carol started a conversation about politics. To an onlooker, however, it might have appeared that way.

"Tommy, do you think Senator McCarthy will stop finding Communists behind every tree now?" Carol asked around Grandma Franklin's vase, which had been placed in the center of the table for the holiday meal and filled with evergreens.

"Oh, Carol!" Bob exploded like a shotgun before Tom could swallow his bite of ham. "How could you ruin Christmas lunch with such an exhausting question?"

"Why is it exhausting?" Patsy asked, calmly coming to her sister's defense. "The President has ordered McCarthy to stop accusing people, hasn't he?"

"Ike can't control him," Dad said from his place at the head of the table.

"I have to agree with you," said Carol's husband. "McCarthy will never change. But he might get less attention now. I think people are getting tired of him. But you're the expert, Tom."

"Honestly, if you all are reading the newspapers, you likely know more about it than I do," Tom said. "But it was the Senate, not President Eisenhower, that made the ruling to censure McCarthy."

"But Eisenhower made a special committee or something to stop him!" Carol persisted. "Because he was accusing some military people of being Communist."

"Oh, back in the spring maybe," Tom said. "As I said, if you read the papers you likely know more than I do. I was still in Arkansas then."

The real reason everyone was in a touchy temper was because Mom was not feeling well and had stepped away from the table. She was in the bedroom, with the curtains pulled over the windows. Joan had gone with her, but Mom had sent her back out to be with the family and preside over the meal. The little nieces and nephews sat in the laundry room, eating their food at a small plastic table.

Perhaps Carol had introduced the topic of politics to get everyone's mind off Mom's illness.

"So do you think President Eisenhower really thinks the Communists are a threat, Tom?" Dad asked. "Joan, is there more coffee?"

"Yes," Joan said, springing up to get it. Poor Joan took Mom's illnesses hard. She transformed her grief into activity, wildly performing as many duties as she could to make up for Mom's disability. Together, she and Dad shouldered the domestic chores that Mom could not do.

Tom had been working in the White House for only a few months and had certainly not discussed Communism with President Eisenhower. He produced art for the White House, not political statements. But no matter, Tom was already learning that at social functions and family dinners, he was now expected to be the authority on President Eisenhower. He usually tried to strike a balance between saying a few intelligent words and exuding an air of secrecy. However, with Sharon beside him today, he did want to be at least a little impressive.

"The President is tired of McCarthy," Tom said, eyeing a green bean on his fork. He took the bite and chewed thoughtfully. "But he is also skeptical of the Russians. We have enough problems here in America that I think he would like to stay out of trouble with the rest of the world as much as possible."

"Like what kind of problems?" Carol asked.

"School desegregation, for one," Tom replied. "The Supreme Court has just ruled that the 'separate but equal' ruling of 1896 is unconstitutional. Eisenhower knows it will be a big fight to get the South to change its ways. The President doesn't want civil war, but he won't let them get away with disobeying a Supreme Court ruling either."

"Well, he picked the justice who made the ruling happen," Carol's husband put in.

"Tommy, tell us about your birthday cake from Mamie!" Patsy said. "Does she really bake a birthday cake for every person who works in the White House?"

Tom laughed and reached for another dinner roll.

"She doesn't bake at all," he replied. "But yes, she's enthused about birthdays. I think she made her staff create a birthday calendar. Then she just orders

Tom at a White House birthday party

a cake from the White House kitchen for that person's department. It's really not such a big deal."

Tom was happy to let the conversation slide on to other topics. He was busy mulling over whether or not to share his announcement. No, he decided, he simply could not share it with Mom absent. That seemed like the sort of thing a person would do if his mother had passed away.

As the others cleaned up the dishes, Tom slipped tentatively to Mom's bedroom. He found her flat in bed. A cotton quilt made of squares from old dresses swaddled her shoulders.

"Are you okay, Mom?"

"Just a headache, Tommy."

"No better?"

"Not yet."

"Can I get you anything?"

"No, I don't think so. Just pray that I can rejoin my family soon."

"Okay, Mom."

Out in the living room, Joan was looking for people to play Monopoly with her. She was the youngest in the family and had always begged her older siblings to play games with her. Bill had received Joan's name in the Christmas exchange and had bought her a game, which suited her splendidly.

"Tom, don't you and Sharon want to play? Pretty soon you're going to get married and move off to Washington and we'll never see you again!" she pouted.

"Joan, you are always matching everyone up prematurely!" Tom exclaimed, swiping at her with a couch cushion. "Want to play, Sharon?"

"We need to sing carols sometime too," Patsy said slowly. A silence fell over the adults, broken only by the children playing with their new toys.

No one wanted to sing carols without Mom.

"Well, let's play the game now and we can sing later," Joan said. "Joe, are you going to play?"

"No, the weather is nice enough that you'll find me outside in the mud throwing my new football with Bob."

"With Bob?!" Bob exclaimed. "Bob just ate too much lunch and won't be moving anytime soon."

Everyone finally found a place. Patsy curled up with the younger generation and read picture books with them. Bill played checkers with Dad, but everyone could tell that Dad was restless and anxious without Mom by his side. Between every game of checkers, he went to check on her.

Finally, late in the evening when Patsy had opened her Tupperware of chocolate peanut butter candy and Joan had brewed yet another pot of fresh coffee, and most of the children were either crying or falling asleep, Mom emerged from the bedroom. Her face was pale, but she insisted she felt much better and wanted to participate in singing carols.

Tom felt as if his happiness was complete. At the piano, he led into "Joy to the World," and everyone joined in. He glanced at the rocking chair and saw Mom's face light up with happiness. He looked at Sharon beside him on the piano bench and winked. He looked at Dad sitting on the edge of his recliner, his wrist snapping up and down as he thrummed the guitar with enthusiasm now that Mom was back in the circle. Soon the last verse of the song thundered in the small living room—"He rules the world!"

Maybe He really does rule the world, Tom thought as he glanced once more at Mom's radiant face. Maybe He really does great things!

"Away in a Manger!" Joan called when the last notes died away.

Tom waited through three more carols, and finally he could stand it no longer. After a rousing rendition of "Hark the Herald Angels Sing," he slid off the bench and stood up. Mom looked at him with surprise.

"I want to announce that Sharon and I are engaged!" he blurted out. He couldn't think of a better way to break the happy news.

Cheers and applause followed. Tears spilled out of Mom's eyes. Dad treated the couple with one of his rare but vibrant smiles. Joan had a fit.

"Matching everyone up prematurely, am I?" she cried, and everyone laughed again. Mom asked what the laughter was about, so Carol had to repeat the earlier conversation. When Mom laughed about it, everyone else laughed all over again.

"I think, ladies and gentlemen," Bill said solemnly, "that this calls for, I solemnly believe, another pot of . . ."

"Coffee!" Joan shouted, running to start it.

"And I'm thinking about those chocolate peanut butter things," Bob added.

"Are there more of those left?"

"Oh, Sharon, what dress are you planning to have for the wedding?" Carol asked. "I just saw a wedding catalog the other day. I would have picked it up if only I had known!"

Tom made many trips home that spring. With Sharon's mom keeping an eye on everything, Tom and Sharon planned the wedding and their new life in Washington. Colonel Schulz had his housing man look for a place for the newlyweds in Washington and found rooms on the second floor of a brick apartment building on Congress Avenue. It was farther from the White House than Tom's O Street home had been, but it had more room.

Tom could not wait for his new life to begin.

chapter eighteen

An Exciting Summer

"**O**kay, Tom," Colonel Schulz said one day a few weeks before Tom and Sharon's wedding. "The Boss wants us to catalog his books and create shelving for them on the farm at Gettysburg. I have assigned the task to Colonel Streiff, but it is not a one-man job. Eisenhower has books at Gettysburg, books in storage, and books in the Oval Office. He has books about art and books about military history and biographies and Westerns . . . Let's see what it says."

Robert Schulz picked the memo off his desk. Tom had just come over to Schulz's East Wing office to eat lunch.

" 'Cataloging and segregating' is what he says." Robert Schulz sanded his mustache with his hand. His buttons still reminded Tom, after all these months, of drawer knobs. "None of the rooms in the Gettysburg house were built specifically as a library. This means we will have to place the books in a number of designated spots throughout the house."

Tom sighed inwardly. He did not consider himself a librarian. He had hated English class with a passion. But he nodded. Perhaps he would get to visit the President's Gettysburg farm, which would be fun. Schulz had earlier spoken of the President's devotion to his Angus beef herd.

Tom knew that the Gettysburg homestead was the Eisenhowers' retirement place. President Eisenhower had always enjoyed studying military history, and the area interested him because of the Civil War battle. Then, as a young officer in World War I, he had been in charge of a tank corps at Camp Colt, an abandoned post on the site of the Gettysburg battlefield. Ike loved the rolling landscape, and Mamie enjoyed the townspeople of Gettysburg. After World War II ended, Ike and Mamie purchased a farm in Gettysburg. It was a 189-acre farm, which they purchased for $40,000. It came with 36 Holstein cattle and 500 Leghorn hens.[1]

"First, though, before we get to designing shelving and all that, we need a list of all the books he owns, with their approximate widths, so we know how much space they will take up. Let's see, when are you deserting us to get married, Tom?"

Tom grinned. Sharon was keeping him well informed on the preparations. There would be orchids and lilacs and a decorated cake. Tom's Grandma Franklin had gifted a punch bowl from the late 1800s that would be used to serve drink.

"But you can't see my dress until the day of the wedding!" Sharon had told him.

Then they would be off on their wedding trip through the southern United States before returning to Washington.

"June 4 is the date, sir."

"Ah, just a few more weeks! Well, work on this list as much as you can until then. The good news is, the Boss is leaving for Gettysburg this afternoon, so it will be a good time to work on the books in his office. Then we need to gather all the books from various other places in the White House and put them in some central location until we can transport them to Gettysburg. Hmmm . . . Any ideas where that should be, Tom?"

"There is a storage room in the basement close to our office that should work well."

"Perfect. And since you are young, your back should be able to handle the work," he added with a smile. "Speaking of your office, I need to make a call."

Robert Schulz picked up the phone receiver on his desk and dialed the operator.

"Mr. Tolley? I am requisitioning your assistant Mr. Kirkman for the afternoon. The President needs some help cataloging his books."

He hung up the phone with a proper clank.

"You want me to . . ." Tom paused. "You actually want me to catalog books in the Oval Office?"

"Yes," Colonel Schulz said. "Don't worry. The housekeepers will be working on cleaning at this time too. Human beings really are allowed to enter, and you will do better than I would. I'm a business-minded man, not a librarian."

Two housekeepers were already at work cleaning the Oval Office. They glanced up at Colonel Schulz and continued their work. Tom saw the one, a little squirrel of a woman, working at the President's desk. She carefully lifted both of his black rotary phones, dusted beneath them, and set them back down.

"That telephone on the far side has a gold dial," Colonel Schulz said, walking across the blue carpet to the desk. "It was given to the President in commemoration of the fifty millionth telephone manufactured in the country."

Tom gazed up at the high blue-gray blinds over the window behind the President's desk. He looked even higher up to the top of the room. The seal of the President of the United States looked down at him from the ceiling, as if wondering why on earth Tom Kirkman was in this room.

Colonel Schulz saw his eyes on the seal.

"Just a few years ago, they had to update that to include Alaska and Hawaii," he said.

"What do you mean?" Tom asked. "Oh, the number of stars?"

Colonel Schulz nodded, sanding his mustache again with his right hand.

"They had to add two more stars to make it fifty. And of course, since it is peacetime now, the eagle on the seal is looking at the olive leaves instead of at the arrows."

"Right," Tom said, and then felt foolish for making it sound as if he were so well versed. He never remembered learning any such thing. Maybe it would be more appropriate to show his ignorance. "Was this room in the original White House?"

"Oh, no," Robert Schulz said. "I'm not the greatest historian myself. I am a business-minded man, Tom, not a scholar. Still, I believe it was—let's see, President Taft perhaps—who expanded the White House. And since there are oval rooms in each floor of the main residence, it was decided to make an oval office for the president too. But really, they say the only original piece left is the fireplace."

Tom looked at the marble fireplace opposite the President's desk. Landscape paintings hung on the walls and over the fireplace. Across the room, past the President's desk, two bookcase niches had been built into the wall. Above these shelves, a shell pattern had been carved into the wall. Matching shells decorated the tops of the windows facing the Rose Garden too.

"Most of these books are general White House books," Colonel Schulz said. "Only a few of Eisenhower's own books are over here on this side."

To his surprise, Tom thoroughly enjoyed the book project. He wrote down each title and author under the appropriate category, as well as the book's width. He didn't exactly enjoy lugging books all over the White House, but after sitting at a desk for months with only a calligraphy pen for weight lifting, it felt like a welcome change.

Tom did continue helping the calligraphers when he could. They were preparing invitations for a White House staff picnic at the Gettysburg farm on July 1. Unfortunately, the calligraphers were not invited. They were not accustomed to getting invitations themselves, but it was still rather perturbing because the picnic was for the White House staff. They addressed invitations to the carpenters, the maids, the engineers, the window washers, and even the telephone operators. Apparently, Mamie had forgotten the calligraphers, tucked away in the basement.

"We will continue this through the summer," Colonel Schulz explained before Tom left for Indiana for the wedding. "There is an architect here in Washington who will be doing all the work on the Gettysburg house. We'll have him draw up some plans for the shelves, maybe in late summer when we know what we are dealing with."

The scent of lilacs inflated Tom's lungs. He shifted, his polished black dress shoes digging into the new carpet. Sharon's mom had insisted on replacing the parlor carpet before her daughter's wedding to Tom Kirkman.

The carpet, a lovely blue, pleased Tom. But nothing could be as amazing as Sharon's face just inches from his.

Thomas E. Kirkman was seconds from becoming a married man. Although he was looking at Pastor Miller as he read the thirteenth chapter of 1 Corinthians, out of the corner of his eye he could see the simple strand of pearls around Sharon's neck and the orchid corsage pinned to her white dress.

"You may now join your right hands," the pastor said.

Tom turned to his bride, his back toward the best man and brother, Joe. Around the couple, the rest of both families blurred before Tom: Sharon's mom, dressed in navy, with a white purse and a corsage of white carnations, with Sharon's dad beside her. Bob, choking inside a navy tie. Bill, eyes on Tom's face. Patsy, dabbing at her eyes with a pink handkerchief. Carol, with her makeup and pearls. Joan, grinning widely, probably thinking of how much fun she was about to have serving the marvelous cake in the dining room. Grandma Franklin, who had gifted Tom and Sharon her 60-year-old punch bowl, now waiting to serve reception guests. Dad, lips parted in a genuine smile, hand clasped over Mom's.

And Mom! She was here too, a picture of beauty, with pink carnations pinned to her navy and white dress. And most important, her face was joyful and pain-free!

"Do you, Thomas E. Kirkman, take Sharon Arthur to be your wedded wife? For better, for worse, for richer, for poorer, in sickness and health, till death do you part?"

Tom looked into the sparkling eyes of his bride.

"I do."

No one in the parlor moved, not even Bob's little daughter Polly, as Sharon's vows followed. Tom and Sharon exchanged rings, and the pastor pronounced them husband and wife.

Wow! So fast! He was a married man. Tom fought to slow down the minutes that raced past. He wanted to memorize the smiling faces and all the wonders of the day.

Tom and Sharon drank punch from the sixty-year-old bowl. They posed for pictures. They ate cake. Neighbors and school friends dropped by to share the cake and punch. They brought gifts wrapped in silver paper and tied with bows.

Before Tom knew it, he and Sharon took the seven cement steps down to the street to Tom's little green Renault, a new car for a new life. In front of the house, the entire family waved them off. They were headed to the South! After that, they planned to go straight back to Washington.

Although the calligraphers had not been invited to the Gettysburg picnic, Mamie had not forgotten Tom. After Tom and Sharon returned to Washington after their wedding trip, an envelope arrived in the mail. It was a note from Mamie Eisenhower, congratulating them on their marriage. It was signed by the First Lady herself.

Congratulatory note from Mamie

When Tom returned to work, Robert Schulz reminded him that President Eisenhower would be going to Denver again after Congress adjourned. The colonel would go with him. During his absence, Schulz hoped that great progress could be made on the library. One day when Robert Schulz and

Colonel Streiff took the architect down to the Gettysburg farm in a military helicopter, Tom was invited to go along. Tom was thrilled—he was doing something even the President couldn't do. Schulz told him the President had not yet been cleared to fly by helicopter, as the Secret Service was still evaluating whether it was a safe form of transportation.

As they lifted away from the airport, Tom was glad to be less important than the President and be able to get such a great view of Washington. Behind them, he could see the Potomac River stretching away toward Chesapeake Bay. Fort Belvoir was also that direction, although he could not pick it out. Ahead of them to the left, the snaking, narrower portion of the Potomac wound into the green smudge of the Appalachian Mountains. Ahead and to the right, the city of Baltimore glistened. All too soon, the helicopter approached the Gettysburg farm. Tom saw a large barn and a pasture dotted with Black Angus cattle. In front of the barn, Robert Schulz pointed out the house that was the residence of the Secret Service when the President was at the farm. The main farmhouse, where the Eisenhowers stayed, had been expanded and remodeled, giving it fourteen rooms.

The military men strode purposefully through the house with the architect, measuring and making plans. There were several options for the books to be placed around the house. A painting studio on the third story could house the President's painting books. The second floor sitting room and the rose guest room both contained shelves, and more could be added. Tom promised to help the architect and Colonel Streiff in any way he could while Colonel Schulz was in Denver with the President and First Lady.

A few weeks later, Tom rolled over in bed and let himself rest just a little longer, basking in the luxury of a lazy Sunday morning. Sharon had left to go to a co-worker's house for a ladies' brunch, and the Congress Street apartment was perfectly still. They had been married a little over three months, long enough to have set up housekeeping, but not long enough to have a routine established. Tom and Sharon liked their apartment and had many happy moments arranging it. Sharon had gotten a typing job in the office of one of the Representatives on Capitol Hill.

Tom finally rolled out of bed and threw the covers in the direction of the pillows. He didn't make the bed exactly, but it was a significant gesture in that direction, he decided. He walked to the kitchen and filled the coffee percolator with water. After spooning coffee grounds into the metal basket, he set the pot on the stove to heat. How nice it would be to get an electric coffee pot! Maybe they would buy one at Christmas.

He crossed the linoleum floor to the entrance hall and opened the front door. Snatching up the morning paper, he retreated to their one brand-new piece of furniture—a green velvet couch which stood a few inches off the floor on tapered wooden legs. He sprawled on the couch, resting his head on a pillow on the couch's low arm and pulling up his mother's yellow and green crocheted afghan. It would be a few minutes before the coffee finished. Just enough for a quick pass through the *Washington Post*.

But it didn't take even a quick pass for Tom to see the shocking headline: "PRESIDENT ADMITTED TO FITZSIMONS ARMY HOSPITAL."

chapter nineteen

Rest and Relaxation

Tom sat upright on the couch, throwing off the afghan. His eyes scanned the article. The President had suffered a bout of indigestion on Friday while playing golf with friends, the article said. On Saturday, he had awakened feeling ill, and Mamie had summoned Dr. Snyder. Around noon, he had suffered a heart attack and was admitted to the hospital.

Tom stared at the paper without focusing, his eyes blurring the words before him. *Was President Eisenhower seriously ill? What if he died?*

It was clear what would happen if he died: Richard Nixon would become President. Tom shook his head and rubbed his forehead with his hand. Nixon did not seem like president material. Tom had never met him, but he knew he was young. And from the gossip Tom had heard, the vice president was not well-liked.

Stop thinking about Eisenhower dying! Tom told himself. *People have heart attacks all the time and get over them.*

The next morning, the White House staff huddled in clusters along every corridor and hallway, exchanging news that they had heard or read about the President. The clusters made their way to the Usher's Office. Everyone knew that Mamie communicated with the ushers even when she was away. Tom and Sandy Fox stood there together, Tom with his coffee and Sandy with his morning pipe. Even Adrian Tolley had unraveled his indestructible routine so far as to stand outside the Usher's Office, listening in. There would be no admonition for being late today.

"I think he'll be okay," J. B. West said. Chief usher Crim, as prim as Adrian Tolley, let him do the talking. "Mamie called in yesterday just to make sure we knew what had happened. Vice President Nixon is acting as President while Eisenhower recovers."

It was extraordinarily quiet, as if each staff member were sending up a prayer for the President.

"I read that he had indigestion on Friday," one of the chefs finally mentioned. "I wonder if it was really his heart attack starting."

"It could be an allergic reaction to the Colorado chefs," Tom suggested helpfully, and everyone laughed.

"Laughter is the best medicine," Sandy Fox said. "Let's hope Ike gets plenty of it, or we will all be working under Dick Nixon."

"Don't say that," a housekeeper said tearfully.

"Come, come!" Mr. Crim interposed. "Most of us have lived through a number of administration changes. We are the staff of the White House, not of any particular man who lives in it. We are strictly, solely, and selflessly devoted to whoever lives in this house. We have been through change before, and we will go through change again. We will do so carefully, courageously, and confidently."

Tom had not known Mr. Crim to be such an orator. His was the voice of experience and wisdom, and the others nodded. Everyone, Tom suspected, was thinking of President Roosevelt's sudden death. It had been ten years, but many of the staff had been in the White House over a decade.

"And besides all that, Mr. Crim," came the majestic voice of Adrian Tolley, "we have every reason to believe that President Eisenhower will recover."

"Very true, Mr. Tolley, very true," said Mr. Crim. "Now, I believe the President and Mrs. Eisenhower would want us all to get to work."

Chatter and laughter soon infused the workers as they hurried off to their respective places.

Tom continued to make occasional trips to Gettysburg. Colonel Streiff trusted him and liked to have his opinion as they measured and planned for the Boss's books. Tom grew acquainted with Eisenhower's Angus cattle, as well as Heidi, the beloved dog that belonged to young David Eisenhower. He learned to know General Nevins, the manager of Eisenhower's farm.

"Listen to this, Tom!" General Nevins exclaimed irritably one day. After a bout of sickness, the general was sitting outside in the fresh air going through mail from the President's secretary, Ann Whitman. Ann was in Colorado, where the President had been vacationing and was now recovering from his heart attack.

"Two people have written to the President and offered gifts for the farm. Ann asks if I will give my opinion of what we want at Gettysburg. Option one is a self-adjusting farm gate that would be 12, 14, or 16 feet in length. Option two is a flock of white geese. She says she thought it was a cackle of geese."

"Let's have the self-adjusting gate!" Tom said brightly. "That sounds interesting."

"Wait, there's more," General Nevins said, reading now. " 'I am holding letters on these. Both would-be donors sound a little off the beaten track.' "[1]

Tom chuckled. "Maybe they are the ones who need self-adjusters, not the gates," he suggested.

"Tom, write me up a return letter, would you? My secretary is out for the day. Tell her we need neither, and bring it here for me to sign."

The news from Denver grew ever brighter. In late October, the newspapers were full of photos of the President meeting the press on the roof of the hospital. He wore red pajamas gifted to him by the press corps. Gold stars studded the collar tabs and the words "Much Better, Thanks" were embroidered on the breast pocket. By the beginning of November there was talk of the President returning to Washington. On November 11, the President arrived. The White House staff lined up at the south entrance to greet him. Once inside, the President doggedly climbed the stairs to the second floor instead of taking the elevator. His doctor had recommended he take the stairs.

The President and Mamie retreated to Gettysburg to recover. Tom's work kept him mostly at the White House helping Robert Schulz, but he sometimes went down to Gettysburg to work on the book project and prepare sketches for the President there. Tom researched Dutch and English paintbrushes and helped procure the canvases that the President most enjoyed. He made sketches of the new bookshelves and labeled the categories of books that could go on each shelf.

When they finally returned to Washington in January, Mamie canceled the social activities. Since the President was taking it easy, Robert Schulz's responsibilities grew. The Calligraphy Office was slow, so Tom often found himself helping in the colonel's office in the East Wing. He made coffee, took down dictation, organized files, or ran messages to Dr. Snyder. He continued to visit Gettysburg occasionally.

Dr. Snyder had ordered Eisenhower to paint at least one hour every afternoon as a relaxation technique. On slow afternoons in Robert Schulz's office, the colonel sent Tom up to the second floor to prepare more sketches for the President. He always repeated his admonition to Tom to protect the Boss's privacy and keep his mouth shut.

When he was at the White House, the President's grandson, David, often sat with his grandfather while he painted. David occasionally brought his toy horses and cowboys to play with on the floor of the painting room. This made Tom think of Billy back home at Grecco's. David also talked to Tom about Heidi, the dog at Gettysburg.

Dr. Snyder or his assistant Dr. Tkach often came in during the painting time to check the President's blood pressure.

One day Dr. Snyder called Tom into the hall outside the painting room.

"How's your mother, Tom?"

"Thank you for remembering," Tom said. "She has her good days and her bad days. Have there been any advances in blood pressure medication?"

"I'm sorry, Tom. Nothing safe has been found yet."

Tom's heart sank, but he nodded and thanked Dr. Snyder.

Tom fell into a comfortable routine with the President. While he sketched silently, the President painted silently. Then Eisenhower would begin to ramble about the friends and foes of his life. He talked about General Omar Bradley, and how glad he had been for his presence during the war in Europe. He talked about the tiny house in which he had been raised in Abilene, Kansas.

"We were poor, Tom, poor," the President commented as he daubed his brush into a pool of yellow paint. He added a tint of red and swirled the paint together to make a shade of orange.

"My family lived in a chicken house briefly during the Depression," Tom said.

"Ah, yes, tough times!" the Boss replied. "We were over in the Philippines with General MacArthur through that time. And MacArthur . . . he was a case."

The President squeezed more red onto his palette. He was working on a fall scene and looking for the right leaf color.

"I tell you, Tom, do you know who Grandma Moses is?"

"The folk painter, I believe?"

President Eisenhower snorted. "If you want to call her a painter! She gave us a painting called *Fourth of July in 1952*, but I couldn't stand it. I really could not. The only good thing was it gave me courage that I might be a better painter than I thought I was."

The President added more red to his palette.

As often happened, a pun popped into Tom's mind. *No, no, do not tell jokes to the President,* he told himself. *That would not be appropriate. Just shut up and draw.* He bit his lip to keep himself from smiling, but the temptation to share the pun stayed. *How will I ever know if the President likes jokes if I don't try one on him?*

Eisenhower stirred his little pool of paint and went on. "I think one of the ushers took the painting and hung it in his office. Recently she did a painting of our Gettysburg farm. As a gift, Tom. That one is meaningful, at least."

"Maybe," Tom said, positively unable to resist any longer, "she's like the leech—decided to be an artist because she was good at drawing blood."

The President threw back his head and laughed so loudly that Tom was worried Dr. Snyder would burst into the room and permanently bar Tom from it.

"That's a good one, Tom, I must say," the President said when he recovered.

"Drafting school puns," Tom said. "Old artists never die, they just withdraw from the scene."

The President laughed again, clearly delighted.

"That one sounds like a nod to my old friend General MacArthur," the President said. "Old soldiers never die, they just fade away. Great talker, MacArthur, always knew how to get on the good side of people. I worked for him for many years. He was a study, that man was." Eisenhower paused and daubed a bit of orange onto a limb of the tree. "He was a study. Made out to be such a great general, but there were some things going on, there were."

Occasionally, Tom said "Uh-huh" or "Of course," and Eisenhower went right on. When Tom finished the sketch he was working on, he put his pencils into his case and shut it.

"Got a parting pun for me, Tom?" the President asked.

"Try not to paint yourself into a corner, Mr. President," Tom said, eyeing the brightly colored tree in the corner of the easel. As Tom left the room, President Eisenhower's chuckles followed him out the door.

It looked as if the President was going to recover from his heart attack. At any rate, it was time to stop worrying about Eisenhower and start thinking about the future of his own family.

In just a few months, in the spring of 1956, Tom was going to become a father.

chapter twenty

Showing Off a New Son

On May 22, 1956, little Jeffrey Scott entered the world at 1 a.m. The baby entranced Tom. He realized he had never sufficiently appreciated the fragile condition of newborns. But then, maybe he had never seen a baby so new. He gazed at Jeffrey with an awe that bordered on terror. The joints of Jeffrey's arms and legs surpassed any engineering perfection Tom had ever seen.

The piercing cry of his son frightened Tom. Was it possible he had a deadly disease the doctor had failed to detect? But the nurse assured him over and over that baby Jeffrey was in the best of health, and Sharon laughed at Tom despite her exhaustion.

Tom held his son and watched the delicate movements of each finger and toe, unable to fathom that outside the hospital window the rest of Washington was proceeding as normal. Tom felt like rushing out into the street, to the White

House, to Congress, to the Supreme Court, to the top of the Washington Monument, and shouting to all the world that the most amazing thing had happened.

Little Jeffrey Scott had entered the world.

Sharon's parents came to the city a few days later on the pretext of helping Sharon adjust, but clearly motivated by an unrestrainable desire to see their new grandchild. Tom wished his mom could come as well, but he did not think she would be strong enough to make the trip. And Dad would never leave her alone. So Tom and Sharon planned to spend most of August 1956 in Indiana visiting their families and showing off their new son.

In August, they took their little car to Indiana. Tom swelled with pride when he placed his almost three-month-old son into his mother's arms.

"Oh, Tommy!" Mom exclaimed, as happy tears spilled from her eyes. "What a handsome little man you have!"

For the rest of his life, Tom remembered his mother this way. It was her best moment of the otherwise difficult month of August. Unable to take part in the family fun, she retreated to her bed more and more. The headaches crippled her.

Tom prayed harder, and with a desperation he had never felt before.

Later that fall, Tom, Sharon, and Jeff returned to Indiana for Thanksgiving. By now, Jeffrey was six months old and of course the smartest little man on the planet. He did cry an unfortunate percentage of the car trip, but it was worth it. When they arrived in Indiana, all the aunts and uncles and grandparents and cousins squealed and fought to hold little Jeffrey.

Grandma Kirkman did not fight and squeal, because she stayed in bed again with her terrible headaches. Tom sat beside her the afternoon of Thanksgiving Day, speaking quietly to her.

"You'll be up and feeling better by Christmas, Mom," Tom said. "We'll come back then. Sharon is going to stay here in Indiana for a few more weeks, but I need to go back to Washington."

"Are you taking the car?"

Mom's words came out like the lightest touch of a feather, barely recognizable.

"I'll leave the car so Sharon can get around," Tom said. "I'll hitchhike. I've done it before plenty of times."

"Okay, Tommy. I wish I could come to your birthday party at Patsy's tomorrow. I will if I feel better."

"I know you will, Mom, if you can. You know Patsy will throw a great party!"

Mom smiled faintly and then coughed.

"Happy birthday a day early, Tom. I can't believe you are twenty-two already!"

Patsy did throw a party, and it would have been perfect if only Mom had been there. At least Mom had convinced Dad to attend the party by telling him she would be sadder if he stayed home and missed it than if he went. Dad hated to leave her, but he went in the end.

Tom would have been happy enough with Thanksgiving leftovers, but no such thing was acceptable for Patsy. She served pulled pork sandwiches with homemade barbecue sauce and green beans from her own garden. A tray of cheese and pickles circled the table, and then a bowl of nuts and mints. Then there was a quivering jello monument piled high with cottage cheese, which Tom assumed was dessert. Coffee and Coke flowed in abundance, and everyone ate as if Thanksgiving dinner had been not yesterday, but many days in the past.

At the end, Patsy arrived with her crowning achievement, to a chorus of oohs and aahs. She had made a birthday cake shaped like the White House. She had made the peaked roof above the North Portico, with four pillars and eight windows on each side and outlined with light gray icing. Counting the central windows between the pillars and the front door, each of Tom's twenty-two candles had a window to stand in. Tom thought the cake was perfect. Everyone found room for more food and enjoyed the cake, along with a scoop of ice cream.

"I won't be able to fit into any of my clothes when we get back!" Sharon lamented.

"Not sure if I will either," Tom agreed. "Maybe we should go find a paint store."

Sharon shot him a confused but unsuspecting look. "Why a paint store? To paint ourselves so we look better?"

"No, I just heard we can get thinner there."

Stuffed with food as they were, everyone around the table howled with laughter. Sharon laughed until she cried.

It was a wonderful meal, but Tom missed his mother's smiling face. Before he left to hitchhike back on Sunday afternoon, he went to sit with her again. As he got up to leave, he bent down to kiss her on the forehead.

"I love you, Mom. I hope you feel better soon."

"I love you too, Tommy. Be safe."

Part three

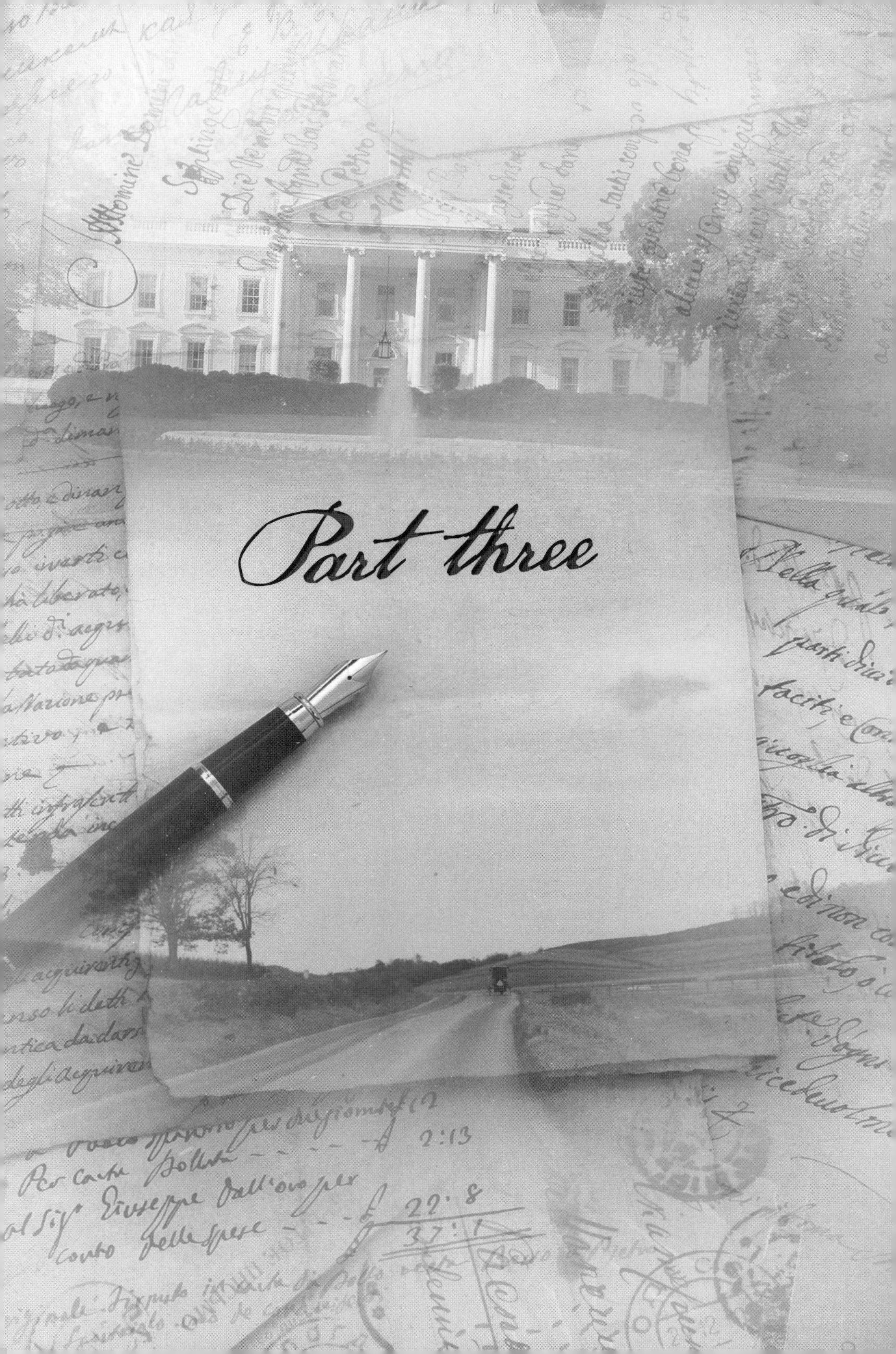

chapter twenty-one

The Phone Call

Tom was feeling down, and he wasn't sure why.

Had it really been only two years since Colonel Schulz had first brought him to the White House? It seemed like two decades. Tom was now a married man—and he even had a son! For a while, he had thought life was too perfect to ever feel sad again. What could be better than having a wife, a son, and a job in the White House?

But Tom had discovered that married people can also have dark days—even if they work in the White House. Since returning to Washington, he had felt even more gloomy than usual. He struggled to understand his feelings, but he suspected the growing distance between him and Sharon had something to do with it.

I need to talk to Mom, Tom told himself. *Over Christmas, I'll have a nice, long talk with her. Sometimes life is too big to solve on my own.*

"Tom."

It was Millie, one of Robert Schulz's secretaries, speaking from the door of the Calligraphy Office. Tom knew her voice, but he was so engrossed in the invitation he was preparing that he kept his eyes glued to the stiff paper.

President Eisenhower was playing golf in Augusta, Georgia, and Robert Schulz was with him. Not so the calligraphers, whose backs were bent beneath the weight of holiday invitations and name cards. Still, Tom could hardly begrudge Eisenhower a vacation after his strenuous campaign and re-election to the presidency.

Although the President's vacation to Augusta seemed like a reprieve of social events, it only magnified the events that would take place when he returned. The President was expected back on December 14. On the seventeenth, he was planning to host a luncheon for the young prime minister of India. On the twentieth, the President and Mamie planned to host a Christmas party for the White House staff. In January, there would be the inauguration and the dinners and social events surrounding it. It was a busy season for everyone, but especially for the calligraphers.

Tom did not look up until he reached the end of the word and lifted his pen from the paper and into the wooden pen case beside him. Shaking his head and running a hand along the back of his neck to relieve a knot, he finally looked up at Millie, still standing at the door.

"There's a telephone call for you in Colonel Schulz's office."

"Is it Colonel . . ." Tom let his hand fall from his neck to his desk, but decided not to ask the question. It was likely Colonel Schulz himself wanting to talk to him. It did seem a little surprising that he had not just sent a message through Millie. But strange things happened all the time in the White House. If Tom had learned anything, it was to never be surprised.

He had already wasted precious moments of the caller's time, so he jumped to his feet and headed out of the Calligraphy Office. With Millie following, he went up the stairs two at a time to the Center Hall. No one was there. With all the important people gone, there was no fear of being seen.

As they hurried down the domed Center Hall on the ground floor, each of the beautiful, sweeping domes seemed to be looking down specifically at Tom, filling him with a sense of dread. *Something's wrong,* he told himself. *Who could be calling me?*

Each pillar and window that flashed past was like a messenger reinforcing his troubled thoughts. *Something's wrong. Something's wrong.* Into the empty East Wing they rushed, oblivious to all the Christmas decorations everywhere. Finally they came to Colonel Schulz's office.

Millie motioned Tom into the colonel's office. "I'm leaving for home," she said. "Make sure to close the door when you leave."

Tom picked up the receiver of the black rotary phone. He heard the voice of the operator making the transfer.

"Hello?"

"Tom."

It was his father.

At the sound of his voice, a chill coursed through Tom's body. Why was Dad calling him at the White House? Dad seldom called him even at his home, and he had never called the White House.

Never.

Dad's voice, though recognizable, wavered slightly as if a strong wind blew against his steel personality. Tom could see his dad standing beside the telephone at their home. He could see the plastic receiver and the rotary face. He could see his dad's tightly curled black hair stacked like a dome on top of his head, crowning his powerful frame. And somewhere behind him, Mom would be there.

Tom gripped the receiver harder. With the other hand, he gripped the side of Colonel Schulz's desk. He saw, as if in a dream, a vein stand out on his forearm.

"Dad. How are you?"

Tom clung to the question, ridiculous as it was, as if it were a life vest. Perhaps, perhaps . . . if he asked a normal, innocuous question, he would get a harmless answer.

"Tom," Dad said again. This time it sounded as if he would go on, but instead of going on, Tom could hear him gulping in a large breath of air. Finally he continued, "We're at the hospital."

In a flash, Tom's cozy picture faded. His father was not standing beside the telephone at home. He was not across from the kitchen where Mom sang and shook parsley into the boiled potatoes. He was not beside Mom's rocking chair and the basket of yarn where she would be working on a Christmas project.

No, his steely-eyed father was standing somewhere in a sterile hospital room, holding a strange phone receiver in his hand. Somewhere behind him, instead of Mom cooking supper, nurses and doctors were rushing about taking care of sick people. Stethoscopes were pressed to hearts. Fingers rested on wrists, seeking pulses. Broken bones appeared under X-rays. Needles broke through skin, seeking veins. Children screamed.

Somewhere, there at the hospital, motionless forms lay under white sheets. People died there, despite all the medicines and medical equipment.

Why doesn't Dad speak?

"I think Mom's having a stroke. You had better come home."

Tom's eyes blurred, and as he squeezed them shut an angry cascade of colors seemed to course through them.

"Tom? Did you hear what I said?"

"Uh, Dad. Yes. Yes. Are Sharon and Jeff with you? Tell her I'm on my way."

Tom hung up the receiver, his eyes still clenched shut against the world. But the whirlpool of color would not stop anyway, so he opened them.

Tom turned, his shoes digging circular furrows in the carpet. *Schulz.* He would have to talk to Colonel Schulz to get permission to leave. And what would Mr. Tolley say about him being gone during the busy season?

He walked around to the front of Colonel Schulz's desk. Normally he wouldn't sit in a superior's chair, but he knew Schulz wouldn't care. Tom sank into the chair, reached for the phone again, and spun the "0" on the rotary dial. The White House operator answered.

"Colonel Schulz," Tom said. "Can you get me to Colonel Schulz?"

The operator paused for a moment.

"Is this Tom?" she asked, recognizing his voice.

"Yes."

"Okay, let me try reaching him. One moment."

The seconds turned to minutes. Since it was evening, Tom supposed Schulz was either at a dinner party with Eisenhower or still on the golf green. He probably wouldn't be in the greatest humor to be called away from either. But Tom didn't care. His head in his hands, he waited as in a trance.

"Colonel Schulz." He heard the trumpet-like voice of the colonel as if coming from the other end of a tunnel.

"It's Tom."

"How are things in Washington, Tom?"

If the colonel was annoyed, it was not evident in his voice.

"Uh, doing well, Colonel," Tom said. "But I-I just—"

Tom stopped, panicked. His voice was breaking, something he had not expected. He could not—he would not—cry while talking to the colonel. He swallowed hard and bit his lip until he could taste blood. Somehow he had to get himself under control.

"I received word that my mother is ill," he said, forcing the words out hastily so there would be no time for his voice to break. "They think she is having a stroke. My dad is requesting my presence at once." *Requesting my presence.* That was a good line. Tom congratulated himself on remaining formal, detached, and military.

"Ah, Tom," Colonel Schulz said. "So sorry to hear that." He paused, and Tom could picture him sitting in front of the telephone as erect as a chest of drawers, though likely dressed in golfing casuals rather than in his formal military jacket.

"Look, Tom, you know it's fine with me if you go, but you have to get permission from Tolley. I'm not a calligraphy man, but I know you are busy this time of year. Get permission from Tolley and take a few days. That's no problem."

"Okay." Tom breathed his first sigh of relief. "Thanks, Colonel. I'll talk to Mr. Tolley."

"Take care, Tom. Let me know how your mom is doing. I'll say a prayer for you."

"Thanks."

"Say, Tom, there's a bottle of Scotch in my cupboard above Millie's desk. Take that, Tom. Please. You have a long night ahead."

"Uh, I can't—"

"Take it, Tom. You know I'm a businessman, not a counselor. But you have a hard night ahead. You must take it."

"Thank you."

Colonel Schulz was often the man to accompany President Eisenhower to church. Tom was sure that Schulz meant what he said when he assured him of his prayers.

Who Tom was not sure about was God Himself. Sitting there in the colonel's chair, the very thought of God exploded like red flames across his consciousness. He leaped out of the office chair and hurried across the room to the cupboard above Millie's desk. In a blur, his eyes took in Millie's perfect family photo of herself, a few sisters, and her parents. Her mom was smiling and cheerful and didn't look like she was ill. *Why can't my life be perfect like that?*

Desperate for relief, he yanked open the cupboard door and pulled out the fat glass bottle of White Label Scotch. Behind a stack of paper napkins, he found several cups made of Styrofoam, the newly invented material that didn't soak up liquid like paper cups did. He snatched up one and hurried back to the office chair. He poured hurriedly from the bottle before he could think of the irony of what he was doing.

Here he was, turning to drink to make himself feel better because his mother was ill. But it was something his mother would not want him to do. And his father, who had watched his own father kill himself with whiskey, had never tasted a drop of alcohol. Now, here, in a lonely office in Washington, their son was pouring himself a glass of Scotch.

"Distilled and bottled in Scotland." Tom read the label as the liquid burned a slow track down the back of his throat. *"Under British government supervision."*

Government supervision.

Power. Power everywhere. Governments watching over their constituents. Where was God then? Could He not govern? If the British government could keep an eye on distilleries in Scotland, could not God heal one woman in the hospital in Bedford, Indiana?

"God, I asked you to heal my mother!" he cried aloud to the empty office. He would make a deal with God. It was an act of desperation. "Please, God, heal her this time! Just give her ten more years and I'll give my life to you! I'll do whatever you want me to do for the rest of my life. But please, heal my mother tonight!"

His voice ended on something close to a scream. He would never have spoken aloud in this office, but for the absolute certainty that he was alone. Angrily Tom rose. He recorked the bottle and replaced it. He hurled the cup into the wastebasket beside Millie's desk. The few remaining drops of Scotch dripped onto the merry snippets of greenery that Millie had discarded after arranging her Christmas decorations.

Everywhere around him was all this cheer and joy. The decor and merriment would kill him soon, Tom thought as he burst out of the colonel's office. He had to go talk to Adrian Tolley. He had to catch him before he went home. He closed the door behind him and hurried through the East Wing. At every turn, there was more of it—joy, peace, blinking lights, flashing snowflakes, stars . . . How could everything look so cheerful and happy when his mother was sick and in the hospital?

As he rushed down the colonnade of pillars, he thought of the man who had been president two presidents back. No. He would not, WOULD NOT, think of President Roosevelt. No, not even when he was walking in the very house where Roosevelt had walked before his blood pressure had killed him. He would not think of cerebral hemorrhage, the horrible brain bleed that had taken his life.

Tom soon arrived, flushed and breathing fast, in the Calligraphy Office. The blinking Christmas tree was the first thing to greet him. Tom quickly unplugged it from the wall. He couldn't stand the obnoxious thing.

Sandy stared at him.

"You already tired of the holiday season before we even hit the middle of December?"

Tom grimaced and sank into his chair like an old man. Only then did Mr. Tolley look up.

"Mr. Tolley, I need to go to Indiana yet tonight. I mean—" Tom regretted his choice of words. "I mean, could I please have a few days off?"

The words fell from his mouth like cotton before the marble presence of Adrian Tolley. Tom felt his shoulders sag. Why had he ever thought that Mr. Tolley, an icon of form and duty, would allow him to leave suddenly in the busy season? Tom's eyes fogged over.

Adrian Tolley raised his hand slowly from his page. He took off the nib and placed it on a grooved wooden tray. He turned to Tom and raised his heavy eyebrows.

"And what could be so urgent in this busy season, Thomas?"

Behind Tom, Sandy remained silent, which was most unusual. Both men had sensed that something was wrong.

"My mother is ill," Tom said. "My dad thinks she is having a stroke." He felt tears threatening at the back of his eyeballs, but he controlled them.

Mr. Tolley carved a few Italian oaths into the silence. Then, "We'll make it, Thomas. Just go."

"How will you go?" Sandy asked. "By car? By train yet tonight? I don't think there'll be many more trains leaving tonight."

Tom stood, shaking his head.

"Sharon has the car. I'll just pack a bag and hitchhike. I've done it before."

chapter twenty-two

The Drive

On Pennsylvania Avenue, Tom splurged and hailed a cab. The buses just took too long, and he could not afford wasted time tonight. Getting the cab to stop at his home, Tom bounded up the stairs of the brick building two at a time. Going straight to the closet, he pulled out a small brown suit-case and popped open the metal clasps. Quickly he threw in several changes of clothes. Pulling some cash from a dresser drawer, he shoved it into a sock and ran back down to the waiting cab.

"Take me to the edge of the city on Route 50," he told the cabbie. "I'm going to hitchhike from there."

"A bit cold to stand outside, sir," the cabbie observed. "But I take people wherever they wish to go."

Tom hadn't noticed the cold. He looked at his outfit and realized that he had not thought of throwing on a jacket. As the cab bumped through thinning traffic, Tom saw the Potomac River to the left, sparkling with upside-down images of the lighted city. They crossed the Arlington Memorial Bridge and continued through the city to Route 50.

"The gas station will be fine," Tom said. "I'll find someone there to give me a lift."

"Five dollars," the cabbie said.

It seemed exorbitantly high, but Tom had made him wait. He handed over the bill without a word and stepped into the night. He walked to the vehicles parked at the fuel station and glanced at the plates. Virginia. Maryland. Pennsylvania. Iowa!

"Sir, are you going all the way to Iowa tonight?" he asked the driver of the pickup.

The driver held a fat, stinking cigar between his orange lips. With a meaty hand, he took it from his mouth and looked Tom up and down.

"If my rig holds I should be there by morning," he said. "You looking for a ride?"

"Just to Indiana. Can you take me?"

"If you can find yourself a place, get in," the man said. He returned the cigar to his lips. Tom went around to the passenger side door and pulled. It opened with a scream of rusty hinges and an avalanche of empty bottles. One of them hit the pavement and shattered into small pieces.

The driver couldn't pronounce the "b" sound around the cigar, and it came out as "m." "If there's plastic mottles, I always muy plastic now," he observed around his cigar. "Greatest invention since the telephone."

Tom started to walk away to look for a broom, but an attendant arrived and waved him away. Tom took the liberty of throwing as many bottles as he could into the trash can beside the gas pumps, then settled into the ragged passenger seat. From the smell inside the truck, he got the distinct impression that the driver had a dog who often accompanied him.

"What mrings you out so late tonight?" the man asked. He put the truck in gear, and it moved forward with a shudder. *Maybe it's having a stroke too and won't survive the night,* Tom thought morbidly. From the wide running board, Tom estimated the pickup was a 1930-something model. It was certainly older than Tom's old Plymouth had been. It was probably as old as Tom himself.

Tom explained that his mother was sick. He gave no additional details, and really did not want the man to keep talking. But he didn't want to be alone with his thoughts either. It was a hard decision.

"I'll probably try to get a little sleep," Tom explained.

The man pulled out onto Highway 50.

"If you can sleep through them West 'Ginny hills, you'll be doing better than most," he said. "Not even my dogs can sleep in them hills."

Tom turned his head to look into the bed of the pickup. So there *were* dogs. How had he missed seeing them when he climbed in?

"Dropped 'em off in Virginny," the man said. "I haul huntin' dogs from a dog kennel in Iowa."

The man reached his thick hand toward a bulging paper bag below the gear stick. Tom saw the heavy black curves of his unwashed fingernails even in the dim light. The hand dipped into the bag and came back out crammed with saltwater taffy. With the expertise of dedicated practice, he used his thumb to scoop open the wax paper around the candy. With at least five pieces still in his hand, he removed the cigar from his mouth and flipped in the opened candy. The cigar-stained teeth bit into the taffy with a smacking sound. He did not go to the trouble of muffling the sound by closing his mouth.

"If you want some, help yourself," the driver said through the candy and a shower of saliva.

Tom had not loved saltwater taffy before, and he was now certain he never would.

"No thank you." He pulled a thin pack of Swan cigarettes from his pocket and lit one. Recently he had begun smoking more, and he found it calmed his nerves and settled his stomach on occasions such as this. The driver made him want to vomit.

It was a terrible night.

As much as Tom longed to escape into the cool oasis of mindless sleep, it was out of the question. He couldn't even rest. The old truck cab was impossibly narrow, and the sharp angles of the truck seat formed Tom's frame into a disabling L-shape. Every time the driver shifted or dipped into his bag of taffy, his elbow rammed against Tom. A sinister rattle in the bowels of the truck convinced Tom it would not get them through West Virginia.

The West Virginia road fought the old truck. When the truck tried to speed up, the road threw a curve out of the darkness. When the truck finally straightened, they would hit jarring potholes, each one jabbing the seat springs into Tom's spine. Tom had never before experienced the slightest difficulty with motion sickness, but tonight he felt ill.

Tom regretted that he had not asked his father for more details. What did it mean that Mom had a stroke? Did it mean that her smile was lopsided, or that she could not move one side of her body? Tom remembered that his childhood Sunday school teacher had experienced a stroke like that. She had never taught Sunday school again, but she had lived and learned to do everything with one hand. And even though she had a hard time pronouncing her words, everyone loved her anyway. It wasn't too bad.

Or did it mean Mom had a stroke like Franklin Roosevelt had, a cerebral hemorrhage? In vain Tom attempted to push aside the thoughts about the death of the beloved president. He remembered hearing the news on the radio at Grecco's. He remembered Mr. West the usher telling about Mr. and Mrs. Truman rushing to the White House pale and shaken at the news that the President had died and Mr. Truman had just become President. He remembered his description of Eleanor Roosevelt, pale but efficient and speedy as ever, making decisions about the funeral. President Roosevelt's body had lain in state in the East Room, the sixth president's coffin to be placed there.

Coffins. Funerals. Lines of people paying their last respects. No, that could not be his mother. God would heal her, God would give her ten more years. He would have to, or Tom would never speak to Him again.

Or . . . his dad had said he *thought* she was having a stroke. Maybe it wasn't even a stroke. Maybe it was only a very bad headache . . .

But no. Dad was, above all things, not a hysterical man. He would never have called Tom home for a headache. In his heart, Tom knew the truth.

"If this old truck don't fall apart 'fore we get there," the driver croaked, "I'm gonna pull up at the gas pumps right inside Ohio across the river. I comes this way a lot and they 'mout the only good place that's open until midnight. If I wanted to get robbed, I'd get gas here in West 'Ginny, but nope, I'm going across the river."

With a scream, the old truck motored up the suspension bridge over the Ohio River. On the other side, a lighted Standard Oil sign welcomed them. A pole light barely illuminated the words on the side of the building: TIRES. GREASING. TUBES. When they came to a stop, Tom slowly unfolded himself from the seat. At least they had made it to Ohio. The next state was Indiana, and Route 50 would take them straight into Bedford. For now, he would escape the confines of the truck and hopefully find some coffee.

"Mister," squeaked a feminine voice at his elbow, "My husband died three weeks ago and I have seven little children. I'm trying to collect money to buy food for my family. Can you spare a dollar?"

The voice came from the depths of a ragged shawl, and Tom smelled accumulated body odor. He didn't believe the story; he had entertained too many beggars in D.C. not to be able to spot the carefully-crafted nature of the story. For one thing, was it possible to have seven little children? However, he did not have the mental energy to formulate a refusal. He handed her a dollar and headed into the fuel station, sighing.

"Any coffee, sir?"

The attendant behind the cash register was a teenager, probably working evenings after school. He reminded Tom of his own days as a gas station attendant. "Might be a bit cold. It was brewed a few hours ago," he said.

"I'll take it."

The old pickup's inhospitable smell struck Tom afresh when he climbed back inside. Dogs. Cigar. Body odor. Soiled truck seats.

"If I wouldn't get paid for driving," the driver complained, "I wouldn't go anywhere with these gas prices." "Always goes up and up. Pretty soon we'll be paying thirty cents a gallon."

Tom sipped the lukewarm coffee slowly. A true coffee lover, he drank coffee any way it was prepared, without discrimination. However, this cup offended even Tom. Had it somehow been mixed with the 25-cent gasoline?

As the truck blustered on through Ohio, Tom tried to sleep.

Beside him, the saltwater taffy squeaked and smacked through the yellow teeth of the driver. Before him, the sickly headlights bobbed with the shaking of the truck, revealing little more than the weeds on the side of Route 50. From the passenger window, Tom could see stars, bright and cold.

Was anyone behind those stars? Or was it just a black void of nothingness reaching on into infinity?

I'll know soon, Tom told himself grimly. *I'll know if there is a God. And if He cares.*

chapter twenty-three

The Hospital

December 6, 1956

The dreams were worse than the sleeplessness. As Tom finally dozed off, images flashed across his unconscious mind like war planes dropping atomic bombs.

President Roosevelt, dying. Mom standing at Tom's bedside, crocheting a funeral blanket for him.

As the pickup hit some gravel on the side of Route 50, Tom awoke, relieved. On the outskirts of Cincinnati, the driver pulled off at a closed fuel station. He pulled a metal fuel can from the bed of the pickup and refilled the tank.

Smelling of gasoline, the man crawled back behind the wheel and instantly dipped into the bag of taffy.

"James Candy Company," he said. "If it ain't James, it ain't good."

Tom stared out the windshield, confused. Finally he realized that the man was talking about the brand of candy he liked. Tom made a mental note to avoid James Candy Company at all costs.

He drifted off to sleep again. This time there was a funeral in the Diplomatic Reception Room at the White House. Lines and lines of people stood outside waiting to be let in. Tom was in the line, waiting behind the people ahead of him. Robert Schulz, in full dress uniform, was handing out saltwater taffy to the waiting crowds. But once Tom got his candy, he found it was dog food, not taffy. Finally he got to the coffin with the United States flag draped over it. He had to stand on tiptoes to look in, and he was holding Jeff, getting ready to point out the face of President Roosevelt. But then, as his eyes fell on the face in the casket, he saw it was his mother.

"Can you tell me where the hospital is in Medford?"

Tom jolted awake. It was the driver, talking around his cigar. Behind them, he saw that the eastern horizon was slightly green, the sign of first light. Ahead of him, he saw the city of Bedford. He was home. No coffin. No funeral. Just the gray stone churches of Bedford rising before them.

"Oh, I'm sorry, take a left on Main Street after the town square," Tom said, wiping a hand across his eyes. "You can drop me off beside the road. I'll walk in."

Tom fumbled for his wallet. He handed the man a $5 bill. It would nearly fill his tank again.

"Is that enough?" he asked.

"If I'd be doing this to make money," the man said, "I'd offer you a metter truck. Keep your money and muy your mama some get-well present."

"Thanks," Tom said. "Safe travels."

The Bedford Dunn Memorial Hospital, like many of the churches and public buildings in Bedford, was constructed with Bedford stone. The early morning sunlight glistened on the gray stone as Tom stretched himself and headed for the front entrance, still clutching his brown suitcase.

Surely the news inside couldn't be too bad.

At the front desk, a receptionist yawned and paged through a book to find the room Tom was looking for. She pointed Tom to an elevator across the lobby, half hidden by a giant Christmas wreath and a pile of presents wrapped in tinsel.

Surely everything is okay, Tom told himself. Surely the receptionist would not be half asleep if someone were dying here.

Tom stumbled off the elevator.

"Tommy!" Patsy jumped from a chair in the waiting room. "You made it! How did you—"

Tom saw that her eyes were red. Behind her, Joan and Joe slowly rose to their feet, shaking off sleep.

"I hitchhiked. Patsy, how's Mom? Where's Dad?"

Patsy sighed.

"Dad's back in the room with her. I'll take you back. She's . . ." Patsy shook her head. "She's not doing well. She won't even open her eyes."

"What happened?"

Joe and Joan gathered with their older siblings.

Joan, who had been at home with Mom, told the story. "Mom felt better after Thanksgiving, then one day she sat up to fold laundry. I don't know why she did that." Joan began sobbing. "I could have done it myself."

"Joan, that's not what caused this," Patsy protested.

"Then she said she had a terrible headache. And she just fell back in bed," Joan finished, sniffling and swallowing.

"It's—" Patsy swallowed. "The doctor thinks it's one of those—you know like President Roos—"

"Yes, I know," Tom snapped. He instantly felt bad, but he just could not take it. He could not bear the name "Roosevelt" right now. "I need to see her."

"Come," Patsy said.

The sterile white walls of the hospital corridor repulsed Tom. The golden Christmas stars dangling from the ceiling of the critical care waiting room offended him. The calm "good morning" from the pretty nurse behind the nurse's desk enraged him.

How could she just say "good morning" as if that made the world better? How could she not be weeping at the disaster of the night? How could she look so casual, as if all was well?

Then they were in the room, and all was over, in Tom's mind. From the moment he saw his mother lying among the hospital linen, her eyes closed and her fingers still, he knew she would not recover. The needle in her forearm, dripping some ineffective medication into her veins, mocked their hopes. The blood pressure cuff around her opposite arm brought all the previous doctors' visits rushing back to Tom's memory. Never, never, had the doctors been able to solve his mother's condition, and they could not do it now. What was the use of fancy blood pressure cuffs and precise metal dials? What was the use of knowing how high her blood pressure had been all these years when it had not helped to cure her?

Useless! Useless! Useless! beeped the monitor at the bedside.

"Tom."

He felt his father's hand on his shoulder.

"I'm glad you made it, Tom."

Tom saw that his father seemed to have aged by many years since he had seen him on Thanksgiving. *But perhaps the same thing happened to me overnight,* Tom thought, remembering the memorable ride.

"I should have stayed here after Thanksgiving," Tom said. "It's just, we were so busy. We worked Friday and—"

"It doesn't make a difference, Tom," Dad said. "Don't blame yourself. No one knew this was coming."

Tom walked to the bed as if in a dream. Sitting in the chair his father had vacated, he took his mother's hand in his. He leaned his forehead against her hand and gave way to sobs.

Tom had thought that nothing could be worse than the long ride from Washington. He had thought that at least when he arrived in Bedford he would know what was going on. But now he was here, and he still didn't know. No one else knew either. Not his father, not the nurses, not the doctors. Not even Mom's old cardiologist knew.

The red-haired cardiologist on duty was the one Tom remembered from that office visit years ago. The doctor still ran his hands through his hair as he talked. He was still long and gangly and tended to look at the floor a lot. He was still dressed almost entirely in brown. The button strip of his shirt was still crumpled with wrinkles.

"I'm sorry, Mr. Kirkman," was the most useful thing he could say. "Her heart is still strong, we know that. It has always been too strong. Her brain is what suffers now. I have a neurologist friend in Bloomington who specializes in these cases. I'll call him down."

By midmorning, the young neurologist from Bloomington arrived. He did not think Bernice Kirkman would recover meaningful function. But even he was not sure.

"The brain is, unfortunately, a very reserved organ," he said, polishing his spectacles on his white coattail with an apologetic air. "Brains don't like to give us much information about what is going on inside. We can see on the angiogram that one of the small vessels in her brain burst and began to bleed. But we don't know yet how that has affected her. We know she is still breathing, and this is a function of the brain. But beyond that, we can't say for sure."

"Do you think there is a chance she might wake up?" Tom asked.

The young man sighed. He squinted through the eyeglasses he had just cleaned, as if searching for an answer. "If I had a crystal ball, I wouldn't be a doctor," he said. "All I can say is that sometimes people go into comas, and then a few days later they wake up. Other times they never wake up." He put on his glasses and clasped his hands together at the front of his white coat, his eyes resting on the silent figure in the bed. Beside him, a nurse and a medical student stood with pens and clipboards in hand. But there were no orders for them to record, no medications to prescribe to save the patient's life.

"She's so young," the neurologist went on, shifting his weight inside the oversized white coat. "I'm so sorry I can't give you more help, but let's not give up hope. The nurses will take great care of her, and we will give her every chance we can for recovery." He glanced at the tube in Mom's nose. "That feeding going into her stomach will keep her strong."

But it did not. An hour later Tom was in a dazed sleep on a chair in the lounge when the doctor came to tell the family that Mom had breathed her last. Joe poked him and he got to his feet. A kitchen food cart rattled by, smelling of broccoli. Tom wanted to gag. As if in a dream, he asked Patsy to take him out of the hospital to Sharon and Jeff.

Patsy dropped him off at the Arthur home on Lincoln Avenue. The December sun rose over the icy cold city, casting Tom's shadow before him as he climbed the seven steps to the entrance. Mrs. Arthur met him at the door. Behind her, Tom saw a Christmas tree half decorated.

"Tom!"

Apparently Mrs. Arthur had not known he was coming.

Tom knew he must look awful, but he didn't apologize. He had no small talk in him.

"Is Sharon here?"

"She's just getting ready to come up to the hospital. How is everything up there this morning, Tom? I'm so sorry."

Tom just shook his head and took the stairs two at a time to the guest room.

Sharon, applying lipstick with the help of an oval wall mirror, shot Tom a welcoming smile.

Tom did not smile back. He dropped onto the bed. In a crib nearby, Jeff slapped the bars of his crib and crowed at the sight of his father. Tom jumped up, scooped his son into his arms, and collapsed back on the bed. Sharon put down her makeup and sat beside him.

Tom squeezed Jeff tighter and looked into his wife's questioning eyes, then away to the oval mirror.

"She's dead."

"No, Tom!"

"Gone."

"Oh, no!"

Tom just shook his head.

"I have to get some sleep; I didn't get much last night."

"You look terrible. I'm so sorry, Tom."

Sharon began to weep. Tom sat up, putting an arm around her. He kissed Jeff mechanically and handed him to Sharon.

"You'll have to tell your mom; I didn't tell her. Wake me up if anyone needs me."

He felt he was still in a dream the next day when the family had to sit down and make funeral plans, discussing which songs should be sung at the funeral and in what dress their mother should be buried. He was also in a dream when family and friends walked past the casket, weeping and telling him and his brothers and sisters that "she is in a better place" and that "she wouldn't want to come back."

That's when he woke out of the fog.

Wouldn't want to come back?! Tom thought angrily, incredulously. His tears snapped off and his anger snapped on.

"I need to step away for a moment," he said to Sharon. He slipped through a door that led to a little Sunday school room and then into the back hall of the Baptist church. Stairs led down to the basement, and he could smell chicken cooking. He ran down the steps and let himself into an empty Sunday school classroom. Paper stars of David had been taped to the windows, and a poster of the three wise men carrying their gifts to the Baby Jesus graced the wall under the words, "Star of the East, thou hope of the soul."

Oh, he thought sarcastically, *so my mom is glad to have the church ladies cooking for us instead of being able to do it herself. She's glad that she gets to go off to glory so the other ladies in church, some much older than her, can stay here and play with her grandchildren and have tea parties and sewing bees without her. Really?* Tom doubted it.

He did not really blame the people who said this. No, he would not blame a mere mortal for something God had done.

It was God who was to blame. The God who claimed to have the power to heal, the power to make whole, and the power to bring to life. The God whom Fanny Crosby had written about. Mom had loved the blind hymn writer's words so much. "To God be the glory, great things He hath done."

Really? *Really?*

Tom wanted to shout the question, but he knew he would be overheard. Hot tears pushed out of his eyes, but he clenched his fists and pushed them back. He did not want God to have the satisfaction of seeing him cry.

"Tommy?" It was Patsy, breathless, standing at the door, looking at her younger brother with concern. "Are you all right, Tom? People are asking for you."

"Oh Patsy, God help us!" Tom said, letting his fist fall onto the wooden craft table with a bang. "Are we in this to make other people have a good day?"

Patsy stared at him. Tom sighed, and let his shoulders slump out of their tight posture.

"Sorry," he said, defeated. "I'll come up. I just came down for a drink of water."

Tom retreated into his fog. He had an engaging smile when he chose to use it, and he did his best to put it on at the expected times. Through the visitation, through the funeral, through the songs about heaven, he steeled his heart and closed his ears to the words he heard. Beside him, Sharon wept and wiped her eyes. Tom pulled out his handkerchief and blew his nose and even shed some tears. But he did not want to think.

And then he was at the grave. But instead of watching the proceedings, he mostly looked down—where the toes of his black dress shoes were planted amid clods of brown dirt.

He heard the voice of the preachers talking about God and how the Lord gives and the Lord takes away. He heard the verses about the trumpet sounding and the dead in Christ rising first, and he did his best to shut out the sounds.

If the Bible had been right, then he would not be here standing among the trees and brown lawns of Cresthaven Cemetery. If the Bible had been right about God's goodness and love, he would not be here wondering if Patsy and Carol had left Mom's wristwatch in the casket. If they had, how long would it keep ticking? Would it last through the winter? Through the summer? Through another winter? He did not want to think. His stomach turned and for a second he swallowed hard to keep back the acid rising in his throat.

He focused again on the toes of his shoes, black amid the brown clods.

chapter twenty-four

Edges of Grief

"I don't want to be one of those people who stays in Washington for fifty years while telling people they are living here only temporarily," Tom said, shoving back his dinner plate. "Let's move home after I finish my time and get discharged. Dad needs more people to be around him anyway."

"I like it here," Sharon said. "I like the social life and the energy of the city. Do you think we will come back someday?"

Tom shrugged.

"I don't want to. This is where I was when Mom had her stroke."

"You can't let that destroy you, Tom! I know you loved your mom, but she wouldn't want you to give up on life because of what happened!"

"You don't understand; you still have your mom."

"I'm not saying it's not terrible!" Sharon said. "I wouldn't like it if my mom—"

"I don't want to talk about it," Tom interrupted. He got up and left the kitchen.

Jeff had begun toddling around the apartment now. As Tom watched, he stepped, toppled, plopped in a heap, and got up to go at it again.

If only I could do that, Tom thought. *Just get up and dust myself off and try believing God again like Mom always wanted me to do.* But he did not, and a deep despondency settled over his life.

As Tom and Sharon began to pack, they could sense the growing chasm between them.

They left Washington, D.C., on a warm spring morning when the cherry trees were in full bloom. The birds and the buses woke up together, chirping and honking, each in their own language. Tom opened the back door of the pale green Renault and threw in their luggage. The little Renault was a good car for getting around the city; he hoped it had the stamina to make it all the way back to Indiana. Sharon and Jeff soon fell asleep, and Tom was left with his thoughts.

Tom drove to the end of Congress Street and turned left at the large Hebrew cemetery as he had every morning when he drove to work. This morning, however, the cemetery seemed to be staring at him and his sleeping wife and son. Each of the orderly grave markers looked at him knowingly. *You thought God did great things, didn't you, Tom? We know the truth. Just listen to us, Tom. Your mom is with all the others—cold, in a box in the ground.*

As they passed St. Elizabeth Hospital a while later, Tom's thoughts took another dark turn. *What good are hospitals anyway?*

Farther east, the mighty Capitol building would soon be alive with the members of Congress coming and going as if nothing was wrong in the world. Richard Nixon would soon take his seat as president of the Senate, as vice presidents always did. Although Eisenhower had been vague about whether he would ask Nixon to stay on as vice president in the second term, he had finally committed. Everyone would be watching Nixon, wondering how he would do if something happened to the President.

Would President Eisenhower make it through another four years of office?

Everyone wondered, although he had recovered well from his heart attack a year before. For a while, the President himself had not been sure if he wished to stay in the White House.

On they traveled through West Virginia, then over the Ohio River. Close to Cincinnati, Tom stopped for a second fuel refill. He ran across the street and paid for two cheeseburgers and milkshakes while Sharon stayed in the car with Jeff.

It was late in the evening when the little Renault puttered into Bedford, Indiana. The limestone churches and houses stood by like a welcoming committee as the car drove up Lincoln Avenue.

Sharon's parents had invited Tom, Sharon, and Jeff to live with them on Lincoln Avenue while they looked for a permanent dwelling. The Lincoln Avenue home was just up the road from Grecco's, the pizza shop where Tom had served so many pizzas and washed so many dishes.

Back home, Tom took one path in life and Sharon took another. Smarting with the sting of his mother's death, Tom withdrew inside himself. When Sharon lashed out at him, he spoke even less. Tom and Sharon both loved Jeff, but they learned to avoid each other as much as possible.

Tom took up work at a construction job. The hard labor was good for him. When his hammer struck, he felt the pent-up energy and grief crash out of his soul and onto the lumber. Besides, construction took him back to his childhood, when life had still been okay.

In the months that followed the dark December of 1956, Tom's siblings spoke to one another in whispers at family gatherings, wondering whether the others worried about the same thing. They all agreed: Dad was spiraling into a dangerous depression. And he had begun drinking, the habit he most despised.

"Tommy, he has a glass with him every time I see him!" Patsy wept openly, speaking to Tom and Bill. Joan sat on the floor close by, building a tower of blocks with little Jeff. The family had gathered to welcome Tom and Sharon home. Their father was out in the yard, giving the siblings a chance to talk together. "Do you think it is okay for Joan to live in the same house?"

Bill, as serious and kind as ever, looked down at Joan and frowned. "How do you feel, sister?"

"Dad wouldn't hurt me!" Joan exclaimed, the yellow block in her hand suspended in midair. "He has a heart of gold! But he doesn't say much anymore."

A heavy silence fell over the older siblings. They knew their father did have a heart of gold, at least in the past. But they were not sure that the man now before them was the same one they grew up with. And they were not convinced that Joan was safe.

"Bock, bock!" Jeff said, reaching for the block in Joan's hand.

"Shhh, Jeff, just wait," Sharon said from a nearby chair where she sat with Carol.

But little Jeff had not yet learned the meaning of the word *wait*. His chubby hand reached for the yellow block. He struck the tower and the blocks tumbled onto the carpet.

Just like our lives! Tom thought, watching the blocks scatter. *Mom's death is the hand that struck our family.*

"Joan, I really could use help with my little people," Patsy said. "Why don't you come stay with us for a bit?"

"I can't leave Dad!" Joan cried, bursting into tears. "If I leave, how will he ever function? I'm all he has!"

Reluctantly the older siblings relented.

One night when Sharon was out reuniting with friends, Tom took Jeff with him to Grecco's. The familiar brown paneled walls and the still life artwork soothed him. The same manager was there, and he greeted Tom with awe.

"You've come back!" he cried. "From the White House! Never thought we'd see you in the humble village of Bedford again! Oh, and I'm so sorry about your loss, Tom."

That was the problem. No matter who Tom met, the subject of pain and grief and loss always emerged.

From the WHITE HOUSE *to the* AMISH

But there was a familiar face, someone whose innocence would not bring to mind adult troubles. At least Billy had not changed. He was much taller than he had been, a grown man. But he still wore cowboy boots and a cowboy hat.

While Tom and Jeff waited for their pizza, Billy clomped over to Tom with a wide smile. He pulled a parcel from his pocket.

Tom blinked. It was the yellow horse, wrapped in a tattered napkin. Surely it could not be . . . ? But it was. It was the horse that Tom had sketched for Billy so many years before. Tom felt tears pooling in his eyes.

Billy handed the yellow horse to Jeff, who took it gladly. Then, Billy pulled a napkin from the holder.

"Picchhure?" he asked Tom, spreading the napkin on the table.

"Oh, Billy," Tom said, "I'm really not very good at drawing right now."

But Billy was unswayed. He clomped up to the cash register, selected a pencil, and returned to Tom.

"Picchhure," he said.

Tom played with the pencil for a second, and began to sketch. Almost without his bidding, President Eisenhower's Angus bull appeared on the napkin.

"Picchhure!" Billy said triumphantly.

A few weeks later, Tom was out mowing the lawn around their house. Sharon came running down the porch steps to get him in for a phone call. Jeff wailed in the doorway, confused.

"It's your brother Joe," Sharon panted. "I think something is wrong."

His body tingling with fear, Tom snatched up the receiver.

"Tom, Dad threatened to shoot a police officer."

Tom tried to listen as Joe's words came to him through the phone line. He felt his heart sink and twist with fresh pain. He gripped the receiver.

"Threatened to shoot—what?!"

"Joan came to our house because Dad started holding a shotgun, so I called the police. A couple of officers arrived to talk to him, but he threatened to shoot them."

"What did they do?"

"I arrived and told them he's mentally unstable and that we are trying to get him into a hospital, so they left. But you have to come help us."

"I'll be right over. Where are you?"

"Back at my house, but I'll meet you at Dad's."

Tom kissed little Jeff and ran for the door.

"Be careful, Tom!" Sharon called.

"I will," he said. He jumped into the Renault and stepped on the gas.

As the stone houses of Bedford gave way to the trees and rolling banks of Avoca, Tom could not stop his heart from pounding. He clutched the wheel of the Renault with all his might. Joe had pulled up at the side of the road at the end of Dad's long lane.

"He'll be fine when he sees us without the officers," Joe assured Tom. "But I still don't want to scare him by just driving in."

"Or make yourself a target," Tom said. "Let's just walk in."

Joe was bigger than Tom by now. He had just returned from his time with the Marines. But Tom's experiences still outweighed Joe's, and he was the leader of the two.

"Dad!" Tom called from beneath the apple tree at the edge of the lawn. "Can we come up? We just want to talk."

The huge frame of their father rested on the porch bench where he and Mom had sat almost every evening in the summertime after they had bought the little house. Tom's heart broke to think of the desolation of the empty side of the bench. Only deep despair could have driven their father to fill their mother's empty seat with things both she and he hated. But there it was. Beside Dad, a six-pack of beer rested in the lonely place. In his hand he held a quart of whiskey. And in his mouth, he held words that his sons had never before heard him say.

"You can come up, but I won't let no lily-livered sons of police officers up here, or anyone else. You can come up, but you'd better not interfere with me. I ain't leaving this house. Don't you think for one moment I'm ever going to leave this house. I'll shoot anyone I know before I leave." He glanced meaningfully at the gun standing against the porch rail.

Tom felt strangely unafraid. His life had unraveled so badly that he seemed immune to fear. He strode across the lawn in full range of his father's gun and walked up the wooden porch steps, past the ferns that Mom had transplanted last spring.

"Dad, it's getting cool. Let's step inside."

"Cool—nothing. You just want to trap me." He got up, walked off the porch, and headed around the house to the backyard.

Tom and Joe looked at each other and then followed him.

"Why are you following me?" Dad barked. Turning, he dashed up the steps toward the back door, crashing into it. Glass shattered. Tom saw beads of blood form on his father's bare arm as he yanked the door open and rushed into the house.

Tom and Joe stared. Tom bit down on his lip, tasting blood.

"We have to follow him." Tom stepped onto the wooden staircase leading to the door. "He's out of his mind."

Crunching over shards of glass, they entered the house. Dad sat at the kitchen table, and both Tom and Joe breathed a sigh of relief. Joe had been right. Dad would not likely hurt his own children.

"Dad," Tom began, "we are all worried about you. You don't seem yourself."

"Why do you think I would be myself?" Dad asked irritably. With red eyes he sized up the quart in his hand and took another gulp. A splash of whiskey missed his mouth and trickled down his massive jaw, still carefully shaven.

"I know, Dad," Tom said. "None of us is ourselves with Mom gone. But we think maybe if you would just see a doctor—"

Tom got no farther. With a terrible oath, Dad hurled the quart of whiskey to the floor and ran to a kitchen drawer. In a flash, he had pulled out a long knife.

"Now didn't I tell you I would kill anyone who tried to get me to leave this house?"

"I've got him, Joe," Tom said quietly to his brother, who was closer to the front door. "Run and get help."

Joe slipped out the screen door. Tom tried to edge his way toward the front door as well, all the while trying to soothe his father. When he got close to the door, he leaped for it.

His father, knife in hand, was close behind.

Tom leaped through the door and slammed the screen door on his father. He knew he could hold the door shut, but his father's knife tore through the screen and cut into Tom's thumb. Blood spurted from the thumb onto the torn screen, but Tom held his ground.

"Dad, calm down," Tom said. "There's no point in fighting."

But Dad would not calm down. The police and medics had to remove him forcibly from his house. Not until he was given a sedative at the hospital did he calm down.

As if the drama at home was not enough, the newspapers were full of craziness too. President Eisenhower had experienced a small stroke on a day he had planned to host a state dinner. Vice President Nixon had stood in for him. According to the papers, the President was now feeling much better.

Tom knew the President had had a busy and stressful fall. About the time Dad was taken to a mental hospital, the newspapers had overflowed with civil rights stories from Little Rock, Arkansas. The governor of Arkansas had defied the federal court order to integrate the schools, and President Eisenhower had sent federal troops to the city to see that the order was carried out.

As he read the stories, Tom could picture President Eisenhower in the second floor painting room, mixing paint and mumbling about the governor defying the court order.

Around the time of Dad's hospitalization and the drama in Little Rock, Tom found a job in Bloomington with a radio and television company owned by a Turkish-born man named Sarkes Tarzian. Tom's job was to draw cartoons and work with the development of equipment for radio and TV. He enjoyed his work, and some days he disappeared in his office for hours, unaware that half a day had passed before he emerged for another coffee. He found that the creation of art soothed his grief and helped him forget his troubles.

Now it was December again. Thankfully, Dad was out of the hospital and doing well. He had even taken up a construction job, his lifelong passion. And best of all, he had stopped drinking.

Tom and Sharon had just welcomed a new son, Brad. Tom had named him after General Omar Bradley, one of President Eisenhower's close friends. Tom loved little Brad, and lavishing him with attention helped to dull the pain in his heart.

Unless he was playing with his boys or drawing cartoons, however, Tom was not doing well. He watched the Christmas decor emerge around Bedford just as it had at the White House last year. Tom wished he could skip the month of December and get on with January. Whenever he heard "Joy to the World," he cringed. Where was the One who rules the world with truth and grace? Why had God not answered his prayer?

chapter twenty-five

Modern Times

1957 to 1959

By the time Christmas rolled around again, Jeff was old enough to enjoy the holiday season. He toddled around the house and exclaimed over Sharon's colorful presents, the twinkling Christmas tree, and the fancy gingerbread cookies. His obvious pleasure made the season more tolerable for Tom. Baby Brad, though he spent many hours crying, was a joy to his father. Tom loved to sit in a chair and hold both of his sons in his arms. Sometimes he sang to them. Sometimes he just talked to them. Tom was sure Jeff was more intelligent than any other one-year-old in the state, and he thought he could detect an incredible sense of wisdom in Baby Brad as well.

When the family gathered for their Christmas get-together, however, the loss of his mother hit him full force again.

"Tommy," Patsy told him quietly when they met at the Kirkman coffee pot on Christmas Day, "talk to God about what you are feeling."

"Patsy, Christmas just isn't right without Mom here. Am I supposed to talk to God about that? I didn't even get to say goodbye to her. She was already unconscious . . ." Tom stopped, biting his lip and shaking his head.

"I know, Tommy," Patsy said, her eyes filling with tears. "I know. I didn't either. But yes, Tommy, you *can* talk to God. About that. And about anything else!"

Tom shrugged and turned to the date pudding, which was still on the counter. He helped himself to another plateful and went to watch Joan beat Bob and Bill at Monopoly. Joan's new husband played too, and he cheered her on even when he was on the losing side.

Soon the next holiday arrived with all the usual appropriate comments. *"Happy New Year! Can you believe it is 1958 already?"*

Amazing, Tom thought, shaking his head. *The years pass so quickly, and the world is becoming so advanced.* Scientists had used computers to develop the hydrogen bomb, and now there was talk that computers were to be used in colleges and hospitals. These machines could process information better than advanced calculators. Tom doubted if machines that filled a whole room would ever be common, but it was impossible to predict. New models of cars and spacious station wagons with lots of seating were also appearing on the market. Tom had his eye on one, now that they were a family of four.

The interstate highway system authorized in 1956 by President Eisenhower was beginning to take shape. These new roads did not have many intersections. Instead, roads that met them had to go over the highway on a bridge or under the highway. The highways were all at least four lanes wide, with two lanes going each way. They had ramps to get on and off the roads. Tom had been on one, and the speed of travel by this route was nothing short of amazing.

He had also heard about a new restaurant called McDonald's. Though Tom had never seen one, he had heard that the restaurant was becoming known for speedy service, fifteen-cent cheeseburgers, and thick milkshakes. He hoped he would get a chance to visit one someday.

At least Dad was doing better. Tom and Sharon even felt good about letting him hold little Brad. And Brad seemed to do his grandpa a world of good too.

Tom had also recovered some emotional stability and found life more manageable. He had decided to go back to school, and then try to get a job as an artist. Maybe he would stay with Sarkes Tarzian or maybe he would do something even more fun, like make maps. Tom kept only a casual eye on political things. He followed Eisenhower from afar, occasionally reading the newspaper and watching the television when he held little Brad at night. He wondered what he would do without his two sons.

On New Year's Day 1959, Tom listened with extra interest to the radio account of a young man named Fidel Castro who had led a successful revolution to overthrow the Cuban government. Cuba, Tom knew, was not far from Florida.

By April, Tom felt that his life had fallen into a tolerable pattern of work, school, and cuddling his two sons. He and Sharon co-existed and did not fight often. Tom was not interested in God, but being a good American and going to church occasionally went hand in hand. To say one did not believe in God sounded like the Communists, and no one wanted to be mistaken for a Communist these days.

One night when Sharon and the boys were at her mother's house, Tom was reading the newspaper. He read about Fidel Castro's visit to the United States. Eisenhower, the newspaper said, had avoided being on hand to welcome Castro personally. Foreign leaders were supposed to come to the U. S. at the invitation of the State Department, not just show up on their own. Castro had not been invited, so Eisenhower felt no need to welcome him.

Tom was about to lay down the paper when a small side article caught his eye. "NEW HOPE FOR HARDWORKING HEARTS," it said. Tom scanned the brief report. A new medication called Diuril had just been released. Diuril helped the body dispose of excessive fluid. It showed great promise for the treatment of high blood pressure, the writer said.

Tom hurled the paper to the floor in a crumpled ball and strode from the house. He ran down the front steps, nearly tripping over the tricycle Jeff had left on the cement walk. He ignored the wave of a neighbor walking by with a St. Bernard. He turned left, then right, and charged down O Street, blinded by rage.

So God could bring a miracle medicine to treat high blood pressure, could He? With His great power He could solve all problems, like the Bible said, right?

Then why could He not have allowed this medication to come a decade sooner? No, just five years sooner. Even a year or two sooner. The article said trials for the medication had been carried out for a number of months. Perhaps it had already been invented before Mom's death.

This was the final straw in Tom's great burden. He would never go to church again, he decided. He would never make any pretext of respecting or honoring God. He would forge his own path in the world. He would not ask God to do great things for Him, or sing that dreadful song his mother had clung to about giving glory to God.

Perhaps there was a God for others. But for Tom, God had forever and finally gone down with that crumpled newspaper.

Tom looked around. He found that it was nearly dark, and that his steps had somehow taken him past Grecco's. He turned away, not wanting to be recognized by anyone on this awful night. But he had not turned before his friend had spotted him through one of the wide windows.

Billy waved wildly, his toothy grin taking up half of his simple, shining face. Billy was ecstatic to see his old friend. Tom waved shortly and walked on.

He hated himself for not being nicer. He hated Billy for being so happy.

chapter twenty-six

A Certificate from
the Past

1960

"Tom, this came to my house today."

Tom jerked awake and looked up from his recliner. Bill stood just inside the screen door with an envelope in his hand.

It was a summer evening in 1960. Tom and Sharon had picked up pizza at Grecco's for a quick meal. Since Sharon and Tom both worked full time, not a lot of cooking happened at the house. Jeff and Brad, now four and two, raced around outside in the backyard, enjoying the fireflies and the cool breeze after spending the day at Grandma's. Since Tom and Sharon had lived with Sharon's parents briefly, Tom used Bill's address for some of his mail.

The envelope was the size of an unfolded sheet of letter paper. In the top left corner, the return address said simply, "The White House."

He shook himself.

"Thanks, Bill. Let me see what this is."

"Is Sharon home?"

Tom picked up a letter opener. "No. She's meeting a friend."

The letter opener ripped through the thick envelope. A letter and a certificate fell into Tom's lap.

"Ah, it's from Schulz!" Tom said with pleasure. "Shall I read it out loud?"

"Sure," Bill said, seating himself on the velvet green couch that had been in the Kirkman family for years. "If it's not too private."

"Dear Specialist Kirkman:

I have been directed by the President to forward to you the White House Service Certificate. This certificate is awarded under the provisions of Executive Order 10879, 1 June 1960, for services performed in support of the President of the United States during the period 18 October, 1954, to 15 April, 1957. I would like to add my personal appreciation for your fine work and the superior manner in which you have assisted the United States Army in its White House support mission. A copy of this letter has been forwarded to the Adjutant General for inclusion in your official records.

With best wishes, Sincerely, Robert L. Schulz, Colonel, U.S. Army, Military Aide to the President."

Tom looked at the certificate. He read that aloud as well.

"This is to certify that the President of the United States of America has awarded The White House Service Certificate to Specialist Second Class Thomas E. Kirkman for honorable service in the White House."

"I do believe that is Sandy Fox's writing!" Tom exclaimed, pointing to the calligraphy used to spell his name and title.

"How can you tell who wrote that?"

Tom held the certificate at an angle beside the lamp on the end table.

"I can't," he admitted. "But he often did the certificates, and it's so well done I doubt it's anyone new."

Certificate from the White House

"Think you'll ever go back, Tom?"

"No. Why would I? There are plenty of people to take those jobs now. Although I am surprised, they still have time to award certificates in the midst of fighting Communism and Cuba. Everyone is so scared of Fidel Castro all of a sudden, whether justified or not."

"Do you think Nixon will win the election?" Bill asked. He wasn't particularly interested in politics, but he found his brother's perspective to be fascinating.

"How would I know? Just because I worked in the White House does not mean I can predict the vote of America. I didn't particularly like Nixon, but I never worked with him much either. I just don't think he's as nice as Eisenhower. Senator Kennedy has plenty of money, that's for sure. Not sure about the Catholic part though. And he's really young. But so is Nixon, I guess."

"Yes."

Tom paused and reflected over what he had heard in the news recently.

"Well, Kennedy hasn't even gotten the Democratic nomination yet."

"But he will, don't you think?" Bill replied.

"Yes, and I think he'll try to use the Cuba problem in his favor. If Kennedy can blame Eisenhower for Fidel Castro getting cozy with the Russians, and come up with a plan for dealing with the situation, he will get everyone's attention."

Bill frowned. He got up and went to the kitchen for a drink of water.

"Is it fair to blame Eisenhower?" Bill asked. "I guess he did get the nation in trouble with that U-2 plane."

The month before, the Russians had shot down a United States plane as it flew over their country. The United States government said it was a weather research plane.

A few days later, Khrushchev, the Soviet leader, no doubt rubbing his hands with glee, told the rest of the story. The plane had not gone up in flames, as everyone assumed. The Russians had it, and they had found rolls and rolls of photographic film inside. Wasn't that a bit odd for a weather research plane?

And, oh yes, Khrushchev added, they also had the pilot. Francis Gary Powers, who was flying the spy plane for the CIA, was alive and in their custody. He had not taken advantage of the poisonous needle in his possession.

The truth was clear: The United States had been flying high-altitude, high-speed planes over Russia, taking pictures. Eisenhower had known that it was a CIA plane, not a weather research plane—and he had lied.

"Yes, that was a mess," Tom agreed. "But I don't know if it's fair to blame Eisenhower for the trouble with the Communists. Eisenhower didn't personally meet Castro when he came to Washington last April, and some people say if he had been nicer, Castro wouldn't be courting the Soviets now. But who knows? And maybe the Communists aren't as bad as everyone thinks."

"Don't say that in public!" Bill laughed. "At least Joe McCarthy isn't around anymore to accuse everyone of being a Communist."

Just then Jeff and Brad ran in from the backyard. Brad was crying because he had tripped over the root of a tree while trying to catch a firefly. Tom scooped him up and held him until he stopped crying. Jeff ran to his uncle Bill and pulled at his hand, trying to get him to join the firefly hunt.

"You doing okay, Tom?"

The sentence came softly, out of the silence. Tom did not like the question. Bill was probing his heart, probably wanting to know if Tom prayed at night and if he had worked through his bitterness. Tom didn't even want to think about matters of the heart. He had gone to church a few times to hear his brother Bob preach. But not lately. Not after he read that newspaper article about the new medication to treat high blood pressure.

"Oh, I'm okay, Bill. Not a saint like you, but you know that."

A soft chuckle came from the green velvet couch.

"No, I don't know that, Tom. Without Christ we all stand on equal footing as sinners."

Again the silence fell, broken only by Brad's sniffles. Jeff had gone to find a toy horse to show to his uncle.

Tom just nodded. After a pause he began, "I don't know, Bill. The Communists might be right about God. They are not right about anything else, but they might be right about Him. If God would have wanted me . . . Never mind, Bill. I think we just view the idea of God differently. I don't want to talk about it."

Although Tom didn't want to talk about it, his thoughts were not so easily controlled. *He just doesn't understand. He doesn't know how I prayed for Mom to be healed. He doesn't know how I prayed for new treatments for high blood pressure. And how God answered my prayer—two years too late.*

Smiling through his bitter thoughts, Tom found a package of chocolate sandwich cookies and passed them to the boys and Bill. Then he gave them each a glass of milk. For the rest of Bill's visit they stayed on safer subjects.

Tom continued to follow the news through the rest of the summer of 1960. As expected, Senator John Kennedy and Vice President Richard Nixon were soon battling each other for the presidency. True to Tom's prediction, Kennedy painted Eisenhower and his administration as hopelessly outdated and behind the times. He blamed the tensions with the Soviet Union and Cuba on Eisenhower.

Cuba, in particular, had turned into a kind of tug of war. It started when Cuba asked the United States oil companies on their island to refine Soviet oil for them. When the companies refused, Castro took their property. In retaliation, Eisenhower reduced the United States' sugar purchase from Cuba. Castro then responded by taking more property and selling the sugar to the Soviets, with whom he was making a definite friendship. It was a game of cat and mouse.

National polls had already shown that a majority of American people had an unfavorable impression of Fidel Castro. Now, a July poll revealed that 50 percent of Americans thought the Cuban leader would be gone within a year.[1] Kennedy, who had once suggested that Eisenhower should have been nicer to Castro, now took the stance that Eisenhower was much too soft with Cuba. Kennedy promised that when he got elected, he would deal with the Cubans and remove the threat of Communism from the Western Hemisphere.

In September, fear of Communism grew even stronger among the American people when both the Soviet leader Nikita Khrushchev and Fidel Castro attended a United Nations meeting in New York. They embraced each other and applauded each other's lengthy speeches. Castro called Kennedy an illiterate and ignorant millionaire. Kennedy could not have been more pleased by this attack, because it strengthened his case that the Cuban issue could bring him an election victory over Nixon. Besides, everyone knew that Kennedy was not illiterate. His reputation for reading a thousand words a minute was already making its rounds. He was rich, yes, but everyone knew that anyway.

A few months later, Tom was at work drawing cartoons for Sarkes Tarzian when the secretary came to his studio.

"Tom, there's someone on the phone," she said, looking slightly awed. "If I heard right, he said he's calling from the White House."

chapter twenty-seven

A Phone Call from Washington

1960

Tom finished the shading he was doing. He dropped his pencil onto the cartoon and went to the secretary's phone in the lobby. He assumed the secretary had heard wrong. But if it really was someone from the White House, he didn't care. He would never go back to Washington.

"Hello?"

"Tom! It's Sandy Fox."

"Sandy! How did you find me?"

"Oh, come on, Tom! You didn't think you could run away from the long arm of the executive branch, did you?"

Tom sighed and shook himself. He hated to admit it, but it really was good to hear Sandy's voice again.

"So . . . *why* did you find me?"

"Ah, much better question, Tom. Much better question! It's like this. Mr. Tolley wants to retire. It doesn't matter to him who the new First Lady is, if it's Pat Nixon or Jackie Kennedy. Although I think he might be partial to the Catholic Kennedys, since he's Italian and all. But he knows the whole White House changes with a new First Lady, and he doesn't want to go through more change at his age. So that leaves me in charge here. At least that is what they're telling me."

"And I suppose that leaves you short on help."

"That it does, Tom. It does. We need someone like you." He paused. "Come on, Tom, why not? We know you, and you already know how the White House functions. And we know you can keep a secret."

"Oh, what now? Are we fighting Commies in the calligraphy department too?"

"Yes, we're having Castro for dinner so we can put something in his soup," Sandy chuckled. "See, Tom, that's why they never hire me for sensitive operations like looking after the Queen of England. I say unnecessary things on unsecure phone lines and you don't."

Tom laughed. "It was the Queen Mother, Sandy, not the Queen."

"Yeah, yeah, I know."

"But I had decided I wasn't going back to D.C."

"Oh, everyone decides that between times," Sandy said expansively. Tom could just picture him waving his hand to brush off Tom's previous foolish thoughts. He could see his bright black eyes shining with assurance that Tom would do his bidding.

"When do you need to know?"

"Last week would have been nice," he said. "But next week will do."

"Next week?!"

"I've got your number, Tom. I'll keep checking in! You'll have to come on Inauguration Day, you know."

"Why?"

"Oh, you know, don't you? Well, I guess you haven't lived through one of those yet. Ah, dreadful days. We have to move the old family out and the new one in—all in one day. It's painful, and every single person is needed to make it happen. All over the house, people have to sprain their backs to move boxes and furniture."

"Oh, so I'm getting a moving job too?"

"Just come back, Tom!"

Sharon had enjoyed the charged atmosphere of Washington, so it did not take Tom long to get her support for their return to Washington the next spring. When Kennedy won the election in November, Sharon became even more intrigued with the idea of a young, classy First Lady with a daughter about Brad's age and a baby to be born before her husband took office.

Tom felt a little sorry for the disappointment he knew must

Tom and Sharon, with Brad, left, and Jeff, right, in Washington, D. C., after he returned to the White House.

be oozing through the Eisenhower staff. The secretaries, aides, and Cabinet members who might have continued under Nixon's administration had all lost their jobs. Most of the White House staff, however, would continue to work under the new administration. They could be fired, of course, but most understood their jobs well, did exceptional work, and stayed for years.

In preparation for the move, Tom bought a station wagon, a black Ford. He was quite proud of it. It would do well for their move to the city.

Shortly after the election, John Kennedy's wife gave birth to a son, John. The nation was star-struck by the prospect of a newborn baby living at the White House with his three-year-old sister Caroline.

Tom went alone to Washington to help with the Inauguration Day move and to find housing for his family. He arrived in the city in a snowstorm the day before the inauguration. He helped the Eisenhowers move out, piling the

President's painting supplies and boxes of books into snow-covered moving trucks. He chatted with Sergeant Moaney, his old friend. The Sergeant was a little sad, but mostly relieved to be leaving the White House and going to live a more private life. Tom was a little sad that he did not get a chance to see President Eisenhower, but he was not too surprised. He wished Moaney the best and went to the basement to confer with Sandy Fox.

"What do you know, Tom, we are getting elevated!" Sandy cried after throwing his arms companionably around Tom.

"We—what do you mean?"

"Jackie Kennedy is apparently going to redo the whole house," Sandy said in something close to an awed whisper. "And when Mamie brought her here on a tour in December, she almost scolded us about working down here. She wants us up on the second floor of the East Wing beside the social secretary!"

"Oh! Well, that's good. We need to work with social people a lot anyway."

Sandy and Tom, after checking to see if their services were needed anywhere else, and not being invited to help either with unpacking Caroline's toys or with setting up the nursery for John Jr., decided to work on their own moving project. With the help of a couple of free-floating housekeepers, they transported everything from the calligraphy room up the stairs, down the glassed-in East Colonnade, up another flight of stairs, and into the new room.

"That light through the east window will be transformative!" Sandy Fox gloated. Tom was overjoyed as well.

"Welcome back, Tom," J. B. West, the chief usher said, sticking in his head as he passed their room late in the afternoon, making a round of inspection. "I can't promise you it will be like old times, but I can promise you it will be interesting. Did you hear that the podium started smoking at the inauguration?"

Sandy and Tom, hard at work arranging the tools of their trade, looked at him in astonishment.

"Just some wiring, I guess. But it sure made for some excitement."

"Ah, so there was no plot for the CIA to solve, I guess," Sandy said as if he was disappointed the smoke had not been Fidel Castro or Nikita Khrushchev hiding beneath the stage.

"At any rate, on to business," the chief usher said. "Did you hear they are assigning Arthur Schlesinger an office close to you here in the East Wing?"

"That history guy that's my age and already won a Pulitzer Prize for the book he wrote?" Sandy said. "I thought he was one of the President's aides. Why wouldn't he be over in the West Wing?"

J. B. shook his head. "Your guess is as good as mine, Sandy. I don't know these people. Maybe Schlesinger is more historian than politician. And by the way, Jack Kennedy is younger than I am, and he's President of the United States. The bar is set a little high in this house. But I would say working in both the CIA and the White House, by your age, is about as good as winning a Pulitzer Prize, Sandy."

"Oh, get along, Mr. West," Sandy said, laughing. "You know, Tom," he added after the usher had left, "you could do the opposite."

"Opposite of what?"

"Opposite of me. You could work in the White House first and then the CIA."

"Why would I work in the CIA?"

Sandy furrowed his brow and tapped his head as if he were thinking very hard.

"Maybe because you would be a natural," he said. "Or maybe I'm thinking about it because I ran into my old boss the other day, and he wondered if I had any suggestions for new recruits for him. He needs people who can be relied on to keep their mouths closed at all times."

Tom stared at him.

"Are you joking? You bring me back to the White House and then you—"

"Never mind, never mind!" Sandy said, breaking into a peal of laughter. "Relax, man. I didn't give him your name or anything. Why would I let you go from this office anyway? I'm not giving you up if I can help it."

chapter twenty-eight

The CIA

1961

"Tom, get your coat," Sandy said, puffing into the new Calligraphy Office after a run up the stairs. "Run over to the West Wing. Evelyn, the President's secretary, has an errand for you."

Tom looked up from the invitation he was working on. The social season at the White House had accelerated under the direction of its new first family. The Calligraphy Office scrambled to stay abreast of the changes, even when all hands were on deck. Several other calligraphers besides Tom were in the office now, including a woman Tom had known from his days in Robert Schulz's office.

Tom stared at Sandy. His normally carefree face was tight and unbending. Obviously, Tom was supposed to go now and ask questions later. He jumped up and ran to the West Wing.

"Tom Kirkman," he said at the secretary's door. "Sandy Fox said you—"

"Here."

She stepped from around her desk. Tom had never seen the secretary before. She was a slender woman who looked older than he had expected, maybe about fifty. She had short black hair and a string of pearls at her neck, both of which reminded Tom of the photos he had seen of the President's wife. Her voice was clipped and efficient, as if she had, in two months' time, learned to deal with low-level people such as Tom Kirkman. Behind her, Tom caught a quick glimpse of a typewriter and a stacking file.

"I'll explain later," Evelyn said. "Take this envelope to 2430 East Street. It's about seven blocks west of here. You have your own car, right?"

"Right."

"Okay, go. Hurry. Open the outside envelope once you are through the gates and tell them the President wants you to hand this directly to the person whose name is written on the inner envelope." It was not an ordinary mailing envelope. It was brown and letter-size, with a clasp tightly fastened on the back.

Tom could not remember the last time he had been so confused, but he knew better than to ask questions. He ran back through the Center Hall all the way to the East Wing parking lot.

He found 2430 East Street hidden behind a chain link fence, although the gate was open. A sign posted on the fence displayed a blue seal with an eagle on top of a shield. Curving around the top of the shield were the words *Central Intelligence Agency.*

Tom drove through the open gate.

"ID, please," a security officer in the booth inside the gate said. Tom showed his White House ID, and the man waved him through. Tom drove up the curving drive to an imposing brick building half hidden by trees and a raised bank of lawn. Seven pillars marked the front entrance. He parked and hurried inside with his envelope and up to the front desk.

"Ma'am, the President would like me to hand this directly to—" Tom tore off the outer envelope. His eyes popped. He showed it to the receptionist.

Allen Dulles. The director of the CIA.

The receptionist was dressed in a heavy jacket, and Tom understood why. The lobby chilled him. Besides being cold, it smelled like a strange combination of garden soil, typewriter ribbons, and vinegar. In the split second that it took the receptionist to glance at the envelope, Tom wondered why he was audacious enough to think that he could personally walk up to the director of the CIA.

"To your right," the receptionist replied, pointing down the hall. "Go up those stairs. It is the first office on the left. Announce that you have a message from the President. I'll call to tell him you're coming."

Tom hurried up the stairs. The heavy door was ajar. Tom stood outside, able to hear voices within, one slightly frustrated. He reached out his hand, knocked on the door, and said, in what he hoped was an official voice, "Mail from the President, sir."

"Come in."

The voices stopped. Tom went inside. One man sat in a wooden armchair before the director's desk, smoking thoughtfully. Another stood against a bookcase, arms folded. Behind the desk, Allen Dulles himself sat, putting his pipe back into his mouth.

Tom had seen photographs of the director but could not remember having seen him in person. But he had heard much about the man. It struck him with a kind of surprise that Allen Dulles looked pleasant and grandfatherly. With round, wire-rimmed glasses, thinning hair, and a calm, patient expression, Tom could not connect him with the public image of aggression and imperialism. He was over sixty-five, and he looked tired.

Tom nodded and hurried across the room. He handed the packet to Director Dulles.

The director nodded and waved him off. Tom hurried away, retraced his steps, and drove back to the White House. He returned to the Calligraphy Office and continued with his invitation.

That evening when Tom was almost ready to head home, Sandy came back into the office. Tom was so intent on finishing his project that he barely noticed when Sandy came in.

"Tom, Evelyn just called. She said she expected you to return to her office after your errand."

"Oh, she did?" Tom raised his eyebrows as he searched his memory for what she had said.

"It happened kind of suddenly, me suggesting you to run that errand. I was over there getting a list of names for the certificates we need to fill out, and she and the President were trying to think of someone who could keep a secret to run a message for them, so I suggested you. But just run over there now and touch base with her before you go."

Tom rushed up the West Colonnade and into the West Wing. He was a few steps from the secretary's door when he nearly ran into a Secret Service agent, who glared at him. Behind the agent, President Kennedy walked briskly toward him, chatting with his special assistant, Dave Powers.

"I know, Dave, but I'm just not sure," the President was saying. "I guess we have to let this go for today."

"Okay, see you tomorrow, Jack," Dave said. Tom knew the President was called Jack by his friends and family.

Tom dived for the secretary's door to escape the wrath of the Secret Service agent, only to find the President moving that way too. They nearly collided in Tom's desperation to get out of the way.

"I apologize, Mr. President," Tom said, his face reddening.

Evelyn saved Tom with a cheery laugh.

"Oh, Mr. President, that's Tom Kirkman, who ran our errand this afternoon," she said, laughing. "He never came back, so I told him to return!"

"Pleasure to meet you, Tom. You must not be the curious type?"

"I was just doing what I was asked to do," Tom said. "I didn't think I needed to know the details."

"Just the man we need occasionally, Mr. President," Evelyn said pleasantly.

"Absolutely. A military man, I believe?"

"Yes, sir, I was."

"Ah, as was I," the President said, as if Tom would not know. "Okay, Evelyn, set him up for the polygraphs or whatever the CIA needs so that he can come

From the WHITE HOUSE *to the* AMISH

and go as he pleases. That's one thing we don't have enough of around here: trustworthy people who know their way around town and around the White House. And Tom, if I ever send you to get a message from the CIA, I want it brought directly to me, not even to Evelyn. Got that?"

Tom stared at him, speechless. He wouldn't think of charging into the Oval Office without checking with the secretary.

"Don't worry, Tom, I'll set it up with the Secret Service," Evelyn said. "As long as they know those are your orders, it will be no problem."

"Great," the President said. "Can you cancel my morning appointments? Dave and I need to meet some people."

"Okay, Mr. President," Evelyn said, and Tom noticed she looked tired. "I'll cancel your morning. Go get some rest."

The President looked tired too, even though he had been in office for only a few weeks. Tom thought the lines on his face reflected physical pain. He remembered hearing from Sandy Fox that the President often had back pain.

For security measures, Tom underwent a grueling series of polygraphs and interviews. Apparently he passed them all, because the Secret Service never troubled him again.

From then on, whenever the Oval Office needed a messenger boy, Tom was called upon. He never asked why he was doing what he was doing—he just did it. In mid-April, he suddenly found himself in the West Wing almost as often as he was in the East Wing.

The newspapers, when Tom had time to read them, were full of dire reports on Cuba and a place called the Bay of Pigs. In an attempt to overthrow the government, a band of exiled Cubans had landed on a beachhead near this bay. The problem was, Fidel Castro had been expecting something like this, and he instantly blamed the United States. Although U.S. government officials initially denied involvement in the attack, the truth soon became clear to all.

The CIA, in coordination with the President and his aides, had trained the Cuban exiles and outfitted them with weapons. It really had been the United States trying to start an uprising against Fidel Castro, and it had failed. Whether the CIA or the President should be blamed for the failure, no one seemed to know. But Tom could tell from his occasional glimpses of President Kennedy that he was not well, either physically or emotionally.

It was clear to everyone close to the situation that President Kennedy and the director of the CIA, Allen Dulles, were at odds. Even though the President publicly took full responsibility for the Bay of Pigs mess, he privately blamed Dulles for having a bad plan. The director, on the other hand, blamed the President for canceling the air strikes that had been planned and were considered vital to the success of the operation.

A few weeks later Tom was home with Sharon and the boys at their apartment when a knock sounded on the door. When Tom opened the door, he found a man in a suit and tie.

"Tom, I heard your name today at the office. Can you come see me tomorrow afternoon?"

Tom did not know who the man was, but true to his track record, he didn't ask. He took the envelope and showed up at the enclosed address.

"Do you think you can learn Russian?" the man asked.

And so Tom began to work for the CIA. Sandy had also been in the CIA, so he understood the need for secrecy and loyalty. Tom kept the calligraphy job for a while, and took Russian language classes at night. Finally the training he was receiving became too intense and Tom had to drop his calligraphy job. The CIA worked out an arrangement with the White House to let Tom keep his White House ID. This enabled him to move freely into the White House and the West Wing. Since his face was familiar to the White House police but not to the public, he was the ideal person to carry messages. No photographers followed him. No one knew his name.

That year was a blur to Tom, just as it probably was to President Kennedy. Kennedy had hoped to do impressive things in the White House. Instead, the Bay of Pigs debacle cast a shadow over his entire first year.

It had been a difficult decision, but Kennedy had allowed the Bay of Pigs attack to fail rather than send in the United States military to help them. He was afraid if he sent in the United States Air Force or Navy, a full-blown war would result with the Soviet Union. If the two countries reached for their nuclear weapons, they could wipe each other's civilizations off the face of the earth. But now the Russians were furious anyway because they knew the United States had been behind the invasion of Cuba.

In his dispute with the CIA, the President forced Allen Dulles to resign, although he sent him away with a complimentary speech and a medal.

Everyone across America was worried. Where would they hide if nuclear bombs began falling? At the government's urging, people built fallout shelters. These bombproof shelters were marked by signs with a special symbol: three yellow downward-facing triangles in a circle of black. Tom was given numbered cards to give to his wife and two sons. They must carry the cards at all times. If a nuclear bomb fell, or there was a warning of one, they were to seek shelter immediately. The numbers would give officials a chance to sort people and reunite them with their families—if they were still alive.

Jeff was five now and Brad was almost four. The boys spent as much time as they could biking outside in front of the Arlington, Virginia, apartment in which the family now lived.

"Jeff, Brad," Tom said when he gave them the numbers. "You must always carry this in your pocket, whether you are playing outside or are in the house. At night, put it beside your bed where you can reach it easily."

"Why do we have to have papers?" Jeff asked.

Tom looked at his boys' wide eyes and sighed. What did they know about nuclear threats? What did they know about bombs or Moscow or Cuba?

"If the air-raid sirens go off, you need to run to the shelter. Understand?" Tom showed them the yellow triangles in the black circle to remind them. Both he and Sharon had been over this before, and there had been numerous practice drills across the city.

Both boys nodded solemnly.

"When you get to the shelter with the yellow triangles, a man will be standing near the door. You need to give this paper to him. Then he will use it to help me find you and Mom."

"Okay," both boys said.

The little slip of paper might be the only way Tom would get his boys back if they were separated in a nuclear attack.

In the spring of 1962, the CIA moved into a brand-new building. As Tom stepped into the new building to find his desk, the walls rose about him to high ceilings. On the floor beneath him, Tom saw the seal of the CIA. Etched in stone in the front entrance, he saw Jesus' words: "And ye shall know the truth, and the truth shall make you free."

Tom felt good about fighting for truth. Not the truth of Jesus, but freedom from the devastating effects of Communism. He didn't mind that the Communists didn't believe in God, but he did mind their economic and social structure. He knew they wanted to overcome the West. He knew they wanted to land on the moon and control the world from there.

He was fighting for freedom. It felt like an important and noble thing to do.

Especially now, since Tom had just gotten some news: He would soon be going to Moscow, Russia.

chapter twenty-nine

Moscow at Night

The Russian's limp shoulders hunched over his side of the wooden chessboard. Based on his slouch, his wild hair, and his sweat-stained white shirt, Tom had predicted his new acquaintance would be an easy defeat in chess. But now he was not so sure anymore. He didn't like the concentrated look in the man's eyes, nor the position of the pieces on the board. And he didn't like that he was already down by two pawns.

"Alex Petrov," the Russian had introduced himself as he shook Tom's hand. His grip had felt like the hand of a dying man. Tom looked into the man's eyes and saw guarded pleasantness.

"And I'm Bill Patrick," Tom said, in Russian.

Tom's official ID stated that his name was William D. Patrick, and that he was a calligrapher and transcriber for the U.S. embassy in Moscow. Since the embassy needed a calligrapher occasionally, and since Tom could easily demonstrate this skill, the fake identity fit perfectly.

The man across from him was a clerk who worked in the office of one of the main missile manufacturing factories in the Soviet Union. He worked with engineers and politicians, transcribing and copying for them. He even did some calligraphy. Another CIA operative had suggested that someone should get to know this young man, as he could probably provide up-to-date information on what was happening in the missile world of Russia.

Tom, fresh off his Russian language classes and known to keep a secret to the end, had been a perfect choice.

During the presidential campaign, Kennedy had argued that the United States had let the Soviet Union get ahead of them in the missile race. This had since been disproven by aerial photos, but the United States was still anxious about the details of Soviet arms manufacturing. It was even worse now that Fidel Castro of Cuba, just miles from the United States, was cozying up to the Soviet leader, Nikita Khrushchev. Any information that could be obtained would be extremely worthwhile.

Tom had been informed that the Russian clerk played chess most evenings at the Café Vronsky. Tom came to meet him in the inner ring of Moscow, not far from the office building where Alex worked. The clerk spoke halting English, and Tom was pleased to find that his own Russian was better than Alex's English. Despite his wariness, the game of chess revived Alex Petrov's spirits rapidly, even as Tom's sank.

"Check," Alex said softly, with a clack of his wooden rook.

Tom bit his lip and maintained an impassive face. He wanted his new friend to think he had seen that move coming.

The Russian had just moved his rook two spaces to the right, pressuring Tom's remaining knight. Tom had seen that possibility, yes. What he had not seen was that, with the same move, the Russian had unblocked his white bishop. From the other side of the board, the white bishop put Tom's king in check.

It was a dismal scene.

Should I sacrifice my knight? Tom wondered. No, it was not *should* he sacrifice it. That was not the question. He *had* to sacrifice it. Silently he moved a pawn up one space, blocking the path of his opponent's white bishop.

Tom Kirkman was not accustomed to losing in chess, but here he was, his first week in Moscow, losing. Besides the personal pain of his situation, Tom disliked the symbolism of starting his career in espionage by losing a chess game. He was supposed to be making an important contact for the espionage branch of the Soviet Division of the CIA.

Tom leaned back in his chair and glanced at the waiter scurrying around the café.

He caught her eye, and she hurried over. She was young and wispy, like a breath of air wrapped in a white apron and a white kerchief.

"More coffee, please," he said. He needed to relax.

She nodded, then glanced at Petrov.

"For you?"

He shook his head without answering. His lips folded against each other in concentration, as if mortal concerns like coffee could never derail his thoughts.

Thankfully, the Russian word for coffee was nearly the same as its English counterpart. Tom knew he could not survive long in Moscow without the ability to order coffee.

Even his more extensive Russian, however, was not bad. As Tom always did when presented with a challenge, he had thrown himself into the Russian language classes heart and soul. After a year of intense training, his instructor, a jolly Russian professor with bad breath, had declared that even his accent was nearly perfect.

"Sir, your coffee," the waitress said, pouring a midnight black stream into his mug. Steam clouded into Tom's eyes, almost obscuring that sinister white bishop across the way.

"*Spasibo,*" Tom said.

"Your Russian is quite good," Alex said politely. "Not bad for an American." His sudden talkativeness probably came from sheer confidence, Tom thought.

"*Spasibo,*" Tom said again with a laugh. As long as he had merely to say "thank you," it was easy. He took a long drink of the dark beverage and frowned at the board. He no longer hoped to win. The question was how to minimize the damages.

Tom struggled on for a few more painful turns before finally tipping his king in resignation. Petrov cheerily shook hands.

The chess game was just one of a variety of surprising things Tom had encountered since his plane had landed in Moscow a few days before.

First of all, Moscow stunned him with its beauty. He had known that Western news coverage of the Soviet Union focused on the negatives, but he had still not been prepared for the intense grandeur of the city. It was springtime, and the parks and boulevards burst with flowering trees and new shoots of green.

The design of the city of Moscow had intrigued Tom ever since he had seen it on the map back in Washington. Unlike the sprawling metropolis of Washington, D.C., cut into regions by the Potomac River, Moscow had been planned right on top of its river. The Moskva River snaked through the city with as many twists and turns as the Potomac. But the streets and neighborhoods of Moscow lay over the river like a wheel, the spokes of roads and bridges almost undisturbed by the tortuous waterway.

The hub of the wheel contained the administrative government buildings, the KGB headquarters with its Lubyanka prison, the Lenin library, Gorky Park, Red Square, and St. Basil's Cathedral.

And, of course, the Kremlin, the capitol building. Tom had studied the basics of the complex: five palaces, four cathedrals, all surrounded by the brick red Kremlin Wall and the Kremlin Towers. The wall had been built between 1485 and 1495. He knew that the Russian word *Kremlin* meant "fortress inside a city."

But nothing compared with seeing the Kremlin from the iron bridge above the Moskva River on a quiet stroll in the twilight. Behind him, cars rumbled over the bridge. Tom gripped one of the iron balls on the bridge railing as he took in the expanse of red wall, majestic green and red towers, and the imposing white and gold structures beyond the wall. Against a lavender sunset, the silhouette of the buildings on a hillside stood out like a kind of unexpected paradise. On the left, a huge rectangular office building with a green roof presided over the riverbank. To its right, smaller buildings burst with gold-plated domed towers crowned with crosses. These intricate palaces must have taken the architect longer to plan than the massive rectangular building. Tom wished Jeff and Brad were with him, so he could point out the palaces, the domes, and the river.

Second, the women and children of Moscow surprised Tom. They were everywhere. Women in bright homemade sundresses with cardigans around their shoulders rushed up and down the streets. Schoolchildren in short skirts and shorts walked in lines into museums and libraries. The central mall, while not offering the same variety of merchandise as an American counterpart, burst at the seams with shoppers.

Tom had learned back in America that the USSR still had twenty million more women than men, due to the losses of men in the war. Still, in the news and on TV, Tom only saw Russian men. Not until he walked the streets of Moscow did he learn that women held many important jobs as doctors, engineers, and plant supervisors. They were also paid the same as men for equal work.

Tom's third surprise was that even the men were kinder and more reasonable than Tom had expected. They were . . . well, almost normal. But they were also very gifted. Alex Petrov's slightly sleepy domination of Tom in chess had only reinforced this belief. What on earth could Petrov do with a chess opponent if he were animated and drinking coffee?

Petrov now ordered a coffee, as if his victory should be rewarded. The two men chatted. Petrov mentioned his two small daughters. His wife, he said, worked at the milk bottling plant across town, and they lived in one of the apartments built for those workers.

It took Tom a few minutes to clear his head from the gloom of the game, but he disciplined himself. If he couldn't keep his cool through a bad game of chess, what was he doing working for the CIA?

As if reading his mind, Petrov tossed a question across the table like a camouflaged grenade.

"So what do you *really* do for the United States? You don't just make beautiful letters."

Tom thought he had been prepared for anything, but the man's direct approach stopped him cold. Worse than the surprise, Tom realized uneasily that he liked this man. He wished they were friends back in Bedford. He wished they could meet for weekly chess at Grecco's so Tom could improve his game. He wished he and Alex Petrov did not have to be sworn enemies.

After a moment's reflection, however, he decided to return the directness in kind. He hoped his hastiness would not cost him his position.

"I help compile information about the Soviet missile program," Tom said softly. "We thought you might be able to help."

chapter thirty

The Darkest Place
in the World

Tom walked past the corner bookshop filled with Russian books and translations, huddling deeper into his overcoat. Despite the arrival of spring, a bitter cold wind had settled over the city. He ducked into the front lobby of a white concrete apartment building. He scanned the street and the empty lobby. He noted the telephone booth on the left before stepping over to the radiator on the right. Reaching behind the radiator, he lifted a packet off its position on a metal hook. Immediately he slid the papers up his sleeve. He returned both hands into his pockets, pressing his elbows tightly against his sides so the papers would not drop out of his overcoat. Briskly he walked toward the U.S. Embassy.

Tom and Alex Petrov had a kind of system worked out. They played chess once a week at the café. They talked about their children and families, but Alex had not invited Tom to his apartment. It was too dangerous.

Tom told Alex he wouldn't be staying much longer because he missed his boys. He had agreed to only a few months in Moscow. With Alex's help, he would collect as much information as possible for the CIA, and then return home.

They did not exchange paperwork or money during the chess games, however. They had worked out a dropbox system close to the bookshop, with help from Tom's supervisors. Every day at 2 p.m., Tom took a stroll in Gorky Park. When Alex had information to give Tom, he scratched a chalk mark on the fifth park bench facing the Moskva River. Tom wiped it off, then went back to his office to check if his calligraphy skills were needed to write out more certificates. Sometime later in the afternoon or evening, he headed back to the white apartment by the bookshop to pick up the information from Petrov.

In exchange for copying blueprints and nuclear formulas that came across his desk, Petrov received both gifts and money. The CIA headquarters provided Tom with any American product Petrov asked for. Petrov liked to fish, so he asked for a fishing reel not available in Soviet Russia. Tom joined him for a fishing trip, and provided him with two styles of fishing reels and a box of lures. They spent many afternoons together, fishing and talking in the privacy of the Russian countryside.

Both Tom and Petrov risked their lives. In addition to the grave danger of getting caught by the KGB, there was the nagging possibility that the other person was a fake. Tom and Petrov got along well, but what if Petrov had also been hired by the KGB to find out information about the U.S. through Tom? From Petrov's side, what if Tom were a double agent also hired by the Russians? The possibilities were intricate, endless, and frightening. But the two truly liked each other, and Tom determined to do his duty for the CIA before returning home to his family.

Back at his desk at the U.S. Embassy, Tom opened the packet that Alex had left for him behind the radiator. Tom reviewed the Russian materials with his chain-smoking supervisor, an expert in reading Russian. The packet contained a list of buildings from the Omsk Aircraft Plant a thousand miles east of Moscow.

"Five assembly and machine shops, each 400' x 150', two of which have

longitudinal monitor roofs.

Steam plant, 115' x 50' with adjoining shed, 80' x 25'." [1]

"I think we already have that," the supervisor said. "But we'll send it on to headquarters just in case."

Under the list of diagrams and copied materials lists, Tom found a handwritten note to himself. The supervisor pulled it out and read it quickly.

"Ah, this is wonderful, Tom! He says he will take you on a tour of the uranium mines if you wish to go! Hmmm. I wonder how he hopes to get you in there. As a friend, I suppose." The supervisor shook his cigarette into the ashtray on his desk.

"Maybe there is good fishing close by," Tom suggested. "I assume it is a bit of a drive?"

"Only a few thousand miles."

Any countries researching and building atomic bombs were scrambling to secure sufficient amounts of uranium. Did the Soviet Union actually have lots of uranium, enough for many nuclear weapons?

The CIA higher-ups liked the idea, so it happened that Tom found himself in a cave somewhere in the heart of Russia. He felt a cold so intense that he was not sure if it was still consistent with planet Earth. Had they gone to the moon by mistake instead of the Soviet countryside? Was it really claustrophobia he felt as he looked at the rocky wall of the cavern by the light of a dim headlamp? Or was the oxygen running out and they were about to suffocate?

Two days before, Tom and Petrov had boarded a train, taking along their fishing gear. Petrov had informed Tom that he knew a back entrance into the mines from his days of fishing on his grandfather's farm. He didn't know, but he thought it possible that the secret entrance might be connected to an administrative building that would provide information about the mines.

"The caves used to be prison camps, you know, under Stalin," Petrov said as they stood together in the cold, the dim light of the headlamp reflecting on icy stones. "So it's been under government control for a long time. Shall we turn off the light for a moment? You'll never see such darkness again if you live to be a hundred years old."

Not to be outdone by his sleepy, brilliant friend, Tom agreed. Petrov snapped off his light, and darkness fell over them like a heavy blanket. It was so dark that Tom fought a rising panic. With sheer willpower, he resisted the urge to demand that the light be turned back on. He pushed away the thoughts of what would happen if they lost their light or if a sudden threatening noise let them know they were not alone. At least they would not wander about for long, because he was sure they would be human icicles after only a few hours.

Suddenly something struck Tom on the shoulder blade, and he jumped as if it had been a bullet.

"Relax, Bill," came the soft, laughing voice of his companion. "It's only water dripping from the roof of the cave. Shall I turn the light back on?"

Water?! Tom thought. *Surely it is too cold for water to be in any other form than ice.*

Petrov snapped the light back on. What had seemed dim before now wrapped Tom's body, soul, and spirit in its boundless embrace. What a lovely, warm, friendly thing a small light could be! Petrov shot it up to the ceiling.

"Step this way," he said, as another drop hit Tom. With the light back on, the drop felt more like a gentle pat. "I think there is a mountain stream that runs over us and oozes through the cracks. Ah, look, it has frozen on your coat already!"

"You don't look so warm yourself," Tom shot back. Growing crystals of frost outlined the Russian's eyebrows, and his breath fogged the air around his headlamp.

Tom could not stop shivering as he doggedly followed Petrov into the maze of rock and ice.

"Ah, too bad," Petrov said suddenly.

Ice-cold metal bars glinted in the passageway ahead, planted like sentinels.

"I guess they discovered this back entrance after all," Petrov said. "When I was a boy, we could sneak all the way down this hall and look down into the working pit. I thought perhaps we could do the same and find some paperwork. But this is a dead end, my friend."

That night, Tom boiled water over the woodstove in the fishing cabin while Petrov stoked the fire with more wood. As he threw in pieces of wood, Petrov confessed that, short of getting his hands on more information, his knowledge of the current mining situation was limited.

"I know that this is one of the only sites where the Soviet Union obtains uranium for nuclear weapons," Petrov said. "But I do not know the details, and I do not have an accurate or up-to-date map. I have a cousin who works in the administration of the mine, but I am not close to him."

Back in Moscow at headquarters, Tom slowly thawed out. He reported to his supervisor that the trip had been cold and not particularly helpful. A few days later, however, Tom was summoned to the supervisor's office.

chapter thirty-one

The End

"This cousin of Petrov's sounds interesting," the supervisor said, taking his cigarette from between his lips. "We need a map of the uranium mines and details about how much uranium is available for the missile program. Tell Petrov we will pay a very good price if he can secure us more details."

A chill invaded Tom's bones like a case of delayed frostbite.

"Petrov's work does not relate to the work in the mines," Tom said. "I don't think he has access to such documents."

"You said he has a cousin."

"Yes, sir, I did. But that could be a suicide mission to ask a distant cousin for classified documents."

The director sighed impatiently. He was a big, decisive man used to giving orders and having them accepted unconditionally. And that is what Tom normally did. But this . . .

"Tom. I'm not asking *you* to do this mission. I'm asking you to ask a Soviet missile man to do it. There's a difference. Do this yet, then you can get on your plane and go back to Washington with honor."

The craftily veiled threat fell from the man's lips like a grenade wrapped in tissue paper.

"Yes, sir," Tom said, and left the room.

At the next chess game, Tom broached the subject using the code words the two had developed.

"I'm thinking about my next move," Tom said.

This meant there was a new mission for Petrov.

Petrov nodded.

Tom scrawled the word *cousin* on a newspaper in pencil, then the word *map*. Petrov was silent for a long time.

"That could be a checkmate," he said.

"Don't put your king in danger," Tom said hastily. "Please don't. You will get a lot of points if you succeed, however."

Petrov made a move with his queen. He had been teaching Tom more and more chess moves and tricks, and Tom had actually beaten him once. Petrov was the best friend Tom had in this foreign land. A better friend than his supervisor, by far.

"I will be heading back to Washington soon," Tom said at the end of the game. "My time is over. But I do hope to be back for a visit, and we will play chess again."

"We will play again," Petrov said solemnly as they shook hands in parting.

Tom arrived back in Washington in October 1962. Not long after he arrived home, the Americans discovered that the Soviets were sending missiles to the island of Cuba. This standoff with the Soviets soon got a label: the Cuban Missile Crisis.

The next few months were a dark period in Tom's life. Always after that, he tried to erase the memories of everything that happened during this time.

He tried to forget all the time he spent at CIA headquarters sorting through large volumes of intelligence sent over from spies in the Soviet Union. He tried to forget the futile wait for documents from his friend Petrov.

He tried to forget his nerve-racking flight over Cuba, where he was the photo operator in charge of the camera in the belly of the plane. The camera used a continuously rolling film, so it mostly operated automatically, allowing Tom to watch the island of Cuba flash by below.

He tried to forget that awful night when he was called to assist at the National Photographic Interpretation Center. There could not be enough coffee to sustain the dozens of processing agents working through the night. There could not be words to soothe the stunning nature of the truth when the large rolls of film from the belly of another supersonic plane revealed the awful truth. Those small, harmless looking shapes on the aerial photography were actually long-range missiles that could reach San Antonio, Dallas, or even Cincinnati. The Soviets just might blow Washington, D.C., off the map with a nuclear blast.

He tried to forget going home to Sharon and the boys and telling them they must stay close to the nuclear bomb shelter. The boys' big eyes looked up at him in wonder, and their small fists clutched those all-important papers with those numbers that were meant to reunite the family "if the worst should happen."

Worse yet, Sharon had changed. Her averted gaze and forced civility told Tom something had occurred during his absence. He did not probe. Instead, he buried himself in the urgency of the political landscape. For the sake of the boys, Tom tried to make their home life as normal as possible, but it was clear that their marriage was strained even more than it had been.

Tom tried to forget his glimpses of the key players in the drama. President Kennedy, looking at the black and white aerial photos set up on easels in the newly created Situation Room of the White House, his face pinched with something worse than his back pain. The President's brother Bobby, sarcastic and forceful, the face of the Kennedy presidency. Whereas the President restrained his comments, Bobby felt no need to be polite. Vice President Lyndon Johnson's dour face rarely appeared on the scene, as he suffered the pain of exclusion from Kennedy's inner circle.

Then there was Tommy Thompson, the quiet man Tom had met once in Moscow. Thompson, a humble man who wore baggy brown tweed suits, knew Khrushchev and the Kremlin personally from years of work in Moscow. He had stayed in Moscow when most other Americans had fled. He didn't say much, but when he spoke, his words counted.

At one of the tense meetings hastily convened around the big table in the Situation Room at the White House, Bobby Kennedy turned to Thompson. Bobby, pacing around the table in a tailored suit, eyed Thompson who stood passively on the sidelines in his baggy brown clothes.

"Well, what does the Russian expert think?" Bobby asked with biting sarcasm.

"I am afraid I am not much of an expert," Thompson replied calmly. "If you would have asked me several weeks ago, I would have told you the Russians would not send missiles to Cuba."[1]

President Kennedy knew he should trust this Moscow man with his unusual honesty and candor. When Kennedy said he did not think Khrushchev would take his missiles back unless the United States removed their missiles from Turkey, Thompson spoke up.

"I don't agree, Mr. President," he said.[2]

And so President Kennedy did not bargain with the Soviet leader. He merely asked Nikita Khrushchev to turn back his ships and remove the missiles they had brought to Cuba.

In the end, Khruschev did just that. The nation, and especially the people in the southeastern part of the United States, could finally breathe more easily again. Tom, too, relaxed a little. Perhaps, if the worst danger was past, he could stay in Washington a little longer.

He arrived at the CIA headquarters on the day after the Soviet ships turned back, anxious to resume his normal role and a comfortable routine. He walked through the front doors and over the massive Central Intelligence Agency seal inlaid in the floor. He gazed at the Bible verse that Allen Dulles had gotten carved into the stone wall: "And ye shall know the truth, and the truth shall make you free." He walked on past the square pillars of the main entrance hall. He took the elevator to his floor, refilled his coffee in the breakroom, and went to his desk. Setting the coffee down, he noticed a file with the word "Tom" written on it.

Tom opened it and found a copy of the map of the uranium mines he had visited with Petrov. He did not recognize the name associated with the file. He assumed his supervisor had passed it on to him, knowing his interest in watching for the map.

Delighted, he snatched up the file and hurried down the hall to the supervisor's office. Had Petrov delivered the map under a second name?

The supervisor frowned at his question and referred him to his secretary. Tom walked around the corner to her desk. She smiled and wheeled her chair to a set of tall filing cabinets behind her. As she clicked the metal lock and the drawer squealed open, Tom felt the coldness of the Russian mine seeping through his frame.

"Petrov," she said, picking out a file. She opened it, raised her eyebrows, and looked at the map Tom had given her. She searched her files for that name, nodded, and put both back. She handed the map back to Tom.

"This map is from a different source," she said. "The Moscow branch informed us of Petrov's execution by the KGB."

Tom gripped the edge of the secretary's desk, much as he had gripped Robert Schulz's desk when he got the phone call from his father on that dark winter night before Christmas some years before.

"You were informed—is it confirmed?" Tom asked desperately.

"Yes, the news clipping is in the file," she said. Her smile had grown tentative under the influence of Tom's horrified reaction. "Would you like to see it?"

Tom could not answer. He just shook his head and retreated to his own desk.

He had done it himself. He had sent Petrov to his grave. He had made his wife a widow and his two daughters orphans.

The End

Tom had not pulled the trigger, of course. But what was the difference? He had known the mission was dangerous. He had tried to argue with his supervisor and had been threatened with a loss of his position if he did not follow orders. To save his job at the CIA, Tom had asked Petrov to perform a suicide mission. Then he had walked off to his home and family in the United States.

I deserve to be blown off the map by a nuclear warhead, Tom said to himself. *I want no part of an organization that sends men to their deaths.*

He was done. He walked to his supervisor's office the next day with a letter of resignation.

"Thomas, you have no idea how disappointed we are in you for quitting," his supervisor said.

"You have no idea how disappointed I am in *you*," Tom replied quietly. "Right out front there it says, 'And ye shall know the truth, and the truth shall make you free.' You people know nothing of the truth."

chapter thirty-two

Faces from the Past

1963

In January 1963, Tom went back to the University of Indiana in Bloomington, this time drawing maps for the geological survey. Bent over the wide sheets of paper, drawing elevations with various widths of felt tip pens, Tom found some satisfaction. He loved maps. He loved drawing and sketching. He loved the hills and fields and canyons of his home state of Indiana.

He tried to forget the CIA, the Kennedys, Petrov. He tried to forget Washington entirely. He couldn't talk about it with anyone, so it would be best to forget, to move on.

He tried to forget his mother's death. He tried not to think about the coolness between him and Sharon. They had experienced periods of trouble since shortly after their marriage. But ever since Tom's days in Russia, the wall between them had settled in like a terminal illness.

The boys inspired Tom to keep living. Jeff was six now, and Brad was five.

"Dad, look at me!" Jeff crowed one day. "I'm the Washington Monument." Jeff stood on his tiptoes making himself as tall as possible. He raised his hands above his head and pointed to the sky.

"Me too," Brad said, marching over and imitating his older brother.

"You can't be!" Jeff retorted. "There's only one."

Tom swallowed his laughter, knowing he should keep a straight face and help the boys settle their dispute. His inner being swelled with pride to know his boys were sharp enough to remember the monument he had pointed out to them back in Washington.

"Let's try something," Tom said. "We will all be the Washington Monument. Jeff, you sit on my shoulders, then we'll hold Brad up to be the very top of the tower. Like this!"

It was precarious at best. The three of them strained and balanced until the monument toppled in a chaos of arms, legs, and pillows. Thankfully, everyone was laughing.

One day about a year after the Cuban Missile Crisis, Tom was bent over a map, drawing. In typical fashion, he focused so intently that he hardly noticed anything going on around him. He vaguely heard excited voices outside his office, but they did not register. Finally the secretary burst in.

"Tom, Tom, don't you hear what is happening? The President has been shot!"

Tom's consciousness erupted from the reclusive world of mapmaking when he heard the news of President Kennedy's death. The emotion that poured through him was not so much shock or sadness as utter bewilderment and alarm.

Why? Why do people always die at the wrong time?

"I think I'll take off for the rest of the afternoon," Tom finally said. His co-workers knew he had come from Washington, D.C. They did not know that he had worked for the CIA, or any other details, but they did know he had worked with President Kennedy. They nodded with understanding. Most of them also looked pale.

Could the CIA have killed the President? Tom asked himself as he sped home.

He wanted to be alone. He wanted to be able to think and watch the drama unfold on TV in the privacy of his living room. The boys were still at school, and Sharon was at work. He would have the house to himself.

Ridiculous, he said to himself. *They said it was a lone gunman. The CIA would not kill the President.*

But if not, then who did? Surely someone had to be behind the bullet besides the man who pulled the trigger. Tom had learned enough during his years in the CIA to know that if powerful people wanted someone else assassinated, they would never fire the shot themselves. If the gunman was Lee Harvey Oswald, as people thought, did he represent someone else?

At home, Tom watched photo after photo and heard report after report and smoked cigarette after cigarette. He saw footage of Lyndon B. Johnson climbing aboard Air Force One with Jackie Kennedy. He saw a video of the breakfast meeting in Texas earlier that morning. Jackie, clad in pink, had received the adoration of the crowds. The President had laughingly complained that no one ever cared what he and the vice president wore.

That was a nice touch, Tom thought, *to bring Lyndon Johnson into his joke.* Tom remembered how the President and Johnson got along, which was really not at all. There were rumors that Kennedy was planning to choose a different vice president for his second term of office.

The real vice president of the country was Robert Kennedy, the President's brother. Ever since President Kennedy's other aides had not succeeded in keeping Kennedy out of the Bay of Pigs disaster, Robert had been by the President's side. He had not been with the entourage in Texas, however.

Tom could only imagine Robert Kennedy's dismay when he heard the news back in Washington, D.C. Not only had his brother been killed, but Lyndon Johnson was now President of the United States and would be moving into the White House. Johnson would be taking over his brother's office, sitting in his brother's chair, eating at his brother's breakfast table.

Hours later, when the boys came home from school, Tom still sat in his chair. A cloud of cigarette smoke hazed the room.

"Dad!" Brad said. "At school they said the President died today."

"Yes, boys," Tom said vacantly. "He did die today. Why don't you go out to the kitchen and get some cookies?"

"Is that the president you used to work for?" Jeff asked.

"Yes," Tom replied.

Tom was having trouble processing his thoughts. He felt overwhelmed with sadness, especially when he thought of the little girl and boy who loved to visit their daddy in his Oval Office. Tom had only seen them once, but he knew from having children himself what a terrible blow this would be to Caroline and little John Jr.

He was alarmed too that a lone shooter, acting independently, could pick off a president surrounded by Secret Service men. He was even more alarmed if the shooter had not been acting alone.

And what about Jackie? President Kennedy had taken good care of his wife and family. Tom was sure the President had loved his wife. But why then had she not been the only woman in his life? White House staff were well aware that she was not. That was what Tom struggled with when he thought of John Kennedy as a person.

But he had respected the way Kennedy had pulled himself together after the Bay of Pigs setback. Tom also admired his steely determination to go on despite his crippling back pain. Some people with the same physical problems Kennedy had would simply have refused to do any work at all, much less the most stressful job in the country.

Tom also felt fear. Could Lyndon Johnson really do the job? Tom remembered that same fear when Kennedy had been elected. Things had not always gone well, but Kennedy had grown and learned from his mistakes and moved on.

Tom had no plans to move back to Washington, but Kennedy's death seemed to close a permanent door on Tom's White House and CIA past. He spoke of neither if he could help it. Instead, he turned further inward, working harder and harder at his maps.

"Tom, can we move you to the Indiana University publications department?" his superior asked him one day. "We think you have the talent to advance the periodical we've been publishing."

Under Tom's watchful eye and precise pen, the university magazine blossomed and won an award for excellence. Soon Tom was moved even higher, to a position in the Indiana University Museum.

The days of the past seemed far, far away. Growing up in the chicken house, playing in the log cabin—everything seemed far away.

Then one day a man stepped out of Tom's past and into his office.

Tom was chewing his ham sandwich thoughtfully as he evaluated the sign he was making. Outside in the lobby of the museum, he heard a secretary pick up the receiver of the telephone.

"Hello!" she said. "Ah, yes, he is. Okay, I will let him know."

The secretary came to the door. "Mr. Kirkman," she said uncertainly, "I hope it's okay. I just took a call from a man who said his name was James Diehl. He said to tell you that he will be stopping by."

"Oh, I know him," Tom said. "No worries. Show him in when he comes."

Tom knew who Jim Diehl was, of course. Tom thought back to when he helped Jim and Joe with their solar system science lesson. What could Jim possibly be doing in Bloomington?

He met him at the door of his office.

"Come in, Jim! How are you?" The men shook hands.

"I'm doing well, Tom, doing well. Just dabbling in some art up here."

"I thought you went to school to be an engineer."

Jim laughed. "Oh, I did! This is just a little side excursion. I've always wanted to take some art classes. When I saw your name mentioned with the award presented to Indiana University for their publication, I remembered how you helped Joe and me way back at your log cabin."

Tom smiled and offered Jim a Swan cigarette and a chair. Both men sat down, Tom behind his desk and Jim in a wooden armchair Tom had requisitioned for visitors.

"The real question is, do you remember how to tell when the moon has gone broke?" Tom asked with a smile.

Jim looked startled for a second, then narrowed his eyes.

"I should have known you would spring a pun on me," he said. "Your brother was bad enough, but he always told me you were worse. Let me see . . ." He tapped the arms of the chair, then slapped his palm down in triumph. "It's when it gets down to its last quarter!"

"You have a good memory," Tom said. "But engineers are smart, so I'm not surprised. How can I help you though? I know engineers are busy and usually make their social calls work in their favor."

Jim laughed again. "You've been in Washington too much," he said. "I think you're confusing engineers with politicians. But you're right; I need a little help. I was wondering if I could bring you my art portfolio sometime and have you give me some tips."

Tom assured Jim it would be an honor and invited him over to his apartment.

"Sharon works every Thursday evening," he said. "Why don't you come keep us company? The boys are nine and eleven. They won't mind."

At Tom's place, Jim spread out his work. Jeff and Brad peeked at the artwork over the shoulders of the men, and then returned to the TV show they were watching. Jim and Tom smoked, drank quarts of coffee, and talked. Tom complimented what he liked and helped Jim adjust where he thought improvements could be made.

"Have you done much sketching, Tom?" Jim asked.

Like a flash, Tom was back on the second floor of the White House. He saw President Eisenhower dipping into a rich palette of color, with Sergeant Moaney at the ready to clean the brushes. He heard the President's laughter when Tom shared his puns and heard him complaining about this or that person who was displeasing him. But Tom also saw the impassive, chest-of-drawers figure of Robert Schulz, telling him that he dare not share with anyone that the President's portraits were not entirely his own. He could hear Schulz saying, "I'm not an artist; I'm a man of business."

"Oh, just a little here and there," Tom answered Jim's question. "I worked at Sarkes Tarzian between my times in Washington. Remember that woodpecker with the bent bill?"

"That was your work?"

"That was me," Tom said, delighted to have thought of the woodpecker to substitute for the White House story.

During Tom's second time in Washington, he had seen a news article in the *Washington Post* about a former White House army private who claimed to have sketched for Eisenhower. Tom had laughed softly at the time. He didn't doubt the story, but he could only imagine Robert Schulz's rage at this breach of privacy. It had not become a major news story, and Tom assumed it was nearly forgotten by now. But he would not be the person to talk about the former President's time-saving painting techniques.[1]

"What did you do after Sarkes Tarzian?" Jim asked.

"Well, I went back to Washington," Tom said. "And then after I came back to Indiana the second time, I worked for Indiana University on the geological survey, drawing maps. Then they moved me to the publications department, and now I'm at the museum."

"The publications department is where I heard your name. They said you brought the journal up from almost nothing to winning a *Time* magazine-level award."

"Let me show you something," Tom said, deflecting the praise.

He took a blank sheet of paper, a knife, and a pencil. With the knife, he carefully shaved the pencil. Then he began to sketch, quickly and confidently. Jim watched, awestruck. Penciled shapes began to emerge—flowers, swirls, and intricate geometric designs. Soon a letter appeared in the center. Tom drew as if he had done the drawing a hundred times before.

"I feel like I'm watching a machine," Jim said. "How long did it take you to learn that?"

"Thirty days, eight hours a day," Tom said. "I've got this illness, Jim. If I want to learn to do something, I can't stop trying until I get it. Unfortunately, I can't stick to one thing either. I keep seeing different things I want to master."

"I see that," Jim said. "Your talent is making me think I should give up art. I could never compete with you."

"Oh, no, don't do that!" Tom said. "Art isn't about competition. It's about the thrill of the process. It's too bad it's not possible to make money on all the projects we spend our time on though." Tom looked down at the design he had just done. "When I was in school doing this, I would spend a day just on the backside of the D. One of my classmates once said, 'Don't do the other side of that thing!' I guess they thought if I did both sides, they would never see me again."

Despite Tom's stated tendency of moving from one thing to the next, he found himself staying at the museum and thriving. He loved the historical research part and the display part.

Jim kept dropping by from time to time for art tips and critique. It never occurred to Tom that he might someday need Jim's engineering expertise in much the same way.

chapter thirty-three

The Voice in the Car

1966

There it was again—that giant Christmas tree in the square. The silver star at its top seemed to stare down at Tom. Other Christmas decorations taunted him from every shop window. Ornaments and tricycles and boxes of chocolate-dipped truffles peppered his senses like birdshot.

Tom drove faster, away from the cheer and laughter and the notes of "Hark the Herald Angels Sing," which he had heard faintly through his closed window. Ten years had passed, but this time of year still made Tom ache.

Why did Christmas cheer always seem to come out in its fullest glory right around December 6? Why did people choose the time of his mother's death to advertise God's love for the world?

This year, as always, everywhere Tom turned he saw or heard more Christmas cheer. The newspapers overflowed with advertisements about perfect gifts and featured Christmas dinner recipes and Christmas floral arrangements. He had even seen a photo of President Lyndon Johnson with his wife in front of the White House Christmas tree.

Tom didn't keep track of Lyndon Johnson much these days. Of course, he had thought of the White House on Inauguration Day, after Johnson had finally been elected. Johnson had run against Barry Goldwater and won by a wide margin. He knew that Johnson's position on the Vietnam War was becoming increasingly unpopular, and many Americans did not think the country should be fighting in Vietnam at all. But he really did not know the man. Not like Eisenhower.

As he drove, Tom thought back to his White House days. He was still amazed how down-to-earth President Eisenhower had been. He had never let his power go to his head.

From the newspapers, Tom knew that Eisenhower had asked Kennedy to refer to him as "General Eisenhower" rather than "Mr. President." Tom knew that Eisenhower had also asked Kennedy to promote Colonel Schulz to the status of General, and that President Kennedy had agreed to do so.

Tom had read with interest about the death of Winston Churchill, the British leader who had been Eisenhower's friend and fellow painter. Queen Elizabeth had invited Eisenhower to the funeral. He had gone, and given a tribute to the British statesman. Tom thought about the final words of the tribute, which he had heard on the radio: "And now to you, Sir Winston, my old friend, farewell."

Tom had also read an article about the funeral in *National Geographic*. Tom had noticed that the article about Churchill was directly followed by an article called "Amish Folk." Photos of the Amish in Pennsylvania showed fields of wheat being harvested by horse-drawn machinery. Tom couldn't help but think of the striking contrast between the tools of war and the tools of peace.

Later Tom read of a second heart attack that Eisenhower had suffered in Augusta, Georgia. He also read of the fiftieth anniversary celebration for Ike and Mamie. Whenever Tom saw photos of General Eisenhower now, he had to look twice to be sure he was looking at the same man he had once known.

He looked weak, thin, and tired. Tom had heard that he had sold his Angus herd at an auction in the spring of 1966. Tom thought of the old Angus bull he had admired so much and wondered if he was still alive. He wondered if Eisenhower was still painting, and if he did all of his own sketch work now that he had more time. He wondered if Sergeant Moaney was still as spry as ever, chasing down Ike's golf balls and chopping up onions for the Boss's famous stew.

Tom wondered how Mamie was doing. Did she still have Rose, her personal maid? Did she still decorate in pink and have a closet filled with outfits?

He wondered about little David. Tom could not forget how much happiness David had brought him that evening when the Queen Mother of England had been in the house, and Tom had been invited to dine. Tom had also chatted with David a few times when he visited the painting room. David had started college, Tom read, in Massachusetts. Tom remembered that David's grandpa Ike had wanted him to go to a military college, but David's parents had prevailed.

Well, at least he still has his parents, Tom thought, and just like that, his thoughts made their bitter full circle.

He, Tom, had no parents. He now had two reasons to hate the holidays. Just two years ago, in 1964, the Kirkman children had once again stood in a circle in Cresthaven Cemetery in Bedford. It had once again been early December. They had once again huddled together in the cold, staring at an ornate box that held the body of one of their parents. They once again heard the Scripture verses and the prayers and the reassurance that "in Christ" there was hope. Tom had kept his face stoic and smooth. No one needed to know that he didn't believe a word the preachers said. If other people crowding around the gaping black hole in the earth wanted to make themselves feel better by believing there was a God who loved them, they could do that.

There was one big difference at Dad's funeral. Right at their feet was a gravestone—one that marked a previous grave. The stone was shaped like a rectangle, with a rounded protrusion at the top. A floral design had been etched into the upper left corner of the stone. The girls had wanted that. *As if it matters,* Tom had thought. BERNICE M. KIRKMAN, the block letters said. NOVEMBER 6, 1906 – DECEMBER 6, 1956.

Fifty years. Mom had been only fifty years old when she died.

Now, in 1966, with the world once again going crazy with Christmas celebrations, there were two matching rectangular stones with decorative rounded tops in the Cresthaven Cemetery.

Somehow, these evening drives away from his refuge at the museum often put Tom in an ill humor. The comfort of design projects and calligraphy hands and photo development soothed him with a kind of analgesia during the day. But when he left the museum at the end of the day, the harsh realities of life came back full force.

Yes, he was an important person in the world of academia. Yes, he had a job he loved, and he excelled at his tasks. He loved the smell of the museum: the ink, the old stone, even the ham sandwiches from employee lunches. He loved working in the impressive 1906 architecture, the wonderful carved stairway banisters, the ceiling crossed with heavy wooden beams, and the deep windowsills. The outside of the museum, with its imposing block doorposts, impressive steps leading to the entrance, and arched windows, also stirred fondness in his heart.

He even loved anthropology, the study of the development of cultures and societies. Despite being a deep, dusty topic, it tied directly to his work as curator of the museum. It gave him deep satisfaction to turn up clues to the cultures of other times and places. It thrilled him even more to follow those clues to their source and understand how those long-ago people had thought and acted.

He could barely remember the day when he had needed to look up the word *curator* in the dictionary just as he had looked up the word *calligraphy* so long ago. He might have looked it up when he heard that Jackie Kennedy had appointed a curator for the White House. At that time, he had never imagined himself being a curator of anything, much less of the much-revered museum of Indiana University.

"Tom."

Tom felt the blood drain from his face. His hands clenched the steering wheel so tightly he was afraid he would break either his fingers or the wheel. He knew he was alone in the car. But someone had spoken to him.

"Tom, I've kept my promise, but you haven't."

Tom's mind reeled. There was no question that this was the voice of God speaking to him. There had been no question from the first word, but Tom could not believe it.

But God was speaking to him.

"You asked for ten years of life for your mother. I gave her eternal life."

But that's not the same! Tom screamed inside. *I want her here!*

"What are you going to do?"

Tom's hands shook. God seemed to be in charge. By now Tom had pulled into his parking spot at home. The voice did not speak again.

But those words stretched into the silence like hands, reaching for him—*"What are you going to do?"*

God sees me, Tom realized. *God was with me in this car.*

There was no doubt anymore. God knew Tom Kirkman. God had seen his pain. God had followed his journey. God had been waiting, watching.

It was December 6, the tenth anniversary of Mom's death.

God knew it, and He chose to speak to Tom on that day.

For the first time in his angry battle with God, Tom burst into unrestrained tears.

Part four

chapter thirty-four

The Paoli Jail

1968

Tom looked up from his recliner. A young boy stood in the doorway of the living room.

"Dad, we're going outside for a bike ride."

It was 10-year-old Brad. Behind him, 12-year-old Jeff stood waiting.

How can Jeff be twelve already?

"Okay."

Tom watched as the two boys disappeared with a pounding thunder of feet. The August evening would at least provide a temporary reprieve from the intense heat of the day. Tom looked back at the newspaper.

In the upper left-hand corner of the paper he saw an article about Senator Ted Kennedy speaking out against the Vietnam War. The article said he was "speaking out for the first time since the assassination of his brother Robert in June."

Tom sighed and shook his head, remembering the shock of that day. It was hard to believe—the second Kennedy killed by an assassin's bullet. Tom remembered Bobby well. He had been so young and energetic. He had just begun to unleash the spring-loaded potential Tom had always seen in him.

Tom's eyes wandered to the upper left-hand corner of the paper. He allowed himself to read the advertisement for air conditioning. *Ah, wouldn't that be nice.* Even now, in late evening, the apartment was sticky and hot. The lone fan that buzzed in the corner of the room teased Tom with its occasional and mostly unhelpful breeze.

Tom sighed and told himself to turn the page. There were plenty of things to buy for growing boys, without extravagances like air conditioning. As his hand reached for the edge of the newsprint, his eye fell on another article, in the middle of the page.

"Buggy Reflectors Opposed by Amish."

Tom's eyes scanned the article with mild interest. It was from Paoli, Indiana, a small town south of Bedford. Suddenly his eyes riveted on the words before him.

Jail?

The Amish, the article said, were prepared to go to jail rather than use a slow-moving vehicle sign that they found offensive to their views of simplicity.

In particular, there was a man by the name of Simon D. Gingerich who was scheduled to appear in court on September 6 to be sentenced on the charge of reckless driving.

Reckless driving? Tom thought, astounded. *In a buggy?*

The Amish say the red and orange emblem violates their religious belief against glorifying man, rather than God, the article explained.

Tom read that if Simon D. Gingerich were convicted, he could face up to six months in jail and a $500 fine.[1]

Tom's arms lost their strength, and the newspaper crumpled weakly to his lap.

He was completely confused. He tried to arrange his thoughts, but things just didn't make sense.

First, Tom found it impossible to believe that a person could be put in jail in the United States of America for wanting to live simply. Tom thought of Pearl Harbor, of his brother Bob on the submarine, and of the gruesome Battle of Midway. He thought about D-Day. He thought about his own work for the CIA. All these things had been done in the name of freedom. Since the Russians didn't believe in God and the Americans did, the Russians needed to be stopped and defeated. Even though Tom had not believed in God himself, he had understood the underlying reasons.

Second, Tom sympathized with the police and Judge Rhodes who represented the city of Paoli, whose main interest no doubt lay in preventing accidents. Tom could still remember the awful crunch of running over Tony. Tom had never been seriously injured in a wreck, but Tony had been killed in one. It had given Tom a lifelong fear of accidents with motor vehicles. How horrible would it be to hit a horse-drawn buggy, even if it were empty? And how much worse if it contained a happy family who loved each other and loved God and lived off the labor of their own hands? So, in Tom's personal opinion, the slow-moving vehicle sign was a good idea.

As Tom laid out these two opposing thoughts in his mind, he realized that there was a third side to this puzzling situation—one that intrigued him: *Simon D. Gingerich was willing to go to jail for his beliefs.*

In the year and a half since Tom had heard God speaking to him in the car, he knew he was a changed man. He knew God was real. He knew God loved him. He had talked with Christian people and had great conversations. His sister Patsy in particular had wept when he shared the story of God's voice with her. He hadn't told the story to many people because he knew they wouldn't believe him. But Patsy had.

"Tommy," she whispered. "That's so wonderful!"

Tom loved her for her enthusiasm and simple faith. He loved her all the more because she was the only person in his life, now that his mother was gone, who still called him "Tommy."

But Tom had still not committed himself to any particular Christian church or group. Even though God had awakened him in the car, he did not feel at all clear about how he should be living his life. He had no brothers in Christ because he had no church family. He knew this omission was hurting his spiritual life, and his initial enthusiasm for God was fading.

Of course, it didn't help that Sharon did not share his faith, but that was not really a new thing.

Tom folded the newspaper and put it on the arm of the recliner. He should call the boys in for their baths soon. The bowl of spaghetti from supper still sat on the kitchen table. He had told Sharon he would put it in the fridge when the boys were finished eating.

But something more important than spaghetti or hot baths was expanding inside his chest. Here was a man, Simon D. Gingerich, who knew exactly what he believed—and he was willing to endure any hardship in defense of those beliefs. Simon Gingerich's faith was so much bigger than a place he went on Sunday. Just from the short article he had read, Tom was sure that this man had a security and a peace that he himself did not have.

I have to meet this man, Tom told himself.

He rose from the recliner a different man from the one who had sat down an hour earlier. He had sat down tired and dull and disinterested. Even the endless chatter of politics had little meaning to him anymore. He rose with something inside him that he had not felt for years. What was it? Whatever it was, the feeling in his heart reminded him of his hopeful days as a teenager.

It wasn't hope, exactly. It wasn't even happiness or peace or joy, or any of those other traits listed in Galatians as the fruit of the Spirit.

Curiosity. That's what it was. An interest in something that promised to take Tom to a place he had never been before.

Yes. He would go meet Simon D. Gingerich if it was the last thing he ever did.

Tom continued to watch the newspaper closely over the next few days. Finally, on Saturday, September 7, he found it.

"Buggy Driver Convicted as Slow Mover."

Then, a week later:

"Amish Man Jailed After Refusing to Pay Fine."

Simon D. Gingerich was in jail.

With disbelief, Tom reviewed the case. People who were fined in Orange County were permitted to pay off their fine by going to jail. They could decrease the fine by five dollars a day, so Simon Gingerich would need to be in jail for at least twenty days.

"I'm going to Paoli," Tom said to Sharon.

"Okay," she said without asking why.

Tom climbed into their 1967 Chevy Biscayne station wagon. It was Monday evening, and he couldn't wait any longer to meet Simon. He turned the key, and the dark green car rumbled to life. A light rain collected on the windshield, so he switched on the wipers and the lights. Before pulling out onto the road, he snapped a flame from his cigarette lighter and lit up. Smoking was something he still did a lot, especially when he was nervous.

In Paoli, Tom drove past the Standard Oil gas station and around the square with its beautiful courthouse and its fine cafe that he knew was famous for homemade pie and fresh coffee. He turned right at the south intersection of the square and drove down the hill. He had been told the jail was located at the bottom of the hill, close to the creek with the one-way bridge.

Tom turned right and pulled up with some astonishment at the building to which he had been directed. He checked the sign a second time. Yes, it said "Orange County Jail." It looked exactly like a house. It had a front porch with wooden steps leading up to it. One side of the house had two stories, with a tall chimney and a porch swing by the front door. The one-story wing on the west side of the house had its own separate door leading out to the porch. This, Tom concluded, must be the jail. He put the gear stick in park and climbed out of the Biscayne.

A man whom Tom knew must be Sheriff Farrell Fields stepped from the house. Behind him, his wife peered out after him. The sheriff settled himself on the wooden porch swing, with a silent glance at Tom. His wife then stepped out to join him.

Tom got the impression that the sheriff wasn't overly friendly. He looked down his long nose at Tom, and waited for him to approach. Beside him, his wife looked very much like a crow, Tom thought. She watched Tom approach with small beady eyes and short, jerky movements of her head.

The sheriff still had not spoken, so Tom spoke first.

"I'm here to visit Simon D. Gingerich," he said. "I understood—I understand—there is a jail here."

The sheriff still said nothing, but now he jutted his left thumb down the porch to the second entrance Tom had seen.

"I go in at that door?" Tom asked, confused.

"Yup. You aren't one of these newspapermen, are you?"

Tom looked down at his hands, as if checking to see if he was holding a pencil and notebook. Suddenly he wished he had brought along something to take notes, but he had not.

"No," Tom said. He paused. Would the sheriff just sit there, or would he get up and let Tom in?

"It's open," the sheriff said, as if this were something that Tom should have known on his own.

"It's . . ." Tom faltered. "Not locked?"

The sheriff reached up to scratch his head.

"Nope."

"Okay. Thank you." Tom walked down the porch.

He had the distinct impression that the sheriff would have treated him differently if Tom had let it slide that he had once worked in the White House. But he was not about to share such a detail.

All Tom could think was, *The door's open. Surely not!*

Tom stopped at the door, his damp shoes squeaking.

"Just go in!" the sheriff bawled.

Tom let himself in. There, on the right, was a heavy metal door.

Just as the sheriff had said, it was ajar.

Tom stood gazing at the door, not making a sound. Then he lifted his left hand and rested it on the knob. With his right hand, he softly rapped on the metal door.

chapter thirty-five

Simon D. Gingerich

"Come in," a cheerful voice said.

For a second, the voice surprised Tom so much that his feet refused to move. The voice sounded pleased with its surroundings and bursting with impatience to share them with a newcomer. It sounded like a precursor to an offer of hot coffee and a slice of cake. It sounded like it came from a man in an armchair with his feet high on a footstool, who would beam up at Tom from over the top of a newspaper.

Tom recovered himself quickly. He pulled the door open and walked inside.

There was no armchair, no footstool, no newspaper, and no coffee or cake. On an old wooden table that had once been red, a stoneware plate held a used spoon and fork, neatly placed. Also on the table, a Bible lay open, about midway through the Old Testament, it appeared to Tom. Beneath the table, Tom saw dusty black shoes. Above the table, Tom saw the face of Simon D. Gingerich.

Tom had expected to find a simple, horse-smelling, slightly unkempt man who pretended a deep faith in God to cover for his ignorance. He was not prepared to meet the intelligent black eyes or the slow, inquisitive smile above a neatly combed black beard tinged with white. Tom suddenly felt foolish for simply walking in, without calling ahead and asking if he could come pay the man a visit.

The two men regarded each other without awkwardness for a few seconds. Then Tom took another step forward as Simon rose and reached out his hand.

"My name is Simon," he said simply. "But perhaps you may know that," he added with a decided twinkle in his black eyes that gave Tom a burst of relief and joy. So Amish people actually were allowed to be humorous! From that twinkle, he was sure of it. In fact, he had the distinct desire to start off by trying one of his favorite puns on this man. With an effort, Tom controlled this ridiculous impulse.

"Tom Kirkman," he said, feeling the strength in the man's hand as they shook.

"You can sit down," Simon said, showing Tom a wooden chair beside the table. "I offer you the best I have."

At this, Tom allowed himself to chuckle outright.

"And why do you come to see me, Tom? Is it our Lord's command to visit the 'least of these' in prison?"

Tom smiled, and he suddenly felt as if he and Simon had known each other for a long time.

"No," Tom said. "I . . . I just—"

Suddenly he found it hard to explain.

"I guess—I—read about you in the newspaper. And I—I wanted to know what would make a man go to jail for the things he believes."

"I see," Simon said. He glanced down at the Bible, open before him. "Do you have one of these books, Tom?"

Tom nodded, eager to say that he did, in fact, have a Bible.

"Which church do you belong to?" Simon asked.

Tom could feel his face betraying his disappointment at being asked this question.

"I was raised Baptist," he said. "But I'm not sure where I belong now. Do you believe the Amish church is the only true church?"

Tom instantly wished he had not asked such a nosy, complicated question so soon in the conversation. But Simon showed no irritation. He slowly flipped a few pages in his Bible, then looked back up at Tom.

"Do you know the verse in John 3:16?" he asked.

"Oh, yes," said Tom. "I do."

Simon looked thoughtfully at his Bible. "My Bible is written in German," he said, "but I believe I can say it in English. Correct me if I am wrong. 'For God so loved the Amish church, that he gave his only begotten Son . . .' "

Seeing the telltale twinkle in Simon's eye, Tom burst out laughing. He was thrilled with the little joke.

"Is that what it says, Tom?" Simon asked. "What does it say?"

"The world," Tom said, still laughing. "It says God so loved the world."

"Yes, that is what it says in German too," Simon said, his grin wide. "And as long as the Bible says it, I believe it. God didn't just send Jesus for the Amish people. Now, Tom, would you tell me a little about yourself and your family?"

Before he knew what was happening, Tom was pouring out his story. He told Simon about growing up in Avoca and watching his mother suffer from high blood pressure. He told him about boot camp in Arkansas, drafting school at Fort Belvoir, and about working in the White House. He told him about his marriage to Sharon, about the two boys, about his mother's death. He even mentioned the CIA. The Amish man made no visible reaction.

"I hope I'm not talking too long," Tom said suddenly. He was taking up much more time than he had thought he would.

"I don't have anywhere to go," Simon smiled. "And I appreciate you sharing your story. May I ask, Tom, where you received that scar on your thumb? Or is that question too nosy?"

Tom stared at Simon, amazed at his intuition. "How did you know there was a story behind this?" he asked, rubbing the scar. "And that I was trying to decide whether to share it with you?"

Simon shook his head slowly as if to say he did not know. Tom told him all about his dad's mental illness, his deep grief, his drinking, and then his violence. He told Simon how both of his parents now rested in the cemetery in Bedford. He even told about hearing the voice of God in his car on the way home from his job at the museum at Indiana University. He also told Simon that he and Sharon were expecting another child.

"I can't believe I'm telling you all this," Tom said again, shaking himself. "I never talk to anyone about my secrets. That's why I got those jobs in the White House and the CIA."

"Perhaps you are talking so freely because you never had a captive audience before," Simon suggested, and Tom laughed again. With each laugh, his heart felt lighter.

"I really came to find out about you, though!" Tom said. "What do you do for a living?"

"I'm a simple man of the earth," Simon said. "My wife and children and I have some animals and we raise crops—corn and sorghum and vegetables. We live off the land, Tom. That's the biggest thing that bothers me about sitting here in this jail. It's time to harvest the sorghum. And I had told my neighbors that I would help them harvest their sorghum as well. It will be a very sad thing if I can't make good on my word."

At the mention of farming, Tom's compulsion to share a pun with this man reached new strength.

"Do you know why the farmer called his pig 'Ink'?" Tom queried.

Simon grinned broadly. "I don't think I've heard that one."

"Because he kept running out of the pen," Tom said.

Simon chuckled—a deep, dignified chuckle of pure enjoyment.

"Oh," he said, his breath still coming in wheezes, "what you don't know about that one is that it's truer than you think! We have pigs about every summer, and we can't keep those little animals in their pens. But how about this, Tom: Why shouldn't you tell a secret on a farm?" Simon paused and then went on, "Because the potatoes have eyes and the corn has ears!"

Tom remembered having heard that one somewhere in the old Washington office of the CIA.

It occurred to him that Simon was somewhat like a corn plant: tall, upright, sedate, calm, a bit earthy. Tom saw dirt beneath the Amish man's nails, but he could tell it was not the smudged-in dirtiness of someone who never washed, but the necessary dirt of someone who had just come in from the field.

"I've heard a lot of jokes about sheep," Tom added. "I tried to tell them to my dog, but he'd *herd* them all."

It did Tom so much good to laugh with Simon. It reminded him how he had laughed around the dinner table with his parents and brothers and sisters years ago.

"But Tom," Simon said, "have you really given your life over to the Lord Jesus? Is He a friend with whom you can talk and counsel?"

His transition from farming jokes to this deep question was as natural as stepping from one row of corn to the next.

Tom puzzled over the question.

"Simon, maybe you are asking just the question I need to hear. I believe in God now. And I have been trying to read the Bible. But I don't know if I have really committed my life to Him."

Simon looked at Tom with such kindness and hope that Tom felt tears welling up in his eyes.

"Would you like to? You must be born again if you wish to have peace. If any man is in Christ, he is a new creature," the Amish man said simply. "Old things are passed away. All things are become new."

Tom knew better than to answer casually or glibly. He took in a huge breath of air, then released it slowly.

"I grew up in church," Tom said. "So I am familiar with those verses. But

I guess I don't know what to do to become a new creature."

"There is nothing you can DO to earn salvation," Simon said. "This book here says that if we confess that Jesus is Lord, we will be saved. Tell Jesus that you believe He is God and that you want Him to be Lord of your life. Oh, I'm sure you were taught all this in the Baptist church too, and maybe by your parents."

"I was," Tom said, slowly nodding. "But—" he shook his head, "somehow their teachings went out of my heart when I turned away from God."

Tom let his head fall into his hands for a moment. His wooden chair shifted and creaked.

Suddenly he raised his head and looked Simon in the eye.

"Why would you say there is nothing that we can do to earn salvation? You are in jail because of your beliefs. I would say that is 'doing something.'"

"I'm not in jail to earn my salvation," Simon said. "I choose to live a simple life because I am saved. I think maintaining that simple life for myself and my family is worth going to jail for."

"Oh," Tom said.

He could not remember ever hearing such a clear explanation of salvation. He felt his heart melt in hope. Hope that the Savior who sustained Simon Gingerich could bring peace to Tom Kirkman too.

"Would you like to have me pray with you?" Simon offered. "I pray best in German, but I will try to say the same words in English."

Simon rose, picked up his chair, and brought it around the table beside Tom's. He seated himself there, and with his hand on Tom's shoulder, he prayed. When he finished, he paused and squeezed Tom's shoulder. Tom knew it was his turn.

And there, in the unlocked jail cell of Simon D. Gingerich, Thomas Ellsworth Kirkman gave his life to Jesus Christ.

chapter thirty-six

New Worlds

The Bible was like a huge wonderful world Tom had never really stepped into. Ever since meeting Simon Gingerich and beginning a personal relationship with Jesus Christ, Tom had begun to study the Bible on his own. It was as if his former exposure to the Bible had shown him photographs of that world, but now he was actually inside it. Tom wandered through the world of Scripture with delight, searching this corner and that corner for hidden treasure. Sometimes he found treasures spilling out at him. Other times he had to dig below the surface. Then he would find that he had not even begun to exhaust the adventure.

Scripture, Tom realized as he studied, was like the universe. Just as every schoolchild knows the names of the nine planets, so most Bible readers know the story of Jonah and the Great Fish or Daniel and the Lion's Den.

Some people think that just knowing the story is all one can know. But Tom found that just as the universe stretches on forever, so the Bible continued to expand the more he looked at it. Tom was fascinated. He was hooked.

A few days after Tom spoke with Simon in the jail, a sorghum farmer bailed the Amish man out of jail because he wanted his help with the harvest. The judge allowed him to take care of the harvest, and then come back later to finish the 20-day sentence. Tom visited him again many times, both in jail and on his farm. Finally, one day in Simon's living room, Tom shared the secret that had been growing bigger each day within him.

"I want to join the Amish church, Simon."

Simon was neither flattered nor stumped by Tom's request to join the Amish church. His children had just come in from raking leaves and his wife had fresh cookies for them all. His handicapped daughter, who could walk only with great difficulty, crocheted a blanket nearby.

"You could certainly join the Amish," Simon said in his slow, kind way as he thoughtfully chewed his cookie. "But Tom, like I told you, we read the Bible in German. The preachers speak in German too."

"I learned Russian quickly," Tom said, reaching for a second cookie. "I could learn German too."

Tom looked at Simon's wife as she walked around her kitchen by the light of a kerosene lamp and put a teakettle on to boil. Her bonnet and dark blue dress gave her the appearance of a patient, innocent woman who knew nothing of the ways of the world. But his interactions with Simon made Tom suspect that, like her husband, the woman had more to her than what met the eye.

Tom thought, oddly, that Simon had some remarkable similarities to the late Bobby Kennedy. He had always felt that Bobby was a mass of hidden potential energy. So was Simon. But the difference was that Bobby had reminded Tom more of a trap that was set. Simon's hidden resources were not self-seeking, but worked only for the good of those around him.

Tom also found a fascination with the simple life of the Amish, and he longed to live that life as well. What a wonderful thing it would be not to worry about the modern world! How much better he could focus on the things he loved so much if he didn't have to worry about the politics and bylaws of a university. He had always loved the outdoors, and he loved animals. He wanted horses, cows, and an occasional pig, just like Simon had. He was willing to give up his vehicle and his modern appliances, and just take the plunge.

"I'm sure you could," Simon said. "I have no doubts at all about your intelligence. But in the meantime, there is another church called the Beachy Amish church. They believe many of the same things we believe, but they hold their church services in English. They have English Scriptures and English hymnals. And they drive cars and use modern conveniences like electricity."

Tom promised to look into attending the Beachy church. But only because it would take him a little time to learn German.

"What does your wife think of all this?" Simon asked next, with his characteristic intuitiveness.

Tom sighed. He let his head fall into his hands.

"I haven't talked to her about it. She won't go to church with me no matter where I go," he said. "It's no use for us to try to get along. We just stay together because of the boys."

"And you have a new little one on the way, did you say?" Simon had asked.

"Yes," Tom said with a smile. "I can hardly wait!"

"How do you think Jesus would have you relate to your wife?" Simon asked. "Study that topic. Ask the Lord for direction. Sharon will make her own choice, but perhaps God will restore your relationship."

Tom shook his head dismally. But he promised to try.

A few days after this conversation, Tom felt the still small voice of the Spirit nudging him. He was alone with his wife. Sharon worked at the ironing board, preparing a maternity outfit she had just purchased for a work party.

"Sharon, I know I'm not too good at listening," Tom said.

Sharon looked up, stunned.

"Why are you saying that?" she asked.

"Because I think it's true. I haven't always treated you the best."

The iron puffed a small cloud of steam into the silent air.

"Okay," she said. Tom found her softer the next few days as they passed each other. Yet, despite Tom's appeals, they remained strangers in their own house, as if the gulf between them was just too big to bridge.

Tom told Sharon about his interest in the Amish church and his plan to attend the Beachy Amish church temporarily.

Sharon stared at him as if he had emerged from a spaceship. She said nothing for a long time. Finally she shook her head.

"Do what you want, Tom," she said. "Just don't ask me to go with you."

A few weeks later, little John made his appearance in the world. For a few brief days, Tom and Sharon enjoyed an interlude of shared happiness. They both loved the little boy with all their hearts.

A few weeks before Christmas, Tom visited the Beachy Amish church— alone, as he had anticipated. He found that their beliefs compared to those he had been taught in the Baptist church, although they seemed more diligent in their interpretation of the Sermon on the Mount and some other Biblical passages. Also, they lived more simply, as Tom had noticed during the Christmas season. The church people celebrated Christmas, but their celebrations tended to center on family, the Christmas story, singing carols to neighbors, and of course, good food. Some families didn't even give gifts.

"Dad, do you think NASA will really put men on the moon?"

It was Christmas vacation now, and the boys were taking it easy. Both Brad and Jeff were reading the newspaper. And John! Tom cuddled his tiny son, who was just now pushing his little stocking feet onto the pages of Tom's Bible. Tom had been reading the Creation account. He peeled his attention off the pages.

"Uh, what did you say, Brad? About the moon?" Sitting in his recliner,

Bible in his lap, he looked up at Brad.

Brad repeated his question.

"Well, they've already put a man in orbit around the moon and brought him back, right? Is that what you were reading? So your question is, why couldn't they land a man on the moon's surface, right?"

"Yes. But then what if the astronauts get stranded on the moon? They might starve before anyone could rescue them," Brad said.

Jeff looked up from his horizontal position on the couch nearby. "They would starve from lack of oxygen, not lack of food," he said. "But that's the whole reason they want to try it—because it's difficult and dangerous! Why else do you think Gus Grissom died?"

Little John grunted and shifted his tiny head on his father's chest, his downy hair mingling with Tom's growing beard. Tom broke into a smile of pure delight. *Babies take up the whole universe too,* he thought. John was only one month old. Tom squeezed the baby close to his heart.

"You're right, Jeff," Tom said. Everyone from the Bedford area knew about their hometown boy Gus Grissom and his untimely death in a NASA test flight. "That's what President Kennedy said when the Space Race started. When he said that Americans would put a man on the moon in this decade, he said it would not be because it was easy, but because it was hard."

"I remember when John Kennedy was shot," Brad said knowledgeably.

"Of course, everyone remembers that!" Jeff shot from the couch.

"Brad was only six," Tom said. "And of course, little John here doesn't remember."

"Okay," Jeff conceded. "Everyone except John!"

Jeff and Brad both loved the little boy almost as much as Tom and Sharon did.

Three months later Tom was back in his recliner, once more holding John. He was now a pudgy four-month-old who loved to tangle his fingers in his father's beard.

Jeff and Brad burst into the living room, holding the newspaper they had just retrieved from its box. Tom knew what they were about to show him. He had heard the news on the radio on his way home from the museum.

"Look!" Brad gasped, holding up the headline. "FORMER PRESIDENT EISENHOWER DEAD AT 78."

"Dad, wasn't he the one who had the Angus cows?" Jeff asked.

Tom nodded. "Yes, he was a great man. I'm sure his son John and his grandson David are very sad today. And Mamie."

"Who's Mamie?" Brad asked.

"His wife, of course," Jeff snapped importantly. "She was First Lady then, just like Pat Nixon is now."

"Let me see the paper, boys," Tom said.

He flipped through the pages of newsprint. Photos of Eisenhower's best moments crowded the pages. Pensive waiting at D-Day. Victory in Europe. Elected president after the "I Like Ike" campaign. There were current photos of Mamie, the Moaneys, son John and grandson David, all grieving their loved one. David's new wife Julie was there too. She was the daughter of President Nixon.

What a full year it had been for Mamie. The Eisenhowers had been involved in Nixon's political campaign last fall, in which he had defeated Hubert Humphrey. Besides the political affiliation, their grandson had married Richard Nixon's daughter the month after the election. Now Mamie had lost her dear old Ike.

It had not come as a surprise, at least. General Eisenhower, as he liked to be called, had been at Walter Reed Army Hospital in Washington, D.C., for the last year, trying to rally from repeated heart attacks and pneumonia. Now the general was lying in state for people to pay their last respects. Soon he would be laid to rest in Abilene, Kansas, where he grew up.

Tom put down the newspaper and found himself walking toward the storage closet under the stairway. He pulled out a box and lifted out a stack of papers and a few photos framed in glass. There they were, at the bottom. He lifted them out and set them carefully on the floor, side by side.

As he ran a finger around the edge of the glass, the scenes came back to life again.

"Thomas, it has been a pleasure." Mr. Tolley, of course.

"Happy trails, pal," Sandy Fox had said with a puff on his pipe. "Can we come get cake at your farewell in the East Wing?" This, with an exaggerated wink.

The farewell in Robert Schulz's office had been warm and kind. Tom remembered eating cake and drinking both coffee and wine. He had assured Millie and Colonel Schulz that he would write to them to update them about his life.

"Stop in Mamie's office before you go," said Sandy Fox, who had indeed come for cake.

In Mamie's office, Mamie herself had given Tom two photos, framed in glass: one of herself and one of President Eisenhower. Mamie's photo said in her own handwriting, *"To Thomas E. Kirkman, with my best wishes. Mamie Doud Eisenhower."* The President's said, in his handwriting, *"For: Thomas E. Kirkman, with best wishes, Dwight D. Eisenhower."*

Tom sighed. He carefully returned the glass frames. He picked up a stack of old letters. Opening one, he saw his own name signed at the bottom. Yes, it was a copy of the letter he had finally written to Robert Schulz's office the year after Mom's death. What a dreadful year that had been!

> *Dear Friends,*
>
> *I am extremely ashamed of myself for taking such a long time to write. So much has happened at our house since we arrived in April that I've not had time to do anything but face what seemed to be a daily crisis of some kind or another. The past months have been both tragic and joyful for me.*
>
> *We have a new son born the sixteenth of November. He weighed 7 pounds and 14 ounces. Both Bradley and his mother are getting along wonderfully.*

Now for the tragedy. When we arrived home in April I learned that my father, who had been a teetotaler most of his life, was drinking excessively and was in a state of mental depression called "paranoia." This, according to the doctors, was caused by my mother's death. I suggested that he consult a psychiatrist, but he was immediately opposed to this suggestion because he didn't feel he needed help from anyone. After two charges of assault with intent to kill, the court committed him to a mental hospital in September. He was recently released from this hospital and has worked every day since. His outlook on life is greatly improved. I sincerely hope he continues to make such progress. This, my friends, is an experience I hope you never have to face.

I worked on construction work all summer, but I have gone back to the drawing board. The job is photography, cartooning, and art work in general. The company I work for has a patent on a certain part required in the production of television sets. I will work full-time until January 28, then I will go on part-time. This will permit me to attend school full-time next semester. The company is located in Bloomington, home of Indiana University.

In closing, my wife joins me in wishing each of you the greetings of the season.

Sincerely yours, Tom

In the next yellow envelope, Tom found the colonel's reply, likely typed by Millie. It was dated on Christmas Eve, and Tom laughed. The colonel couldn't even let people off work on Christmas Eve.

Dear Tom:

Thanks from all of us for your letter of 17 December and rest assured that we more than understand why you have not been able to write. We all read your letter with interest and share with you your feelings of sadness and joy at the recent events in your life.

We were distressed with the news of your father's depression and hope and pray that this attitude has improved and that he is on the road to recovery.

And of course we were delighted with your and Sharon's news of the new boy. Our congratulations to you both. Things remain pretty well the same in the office.

I have just returned from a prolonged stay in Paris where I was assisting in the preparations for the President's visit. As usual, Millie and Barbara have been kept extremely busy keeping all of us happy and in harness. All of us look forward to a very Merry Christmas, Tom, and we join in sending you our best wishes for a happy holiday season and lots of good luck in 1958. We certainly hope that your work will permit you to attend school full-time next semester because that certainly appears to be the most important thing for your future at this point.

With best personal regards.
Sincerely,
Robert L. Schulz, Colonel, U.S. Army
Military Aide to the President

Tom wondered how General Schulz was doing. He made a mental note to write to him soon. He wasn't sure that he would go into all the details about Simon Gingerich and the Amish and the Beachy Amish church. But at least he would like to touch base with the general after the loss of a man who had been the general's boss for perhaps thirty years.

chapter thirty-seven

Joining the Amish Church

Tom still wasn't sure what he thought about everything that had happened since September when he first met Simon D. Gingerich in jail. Tom interacted with different members of the church and learned as much as he could from them. Brad went with him to church. One day Tom let Brad invite his friend Floyd home for lunch. Sharon remained aloof. She had no interest in going to the Beachy Amish church. But she offered Tom's church friends hospitality. She cooked a delicious meal of spaghetti and meatballs for Tom, Jeff, Brad, and Floyd.

Tom was not surprised at her lack of interest. This church was different than any Tom or Sharon had attended before. All the women wore head coverings. And because they took Jesus' teachings seriously, they believed in loving one's enemies to the point that they refused to take part in war. Many of the young men of the church had served several years volunteering in hospitals rather than joining the Vietnam War.

Tom spent many hours discussing the topic of nonresistance with his new friends at the Beachy Amish church. Tom had been familiar with the idea of Christ's way of nonviolence ever since Bill had joined the Seabees so he could avoid taking lives. Still, after working with military men in the White House, Tom had many questions. He admired Eisenhower's leadership abilities and Robert Schulz's loyalty to his "Boss."

"I don't think there's anything wrong with respecting the positions of those men," one brother in the church told him. "But we feel God calls the committed Christian to a greater fight. Have you found this verse? 'We wrestle not against flesh and blood, but against spiritual wickedness . . .' "

Not long after Eisenhower's death, Tom heard the shocking news that General Robert Schulz had also had a heart attack. Quickly he sent him the letter he had been meaning to send and told him that he was sorry to hear of the reverses in his health. Using an Indiana University letterhead, he addressed the letter to the U.S. Army Hospital in Fort Belvoir, Virginia, where he had first met Robert Schulz.

> *Dear General Schulz:*
>
> *I heard via radio and television of your recent problems with your heart and wish to express my best wishes to you for a speedy recovery. If I can be of any help to you or your family during your period of recuperation, please let me know.*
>
> *My family and I were saddened upon receiving news of President Eisenhower's death but took pride in the fact that under such difficult times your efforts were apparent in providing comfort to both the Eisenhower family and the nation. You, General, served your "Boss" well and made possible for his leadership qualities to be exercised to the full for the good of mankind. Because I am aware of your role in his ability as a leader, my admiration and respect for you is great.*
>
> *I take pride in the fact that I served under you and appreciate your*

past kindness to me. So, please accept my wishes for a fast recovery
and my regards to your family.

Sincerely,

Thomas E. Kirkman

Curator of Exhibit Design

First, Tom received a brief note from Colonel Richard Streiff, the officer Tom had worked with on Eisenhower's Gettysburg bookshelves. The letter said that Schulz was resting and recovering, but unable to write. Finally, on July 14, 1969, Schulz wrote a letter to Tom. It was short, and Tom suspected that the general had needed to make a form letter to reply to numerous letters.

Dear Tom,

Today, I am working the first four hours daily with the doctor's blessing. I hope as of the fourth of August I will be "perking" full time. I want you to know how much your concern during my hospitalization and convalescence is appreciated. While the doctors can and did perform extraordinarily, without the thoughts and prayers of my friends I know I would not now be back at my desk. I hope you will forgive the brevity of this note, but I did want you to know of my gratitude at the first opportunity.

Cordially,

RLS

Special Assistant to the President for Liaison with Former Presidents

Tom studied his old boss's new title. Since Eisenhower was gone and Nixon was in the White House, General Schulz had a new role. Tom wondered what he would do to facilitate a good working relationship between Harry Truman, Lyndon Johnson, and President Nixon. It sounded like a difficult task.

But not as difficult, perhaps, as the mission going on in space. Two days after the date of Schulz's reply to Tom, the whole world watched as Apollo

11 launched out of Cape Canaveral heading for the moon. On the day that Tom received the letter from Schulz at his desk in Maxwell Hall, the spacecraft was still moving toward the moon.

Tom closely watched the story of Buzz Aldrin, Neil Armstrong, and Michael Collins with hundreds of thousands of other tense viewers. When the men reported watching the earth rise during their orbits around the moon, Tom thrilled with wonder and amazement that God had so enabled man that they could explore this far. When Neil Armstrong and Buzz Aldrin stepped onto the surface of the moon, Tom could not help being just a little bit jealous.

In March of 1972, Tom bought a farm out in the country, a dream come true. Peace filled his soul. Life was simpler, Scripture was alive, and baby John was adorable beyond description. Even learning German was fun.

Tom resigned as curator of exhibit design at the Indiana University Museum. He had enjoyed his time there. He had created a massive exhibit for the Sesquicentennial of Indiana University, and another exhibit called "Culture: Strategy for Survival." He had also facilitated the museum's moving process from Maxwell Hall to its new quarters in the Student Building.[1]

He finished a last exhibit for the museum, called *The Mingling Streams: Cultural Change in Latin America*. In May of 1972, the *Indianapolis Star* announced the opening of the exhibit. "*The exhibition, through artifacts, photographs, and recorded music, illustrates specifically the influences of European religion, music, and technology. 'The Mingling Streams' exhibition was designed by Thomas E. Kirkman, curator of exhibits for the I.U. Museum.*"

Tom put his heart into the exhibit because he knew it would be his last. He carefully created a banner with his best large-letter calligraphy for the title "Once Upon a Time." He took special pains to show how music had been passed from culture to culture. He showed how the African thumb piano, called a mbira, became the marimbula of Cuba and Columbia after African slaves introduced it to them. He showed how the conquered tribes of Latin America had changed their European conquerors too, giving them words such as *maize, tobacco, chili,* and *cocoa.* His pride and joy was the recorded music of native players using the instruments displayed in the exhibit. He also appreciated the full human skeleton an assistant had brought back from a research trip.

Tom had always valued his access to the museum's woodworking shop. Seeing John run around the house and trying to climb up to see things, Tom decided to avail himself of the equipment and make John a little stool. With wood from old shipping crates, Tom crafted a tiny multi-layered step stool for John.

And yet Tom was overjoyed when he officially became a farmer and carpenter. Now he would have time to study German and join the Old Order Amish church as he had wished to do. Now he would have time to tinker with things he had always wished he could but never had time to deal with. Now he would have animals out at pasture. He would buy chickens, plant a garden, and live off the land.

Tom wondered what had happened to President Eisenhower's herd of Angus cattle. He knew they had been excellent animals, and he hoped to find a descendant of them. He remembered that Eisenhower had received an honorary membership from the Heart of Ohio Aberdeen-Angus Breeders Association. He wrote a letter to this organization, and after a long process of being referred from one person to the next, he was given a record of a sale bill of animals that were registered descendants of the Eisenhower herd. From there, he tracked down the farmer who had bought them and was able to purchase a calf from the herd. With an Eisenhower Angus calf on his farm, Tom felt a strange sense that his life had come full circle.

By the next year, Tom had learned German. He also had a team of horses, which he began using to farm his land. He purchased a buggy and began attending an Amish church. This had been his intention from the beginning. Although it was not the same church Simon Gingerich attended, he still wanted to see it through. Since his car didn't have much resale value,

Tom took off the wheels and replaced them with cement blocks. He dismantled the car motor and used it to make a sawmill. He began to fell his own trees and cut his own lumber.

Brad took after his father's love of construction work.

"Dad," Brad said one day when he was fifteen, "may I quit school and start a construction job?"

Tom studied his teenage son. In the Amish culture, quitting school was not only acceptable but expected. But Tom also knew what an outcry would come from Sharon and the extended family if he quit.

Finally he replied. "Brad," he said, "you may quit, but you have to promise me two things. First, you need to agree that you will earn your own money; I will never give you a dime. Second, you need to have a job before you quit school."

Brad agreed and followed both guidelines.

In the fall, Tom went through a private instruction class given by the bishop of the Amish church. The bishop put Tom on a fast track through the church's catechism, called the Eighteen Articles of Faith. Normally the instruction classes were composed of teenagers. With more life experience, Tom could soak up the deep doctrinal fare with greater speed.

The bishop invited Tom to his own house for the classes. The bishop's wife boiled water for tea. She also always served a piece of dessert or a cookie to the men. After the second time of forcing himself to drink tea, Tom asked casually, "You don't happen to have coffee on hand, do you?"

Of course she had coffee, and after that Tom was able to focus on the Eighteen Articles of Faith in the small booklet the bishop gave him. Tom stared in fascination at the names of the men who had signed the articles on April 21, 1632. He had no idea the Amish church went back that far.

Many of the articles aligned perfectly, as the Beachy Amish church had done, with the principles Tom had been taught in the Baptist church. They were nothing new to him. Some of them made him somber, however, like Article Twelve.

"*Matrimony,*" the article was titled. "*We also confess that there is in the church of God an honorable state of matrimony between two believers of the different sexes."*

Tom frowned and sighed. He arranged his beard and finally spoke.

"I don't think my marriage is between two believers," he said sadly. "My wife and I have never seen eye to eye on matters of faith. She didn't have a lot of interest in going to church earlier, and she isn't interested in the Amish faith either."

The bishop, while less personable than Simon Gingerich had been, was a man with kind eyes and wise words. He had a way of pausing before speaking, as if consulting God in prayer.

"We would not see fit to sanction a marriage between two young people in that condition," the bishop admitted. "But if you have done everything you can to encourage your wife in the faith, I don't believe God will hold you accountable for what she chooses to believe. In fact, there is Scripture that instructs those with an unbelieving spouse to stay with that person. Perhaps that person will be won to the faith by the conduct of the believing spouse. Let me read it to you."

The elderly man turned the pages of his Bible to 1 Corinthians 7 and began to read to Tom.

That same evening of study brought them to Articles Thirteen and Fourteen.

"The Office of Civil Government," the bishop read the title of Article Thirteen. Behind him, a kerosene lamp flickered on a side table. Tom reflected how far he had come from the Calligraphy Office of the White House and the lights shining on the Kremlin in Moscow.

"I understand you once worked in government," the bishop said.

"I did," Tom said, scanning the words of the article. "I tired of Washington, at any rate. But I believe from this article, you do not take part in any kind of civil government?"

"That's right," the bishop said. He read Romans 13:1-7, along with a number of other verses. "We are commanded to pray for, respect, and honor the leaders of the land. We are to obey them as long as their commands do not cause us to disobey God. We are to pay our taxes. Will you read Matthew 22:20 and 21?"

Tom found the place and read the verses about the coin. Then he read Jesus' words, "Render unto Caesar the things that are Caesar's, and unto God the things that are God's."

"What about military service?" Tom asked. "I was also in the military."

"That is the next article," the bishop said with a smile.

"I think I already know your position," Tom said, turning the page. "And I am somewhat familiar with it. My brother Bill was a conscientious objector in World War II."

The bishop nodded. "We call it nonresistance," he said, beginning to read from the booklet. *We believe and confess that the Lord Jesus has forbidden His disciples and followers all revenge and resistance."*

Tom pondered this, taking a long sip of coffee. The Vietnam War still raged on. The American public had turned against it, and as a result, had turned against Lyndon Johnson. Johnson had declined to seek a second term. Now President Nixon was left to deal with the war, but it still had not ended. Around the country, students were revolting against the draft. Newspaper and television reporters had captured images of young men burning their draft notices.

"What about the draft card burners?" Tom asked the bishop.

"Well," the bishop replied after a pause. "I do not read the news as much as I ought, perhaps. What do you think about the things you have read?"

"Well," Tom said, "I think if they truly want to follow Christ, they will be respectful to the government and register as conscientious objectors. I don't think burning a draft card is honorable."

"Yes, many of our young men have entered alternative service programs," the bishop said. "But things were not always so. In the past, conscientious objectors have been imprisoned, and a few even died while in prison."

Tom refilled his coffee and picked up an oatmeal cookie. He thought of President Eisenhower, once General Eisenhower, commander of the armed forces in Europe in World War II. He knew what Eisenhower had thought of cowardice.

"How are we to reply to people who say we are using conscientious objector status because we are cowards?" he asked. "Or people who have lost sons in the war and are angry that our sons have not gone to war?"

The bishop paused and tapped a finger thoughtfully on his Bible.

"Sometimes we must pray and ask God for wisdom," he said. "But I think from Jesus' words, we can understand that following God is not for cowards. If we follow Him, we will suffer for His name. Perhaps not on a battlefield. But we will suffer."

Tom thought of Simon Gingerich sitting in prison and nodded. He still didn't exactly agree with Simon's view on buggy reflectors. Yet it was an example of devotion to faith that was "not for cowards," as the bishop had put it.

It was a faith more brilliant than fame or military strategy because it did not rely on the strength of men. Tom wanted this faith too.

It was almost Christmas when Tom completed the Articles.

"What is your wish?" the bishop asked Tom in German on the morning of his baptism. Tom was able to declare the expected response in German. He was of the same mind and doctrine as the Amish church. He sincerely wished to join it.

chapter thirty-eight

The Amish Man
Designs an Engine

It was almost Christmas time. As the baptismal water trickled over Tom's hair and down into his long, bushy beard, Tom found tears squeezing out of his eyes to mingle with the drops of water. He thought of Jesus and the great sacrifice He had made for the sins of Thomas E. Kirkman. He thought of how God had searched for him despite his rebellion. He thought of the irony of God's timing, that his baptism had come during the season of Christmas he once hated so much. He was also amazed to find his son Brad following his footsteps. Brad watched his father's baptism and soon joined the young people's instruction class.

Tom's baptism into the Amish church unraveled what was left of his relationship with Sharon. She could not understand the peace Tom had found within the Amish community. He tried to extend grace to his wife in hopes they could be reconciled. He compromised or gave in entirely on issues he did not feel were a matter of conscience. However, despite moments of peace, the chasm between them grew ever wider.

Most of those closest to Tom were glad to see the change that had come over him, and perhaps not too surprised. They were used to watching Tom follow the beat of a different drummer from that of normal society.

"Tommy," Patsy said. "You are a different person. I can tell! I'm really so happy for you, and I'm glad that Simon led you to a relationship with the Lord."

Brothers Bill and Bob, while attending churches from other denominations, were also overjoyed that their younger brother was serving the Lord.

Tom thought of his mother, and he knew she would be pleased too.

The next summer, Jim Diehl came by to see the horses and the farm and the Eisenhower Angus cows. Tom showed him around and then invited him in for a cup of coffee.

"I'm sorry I can't offer you a smoke anymore," Tom said.

"No worries—I quit myself," Jim said.

They settled in the living room on Tom's armchairs. The TV had been removed.

"Are you following all this rage about the rotary engine, Jim?" Tom asked.

"Oh, here and there. Why?"

"Well, I don't know," Tom said. He took a gulp of coffee as if to fortify himself for what he wanted to say. "Ever since I read that article last year in *Popular Mechanics,* it's been nagging at me. I just don't think the Wankel engine is as great at GM thinks it is. Their president—what's his name, Ed Cole?—just raves about it. Everyone thinks it's going to change the scope of transportation. But I think the Wankel deserves some improvements."

"Well, design your own version, Tom!" Jim said. "Do you still have a copy of that magazine? I think I saw it at one time, but I need a refresher."

Tom got up from the recliner and walked into another room. There, his desk overflowed with papers and magazines. He dug into the pile and miraculously came up with the orange May 1972 edition of *Popular Mechanics.*

He looked up to see Jim watching from the doorway.

"I guess this is your form of organization," Jim said. "If you can find the right thing that quickly."

"Right!" Tom agreed, brushing his beard. "I do intend to clean my office sometime. But I'm so good at *'crastinating,* I think I might go *pro.*"

Jim, wheezing for breath through his laughter, finally found the composure to open the magazine.

"Ah, yes, they were planning to have this rotary engine ready for the 1974 Vega," he said, scanning the magazine. "I don't think that's happening. Let's see, page 109. Hmmm . . . *'You're witnessing the start of a revolution in the auto industry.'* Wow! This writer is confident. *'It's a long way from the first GM Rotary to the end of the piston engine . . . Yet it is going to happen. The Wankel engine is cheaper to make . . . impressive list of advantages: lightweight, small package size, vibrationless running, low noise levels, wide speed range . . .'* "

"Right there in the second column," said Tom, who was standing beside Jim and looking over his shoulder, "Ed Cole says, *'We know what makes it work, and we think we're ahead of everybody else right now.'* "

"Yes, and look at this list of specs down here. They say the GM rotary will include all-iron construction, 100,000-mile-plus seal life, and 24,000 miles or more between oil changes. That's crazy!"[1]

"I know." Tom crossed the room to grab his cup of coffee. It was cold by now, but he drank it anyway.

"Well, I guess they are confident in the design," Jim said. "But hey, if you have a better idea, just do it! You'll enjoy the process. Remember, that's what you told me about art—enjoy the process."

"Hmmm . . ." Tom said. "It seems a little unusual for an Amish man who doesn't even drive a car to work on an engine idea. But why is Wankel using that triangular design?"

Jim laughed. "A lot of things have engines besides cars, Tom. Don't Amish people use sawmills and generators? And besides, when did 'a little unusual' ever stop you from doing what you wanted to do?"

Tom looked sharply at Jim, as if he had just scored a winning shot.

"You have a point," he said.

The Amish Man Designs an Engine

Tom kept up with old friends from the past, but he also gained many new friends among the Amish and Mennonites. He tinkered around at the welding shop of his friend Nick frequently. He shared meals in many Amish homes. To his mild horror, some of them did not serve coffee. This was a trial, but it did not make him leave the Amish church.

Tom quickly developed a reputation in the Amish community for his sincerity. At first, when people heard that a former Washington, D.C., man wanted to join their church, they questioned his motives. But as it turned out, Tom truly identified with their simple lifestyle and their commitment to the authority of Scripture. He earned the trust of one family after the next.

Tom also became known for his humor.

"How's your faith today, Tom?" the Amish bishop asked one morning before church, in his Pennsylvania Dutch accent. The men were standing around outside chatting for a few minutes before going into the building to begin the service. They rubbed their hands and stomped their feet as they talked. It was a bitterly cold day, and they had all come to church by horse and buggy.

"Well, my face is fine, but my toes are frozen," Tom replied cheerily.[2]

Tom learned to plow and cultivate with horses and horse-drawn implements. He worked side by side with his boys on the big jobs. Little John ran all over the farm now. He could escape from Sharon and be gone in seconds. He loved the animals and had a dog named Tony. Tom hadn't named the dog, but he had told John that he had once had a dog by that name. So John had named the dog after his father's dog. In his mind, Tom thought of this new dog as Tony the Second. There could never be another Tony.

Tom took his place in the community. When an Amishman had a building that needed to go up, Tom was there at the barn-raising, helping with the construction. When someone in the community died, Tom attended the funeral, sitting on the backless bench. He joined in wedding celebrations and attended school picnics.

Sharon continued living her own life. She did not accompany Tom to Amish weddings or funerals. But if the boys wanted to go, she did not argue.

The hot summer months were Tom's favorite. He spent long hours outside on the farm. The noises of the horses and the clatter of the farm tools created an atmosphere of peace. Several times this atmosphere of peace was interrupted by an ambush from Tom's two oldest sons, now teenagers. On the hottest days, when construction work started early and ended early, the boys would emerge from the weeds, kidnap their father, and throw him in the creek. Although Tom complained long and hard, his sons delighted him.

In the winter, Tom worked inside on his engine plans. After extensive drafts and revisions, Tom finally contacted his friend Jim to come look at his plans. When Jim arrived, it was another cold day. Tom took him out to a small shop where he had created a wooden prototype of the engine.

Tom wondered if his aversion to winter stemmed partly from the deaths of both of his parents at this time of year. For whatever reason, he hated the cold. He shivered and lit up a kerosene heater. Close by in the pasture, Tom's horses stamped and snorted.

"Can't stay warm anymore," Tom said. "Guess I'm an old man."

"It will be summer soon," Jim said with a glance at the trees.

"No, still bare as poles," Tom said. "And as soon as summer hits, my boys will throw me in the creek again. I keep telling them that someday they'll have boys too who throw them in the creek. It's all in good fun, of course. But look here at my wooden prototype."

Jim hunched down and peered at the wooden parts.

"What do you think, Jim? Could you help me build it? Here are the plans."

Tom unrolled a sheaf of blueprint paper, and began reviewing the plans with Jim.

"Are you hungry?" Jim asked suddenly. "Let's run up to Grecco's and have a pizza while we look these over."

As they drove and chatted, Tom wondered if Billy could still be an employee at Grecco's. It was almost thirty years since Tom had first gone there with his mother. Tom had been back at Grecco's several times recently and Billy had not been there. If he was still at Grecco's, would he recognize Tom in his Amish hat and long, flowing beard?

Tom and Jim settled in a booth and ordered their drinks and pizza. There was no sign of Billy.

Jim's engineer eyes perused the plans. He scanned the blueprints, page after page, much as Tom had looked over his sketches back at the university a decade before.

"I would need to change a few things," he said. "You have the radials at an angle here . . ."

Tom was leaning over to look at the diagram Jim indicated when a voice spoke close to his ear and a hand tapped his hat.

"Cowboy!" Billy's voice said proudly as his hand drummed on the hat.

"Billy!" Tom said. "How are you?"

"Picchhure!" Billy said, pointing at the blueprints.

"That's right, Billy, it's a big picture," Tom said.

The men talked design plans until Grecco's closed, and continued talking about them on the way home.

A few months later, Tom was down at the neighboring steel shop belonging to his Amish friend Nick. A friend of his wanted a custom paint job done on a carriage wheel. The customer wanted it to look bright and cheery and overflowing with flowers. Nick told the customer that he knew just the man for the job.

"Tom, you're a talented man," Nick said later as Tom worked with his palette of colors. Even though Nick had suggested Tom, he was still filled with amazement as he watched him.

Tom spun the carriage wheel and angled his paintbrush carefully to paint another flower.

"Thanks, Nick," he said with an upward glance. "But I just love to do a lot of different things. And I think you are quite talented yourself. Running a steel shop takes intelligence. And it takes something I don't have: sticking to the same skill for more than three months!"

Nick laughed as Tom turned the wheel again.

"I haven't seen any articles in the paper about my work," Nick said, smiling.

"Oh, are you referring to that article about my engine? I didn't know it came out yet," Tom said. "Where did you see it?"

"Had a friend drop it off. You haven't seen it yet? I'll go get it."

"Nick, you've got better things to do than chase after some reporter's addled impressions about my engine project. You know what they say—a journalist is a machine that converts coffee into copy."

"What do you convert *your* coffee to, Tom? Artwork?"

In answer, Tom reached for the paper cup of coffee resting in his aluminum tin of paint tubes. He swallowed it luxuriously.

"Engines, apparently. Let's see what the article has to say. No, really, we don't have to look at it now. I can read it later."

"No, Tom, I find this very interesting, and I need to get you to explain it to me. It's titled *'Ex-Curator Designs Engine.'*" Nick started reading. "*'A radical internal combustion engine, based on designs by Thomas Kirkman, is taking shape in Bedford.'*"[3]

Tom burst out laughing.

"You just can't rein in these writer people," he said. "Radical. Seriously."

Nick went on. "*'Kirkman's concept is a technically fascinating and mechanically simple variation on some rather ancient principles of propulsion. It is a rotary engine with fourteen continuously variable compartments whirling on a central driveshaft. The engine combines some of the aspects of turbine power with the familiar intake, compression, ignition and exhaust stages of the four-cycle engine. But it does not reciprocate, it turns. The engine is unique in construction and eleven patents have been awarded by the patent and trademark office of the U.S. Department of Commerce. One of the patents is for the engine . . . About four years ago he bought a farm near Odon in Daviess County, returning to the simpler life of the Amish faith.'*"

Tom laughed again. The June sun sparkled on several flecks of red paint in his beard.

"Returning to the simpler life. That makes it sound like I was raised Amish!"

"It does indeed," Nick said. "I guess everyone will think you went wild and came back. Okay, going on . . . '*He keeps eight horses for farming and local transportation and adheres strictly to Amish tenets to the point of refusing to have his photograph taken. He professes utter fear of automobiles.*' " Nick looked up. "Did you say that?"

"Yes, I did," Tom said.

Nick read on. Tom had explained his reason for making the engine: In the winter, life grew boring on the farm. He also said that the Wankel rotary engine was not as highly advanced as it could be. Tom thought he could do better. He admitted that he was not an engineer, but a designer. For this reason, his friend Jim Diehl, a tool and die maker, had taken on the job of "chief engineer." The article said Jim was making the patterns and hoped to have the aluminum prototype made in a few months. It mentioned more of Tom's friends from the D & M Tool Company, who were in on the project as well. Tom had reached out to Warren Porter, a contractor, to help him with the mathematics.

"*I've seen nothing so far to indicate the engine won't work,*" Jim Diehl was quoted in the article.

Nick chuckled. "Listen to this: '*Kirkman said, in his Amish way, 'If I thought this were strictly automotive, I wouldn't have anything to do with it.*' "

Tom's brush dropped onto his palette. "In my Amish way," he said, shaking his head. "Do I have an Amish way, Nick?"

Nick just laughed and read on. The columnist gave more details about the history of the rotary engine and the ten working parts of Kirkman's engine.

"Well, Tom," Nick said, "that's fascinating. Do you have the paperwork yet for the patent?"

"No, it's being prepared in Washington, D.C., at a firm I learned about when I lived there," Tom replied. "Bacon & Thomas. They'll mail it out to me within the month, I think."

"What do you think you'll do with it then, Tom?"

Tom spun the carriage wheel several times before answering.

"I'm not sure yet," he said. "When the patent arrives, I think I would like to show it to Ed Cole."

chapter thirty-nine

Ed Cole

Ed Cole had been the president of General Motors. From reading the newspapers, Tom knew he was an immensely personable man. He also knew that he was a businessman who liked to get things done and was a leader who didn't want to be contradicted.

However, Tom also knew that Ed Cole was endlessly enthusiastic about new ideas. He had been found on the floor of his conference room tearing apart engine pieces that didn't work. He was committed to anything that could make his car companies succeed. Ed had pioneered the catalytic converter. He had pushed for air bags. He had championed the Chevy Corvair, which then plummeted into obscurity because of an attack by naysayers who called it unsafe. He had also been enthusiastic about the rotary engine. When he turned 65, he was forced to retire because of GM's age policy. To his chagrin, just before he retired, GM decided to stop their work on the rotary engine.

Ed and a group of investors had purchased 50 percent of Checkers Corporation, a car manufacturing company. Known as a man of many ideas, Ed was elected chairman in hopes he could turn the company out of its slow downward spiral. He had several ideas documented by the newspapers. He wanted to design a cargo plane twice the size of a 747 that could transport fifty Cadillacs from Detroit to Moscow, nonstop.[1] He wanted a fleet of 300 of these, at a total cost of 13 billion dollars. He also wanted to make an engine that ran on water and air.

Ed Cole welcomed Tom into his Kalamazoo office with a guarded smile. A secretary brought coffee. The liquid sloshing into the mugs sounded deafening in the silent room. Tom noted a copy of the *Detroit Free Press* at Ed Cole's elbow with the headline "747s COLLIDE: TOLL TOPS 550." Mr. Cole caught Tom's eye and glanced down at the paper himself. He picked it up and tossed it to the side with a shake of his head.

"Terrible story, isn't it," he said. "Just terrible. Perhaps you are aware that I am a pilot myself?"

Tom wished he had done more research on the man sitting across from him.

"I was not aware, sir."

"Well, just little planes. I fly here to work quite regularly. I am generally alone, so it's hard to imagine how dreadful that crash was at Tenerife."

"And it sounds as if it was a communication error that could easily have been avoided," Tom offered. The article was of two jets colliding on a runway on the small European island of Tenerife. Because of radio static and language variation, a jet was doing its takeoff in the fog, not knowing that another jet was coming toward it on the runway. The pilot had tried to swerve, but it was too late by the time the other plane was visible.

Mr. Cole shook his head again before opening the folder Tom had given him. He spread the papers on his desk and left Tenerife behind.

"You know we just spent $150 million dollars at GM for a rotary engine that amounted to nothing," Ed said.

"I am aware that it had some problems," Tom said. "I beg your pardon, but it's not surprising since you used a Wankel engine."

Mr. Cole looked up sharply at Tom. The backward sweep of Mr. Cole's hair, at the top of a soaring forehead, reminded Tom of J. B. West, the White House usher.

Why on earth did I start out by saying that? Tom asked himself. It sounded arrogant and presumptuous, even though Tom had not meant it that way. He truly believed what he had just said. He tightened his fingers around his cup of coffee and tried desperately to relax. He needed to finish his thought so Mr. Cole would not suspect him of boasting.

"I've included diagrams," Tom went on, "showing the superiority of this engine to the Wankel engine. For example, I didn't like the way the Wankel combustion chamber forced the flame into a smaller and smaller space. So I've made my combustion chamber continuously expanding. And I've made a number of other improvements. I'm sorry the Wankel didn't work out though," he added politely.

"Just last week, GM laid it to rest," Cole growled from his side of the desk. "Done."

The chairman spread the blueprints for the engine across the table. He arranged the pages of explanation. As he flipped from page to page, Tom sensed excitement simmering behind the veiled eyes.

"Now, explain this rectangular seal to me," Ed Cole said suddenly.

"The diagram is on the next page," Tom said comfortably. "You can see that a rectangle will hold its position much better than a triangle."

"Uh-huh! Fascinating. Go on."

"And since the sealing of an engine is such an important factor in fuel efficiency, I feel confident that my Kirkman engine will burn cleaner and more efficiently than its counterparts."

The chairman flipped to Tom's list of possible uses for the Kirkman engine.

"Number fifteen!" he exploded. "Why on God's green earth do you have the automobile as number fifteen in possible applications? After firefighting pumps and generators?"

Ed Cole

Tom had the distinct impression that Ed Cole's voice could fill a stadium without amplification.

"Well, I did put wood splitters after automobiles," Tom said with an amiable grin. "Mr. Cole, I'm an Amish man. I can tell you that if cars were the only use for this engine, I wouldn't have bothered designing it."

For a second, Ed Cole's hand, which had been lifted in the action of flipping over the applications page, froze.

"You're an Amish man?"

"Yes, sir, I am. I farm with horses."

Ed Cole burst into a hearty peal of laughter.

"May I come visit your farm? I'm serious, I'll just fly down there on a free Saturday. But business, Mr. Kirkman, business. I find this fascinating. You are trying to tell me that you think your engine . . ."

Here, he returned his focus to the stack of papers and flipped back to the diagram of the seals.

"You think your engine can actually be cleaner than existing models? Why," Ed Cole swore like a sailor, "those were GM's two reasons for putting the rotary on the back burner. Poor fuel efficiency and high exhaust emissions."

"I don't doubt it with the Wankel," Tom said with what he hoped was a gentle smile and not an arrogant one.

Ed Cole laughed again, as if he could hardly contain his delight.

"Okay, Kirkman, I need to keep this. I need to talk to my board about this. I think Checkers could be on its way up again! Wouldn't I love to rub that under the nose of my old friends at GM! I beg your pardon, Mr. Kirkman. I do apologize. My colleagues can all tell you that I get a little overeager when I hear about new ideas."

Ed Cole sprang up and paced across the room to a bookcase packed with binders and hard-backed volumes that looked like a kind of encyclopedia. Loose papers sprouted among the spines and binders, and a stack of folders had spilled out onto a nearby chair.

"My question, Kirkman, is how am I supposed to explain to my board that this is the idea of an Amish man? Who, by the way, sees fourteen other uses for his engine that he prefers over the automobile?"

Tom smiled and stroked his beard. "Mr. Cole, I would love to manufacture this thing myself and turn it into the wood splitters and generators I envision. But at the same time, I'm just a farmer. I have a couple of great friends who have been working with me on this, but we still don't have the setup required for development and testing. That's why I'm here. Perhaps, if it works for you, it can also work for me on the farm in some other capacity."

Cole came back to the desk.

"And you understand, of course, that if you let us play with it, you can't show it to anyone else?"

"Absolutely. I have the patent."

Cole narrowed his eyes, as if judging Tom's intelligence and understanding of the world.

"I still don't understand how an Amish boy grows up and designs this," Cole said. "I really mean no offense, but I don't know much about the Amish. I read an article about them a few years ago. I thought they planted gardens and drove buggies."

"Oh, we do," Tom said. "But that's not all we do." He paused, trying to connect with Ed Cole as a fellow human being. "I didn't grow up Amish. I've worked in the White House, and I've worked for the CIA. But the most memorable person I've ever met was Simon Gingerich, an Amish man who taught me what it means to be born again and have a relationship with Jesus Christ. That's why I'm Amish now."

Ed Cole's mouth dropped slightly ajar. Tom always remembered him that way, sitting at the desk staring back at him, his J. B. West hair blending with the framed art on the wall behind him. Certificates and awards from General Motors littered the wall, along with several huge maps. All the power and prestige that a man could hope for was represented on that wall.

And yet, in Ed Cole's expression, Tom sensed an odd emotion: envy. Ed Cole was envious of Tom's peaceful, simple life.

The moment vanished. Cole snatched up a desk calculator. "You know I can't offer you as much money as we spent on that other engine. Just a fraction of it, I'm afraid, even if the investors like your idea. I could maybe see my way to getting you 15 to 20 million dollars for this idea. Realistically, it's probably going to be 13 or 14."

Tom looked evenly back into Ed Cole's eyes.

"I'm not a businessman," he said, and suddenly he thought of Robert Schulz. "I do have some professionals working with me. Ultimately, I trust you to give me what is fair."

"All right! Our next board meeting is in two weeks. I'll have my secretary give you a call if we want to set up another meeting. In the meantime, keep this idea to yourself if you want to be considered for the contract."

"Of course," Tom said.

A few weeks later, Tom picked up the phone at his desk on the farm.

"Hello, is this Thomas Kirkman?" a pleasant female voice asked.

"This is Tom."

"I have Ed Cole on the line to speak to you. Here he is."

"Hi, Tom! It's Ed Cole. I want you to know I spoke to the group about your design, and we had a favorable response with the exception of one man. I think we're going to have you come up here and fill out paperwork and go from there. Sound good?"

"Sure!" Tom said.

"All right then, I'll have my secretary touch base with you to arrange a time when I'm back in Kalamazoo."

About a week later, Tom came in from a day of planting his fields and settled himself on the recliner with his newspaper and a cup of coffee.

He read about the death of Sid Collins, a racetrack announcer, found dead in his apartment in Indianapolis. Having received the diagnosis of Lou Gehrig's disease, he had decided to hang himself. Tom turned the page and found an ad for a spring special for carpet steam cleaning for $19.95. He almost turned another page, when he found the face of Ed Cole staring at him from the upper right corner of the newspaper.

Ed Cole's friendly smile and swept-back hair appeared above a single word: "KILLED." In shock, Tom read the short paragraph, which appeared to have been hastily tacked into the paper at the last minute. Yesterday, while flying from his home area to Kalamazoo, the ex-GM president's plane had gone down in a rainstorm.

Another person dead at the wrong time.

Tom froze. His wrists crashed to his knees and the newspaper collapsed. John, now nine years old, looked up from his Lincoln Logs building project in astonishment.

Could this be true? And if so, why? Was it truly just a weather accident? Or did that "one person" who disagreed with spending $13 million on a rotary engine . . .

Tom shook his head. He must not think that everyone was like the CIA.

At least, Tom thought, *I talked to him about Jesus Christ. But could I have done better? Could I have said more?*

As much as he tried to push away the thoughts of conspiracy, his experiences as a spy pressed in upon his consciousness. It would be so easy to kill a lone pilot. And why not, if you could save $13 million?

No, it wouldn't be easy, Tom scolded himself. *It might be easy for the CIA, but not for some random person. Stop thinking like that, Tom. It's ridiculous. This is rural Michigan in 1977, not Cuba in 1961.*

Tom gulped the rest of his coffee and went to the kitchen for more. As he stood leaning against the counter, reality sank in—his idea for a rotary engine had likely gone down with Ed Cole's plane.

chapter forty

Loss and Gain

The next day Tom ordered a May 3 copy of the *Detroit Free Press*, assuming it would have more details of Ed Cole's plane crash. When the newspaper arrived a week later, he pored over the story.

Edward Cole, he read, was flying his twin engine Beagle plane from the Oakland Pontiac airport to his office at the Checker Corporation in Kalamazoo. He had been flying for twenty-six years and had logged more than 3,000 hours in the air. Because of bad weather in Kalamazoo, he delayed his flight about an hour. During the delay, he drank coffee in the hangar office and chatted with the employee there about Checker and about the purple martins in his backyard.

"At the time of the crash," Tom read, *"the Kalamazoo Municipal Airport was reporting a 300-foot cloud ceiling, with one mile of visibility. Because of the bad*

weather, it was open only to pilots with an instrument rating, which Cole had."

So it was a weather accident. Surely.

In the article, a woman from the small town of Mendon told her account of the story. She heard the sound of a plane circling over her house. Her dog began barking incessantly, so she ran outside into the misty day to see what was happening.

"I saw the plane in the sky, kind of soaring or floating and then all of a sudden there was no noise. The engine just quit. It was perfectly quiet. The next thing I heard, there was a terrible boom, like an explosion."

A mail carrier, too, had heard a big bang.

Then Tom saw what he was hoping for: the Federal Aviation Association had been there.

"FAA officials refused to speculate on whether the crash was caused by bad weather, by a mechanical failure, or by pilot error."

Refused to speculate? In Washington, that kind of reply meant *we are hiding something.* Tom shook his head. *What had they really found?*[1]

Tom sighed. Rural Michigan was not Washington. He laid down the paper. He wanted to be talked out of his nagging sense of suspicion about the crash. The article had not succeeded in doing that. Yes, the weather had been bad. The mail carrier had described it as "really misty like the clouds were on the ground."

He would have to assume that was it.

But Ed Cole had twenty-six years of experience flying. And the explosion . . .

No, no, Tom thought. *I have to let it go.*

That night Tom spent several hours studying John, chapter 11. With a green highlighter, he marked his favorite verses. He thought of the death of the man he had known so briefly, yet so recently. Mary and Martha's distress at their brother Lazarus' death comforted him. "But I know, that even now, whatsoever thou wilt ask of God, God will give it thee." He highlighted that verse in John 11:22, and then verse 27. "She saith unto him, Yea, Lord: I believe that thou art the Christ, the Son of God, which should come into the world."

How powerful, Tom thought, *to be able to express your belief in the Messiah right after He came too late to save your brother!*

Work on the engine stalled. Jim Diehl's shop was not set up for engine manufacture, even though he had worked with it extensively. D & M Tool Company had also worked on the project. But Tom realized that without the power of a larger company to develop the engine, it would be difficult to make it happen.

And besides, there was that rankling, bothersome suspicion. No matter how many times he told himself that it was just his connection to the CIA that had distorted his views, he could not entirely resolve the matter. *Had someone killed Ed Cole?*

He completed a careful record of the engine and bound it in a red folder. Using a calligraphy hand, he dated it *Nov. 1977.* He put down his pen. Then he picked it up again and added the words, *Finally, after 5,000 years,* signifying that it was finally done.

Then he took it to the cupboard above his desk and carefully filed it away.

"It already got one man killed," he said to Brad, now a young man of twenty. "I guess I'll just let it go for now."

Tom couldn't help but wonder how things might have been different if the engine had gone into research and development, and the promised money had been paid out to him. As it was, Tom found himself in debt. Sharon, who never had been interested

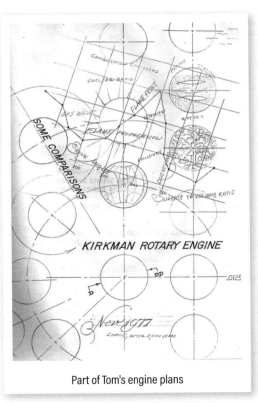

Part of Tom's engine plans

in the Amish church and refused to join Tom in his beliefs, finally left. Although his respect for the Amish beliefs and way of life had not changed, Tom did not feel that he could remain part of the Amish community as a divorced man. He did not want to give the community a bad name. Reluctantly he stopped attending the Amish church services. To recover his debts, he sold his farm and began working for Brad's construction crew.

True to his promise, Brad had not asked Tom for a single dime to start his business. Now Tom found himself receiving dimes from his son, in the form of paychecks.

Tom began to research Indiana history, especially the stories of his ancestors. As he collected information, he hoped to write a book someday.

One day as he was researching, his telephone rang.

"Tom!" It was the voice of a former co-worker from Grecco's. Tom had not talked to this friend for years.

"Have you heard that Billy is in the hospital with pneumonia?"

"Oh!" Tom said. "I hadn't. At Dunn? Thank you for letting me know."

Tom made the trip to the respiratory floor. He disliked hospitals. He hated the antiseptic smell of the surgery floors. He hated the beeping of IV pumps and call lights.

But he had to go.

"Billy," he said softly, after nodding to Billy's elderly mother. "It's Tom from Grecco's. Can you hear me?"

Billy's eyes opened slowly. He smiled.

"Billy, I know God is real, because I heard Him talk to me one day. I know He will be waiting for you in heaven. But Billy, before I heard God talk to me, I saw God in you."

Billy's eyes closed, then opened again.

"Thhhank you," he said softly.

Eyes filling with tears, Tom turned to leave. As he passed the bedside table, he saw the yellow plastic horse, standing amid the tatters of two paper napkins.

In 1983 Tom and a friend bought an old mill on a stream. With the help of Jeff and Brad, the mill was refurbished to run as it had in the old days. Tom ground flour on the weekdays. On the weekends, he invited musicians like himself to play and sing at the old mill. Like his father and mother, Tom wanted music in his life every day.

In the 1990s, Tom determined to design and build a log building. He sketched the blueprints on large sheets of paper, detailing the dovetailing, rafters, and metal roofing. Sometimes he drew on his calligraphy experience. On one sheet of the blueprint, he wrote *"Wall Detail"* in an elaborate calligraphy hand that he had learned from Adrian Tolley in the Eisenhower White House. He drew arrows from the wall section to a magnified view of the wall. He detailed the rings of the poplar logs that he planned to use.

Tom hoped to turn the log building into a deli someday, so he chose his location carefully. After a study of local history, he decided to build it in Avoca, the town where he had grown up. Because he knew his father had sent his siblings to their grandma's place on the Avoca train, Tom was drawn to the railroad towpath. Tom had found that the train that once ran on this

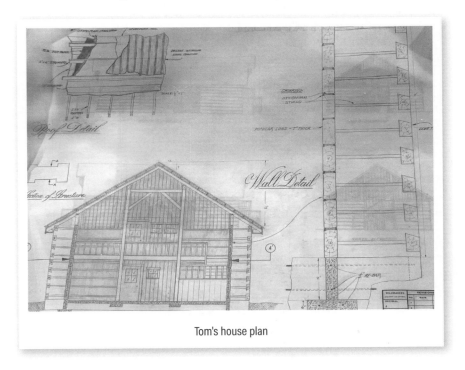

Tom's house plan

track had been called "Old Nellie." To suit these details, Tom drew up a logo for his potential deli. The logo was a train engine steaming up a track. In a circular design around the train, and on the foundation under the track, he arranged the name of the potential business: Kirkman's Old Nellie Deli.

"Tommy, if I were younger, I would come and be your chef," his sister Patsy said. Patsy's interest in Tom's life, and her confidence in his abilities, had never wavered.

When he was finished with the plans, he began to work. By now he was in his sixties, and he knew he might not get another chance to make a building on his own. For this reason, he determined to do everything himself. As he worked, he found his mind going back to his childhood, when his father had built the log cabin to move them out of the chicken house. Using many of the same techniques his father had used in the 1930s, Tom constructed a high, peaked roof, a balcony, and a porch.

He presented his plans to the zoning board, who told him the sewer system he had planned was not up to code for a public building. Disheartened, Tom put aside the logo for Old Nellie Deli. He could not use the log building as a public deli.

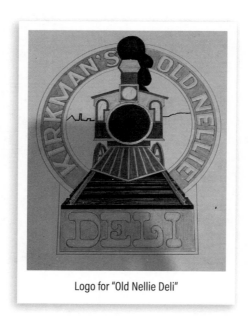

Logo for "Old Nellie Deli"

chapter forty-one

Conversations with Brad

It was while Tom ground wheat at the mill in the mid-1980s that he read in the newspapers that Robert Schulz had died. Again his mind went back to Washington. He thought of Robert Schulz instructing him to protect the story of Eisenhower's paintings.

It would be okay now, Tom was sure, to talk about his sketches for Eisenhower. But should he? What would be the point? Perhaps he would someday mention it to one of the boys.

Over the years, working with Brad, Tom occasionally allowed himself to let a memory slip out to his son. Once, back when they worked together on the farm, they watched a plane from Grissom Air Force Base streak across the sky.

"Wouldn't it be fun to fly in a fast plane?" Brad observed, watching the trail of the jet with interest.

"It's not what you think it is," Tom said dryly. "I remember breaking the speed of sound over Miami. We throttled up from there and flew across Cuba at 1,500 miles per hour, taking photos as we went."

"How can you snap pictures if you're going that fast?" Brad asked in amazement.

"You can't. The shutter just stays open," Tom said.

Then Tom changed the subject as quickly as possible with a question for Brad.

"Why did the scarecrow win the Nobel Prize?"

Brad thought for a few seconds before hoisting another bale of hay. "I don't know, Dad."

"Because he was outstanding in his field."

Tom could not resist packing as many puns into life as possible. He had gotten himself into trouble a few times, with grumpy characters who did not allow themselves to see humor in life. But mostly, Tom felt that his humor provided cheer to those around him. Brad was a great partner in this "crime."

Another time, on a bitter winter day, Brad and Tom worked together on a construction project.

"Wow, it's cold!" Brad exclaimed, rubbing his gloved hands.

"I've been colder!" Tom replied. "In a tunnel in Russia. The water dripped down my back and froze."

As soon as they were finished with the job, Tom and Brad went to McDonald's for a hot coffee. For some reason, Tom thought about the old days when Brad was a little one-year-old. That was the year Tom had first heard about a new restaurant called McDonald's. He had hoped to try the restaurant's cheeseburgers and thick milkshakes someday.

Sometime after the conversation about the flight over Cuba, Brad brought Tom several sheets of photographs he had found online at work.

"Dad, are these some of the photographs you took while flying over Cuba?"

Tom looked at the gray and white images. He saw the faint lines of road-ways, the dark texture of forests, the geometric shapes of buildings, and the missile launch sites. Despite the many years that had passed since he had last seen those images, Tom felt the terror and tension return with a rush. The blood drained from his face.

"Get those out of here," he snapped at Brad. "Those are classified. I don't ever want to see them again."

Brad looked startled, but he promptly took them away. As he retreated, Tom felt his heartbeat return to normal. He paused to consider the situa-tion. After all these years, perhaps the photographs had now been released. Many of the people Tom had worked with then had already passed away. And Cuba, while still under the leadership of Fidel Castro, was no longer a threat.

But still . . . he had been trained. He would not have those photos in his sight.

One day Brad had a story to tell his father.

He had been driving the countryside with his wife and children, as a stress reliever. Both Brad and his wife were troubled about a certain situation in which they found themselves.

"I didn't even know where I was, Dad," Brad confessed.

As he drove, Brad looked over at a field beside the road. He saw a water wheel in a creek. The wheel turned a crankshaft that ran up a hill to a small cluster of buildings. The buildings were at the end of a long lane. Interested in the mechanics of the operation, Brad drove up to see what he could find.

There, in a building at the top, an Amish man sat at a sewing machine sewing a shoe. Brad got out of the vehicle and just stood there and watched him, intrigued.

Finally the man looked up at him and said, "What's troubling you, young man?"

"Nothing is troubling me," Brad replied. "I just drove by, and I am mechanically minded and I'm nosy. I wanted to see what you are working on." The sewing machine hummed a little longer. Then the man raised his head again and gazed at Brad with a look that went right through him.

"It's clear that something is troubling you," the old Amish man repeated.

Brad found himself suddenly spilling out the entire story of the struggles he and his family were having.

"There are murderers in that place," the Amish man said. "You've got to get out of there."

Brad looked at the man behind the sewing machine in astonishment.

"I know every one of those people, and none of them are murderers," he said.

"I mean that they have troubled your soul," he said. "You need to get away from them."

Brad digested this for a while. Were they associating with people they shouldn't be?

"What's your name?" Brad asked, suddenly remembering that there had been no introductions.

"Simon Gingerich," the Amish man said simply.

"You can't be serious," Brad said.

"I believe I know my own name," the man replied with a twinkle in his eye.

"But—I suppose there are a number of Simon Gingerichs. Surely you aren't—my father Tom Kirkman talked with a Simon Gingerich who was in jail. He taught him about the New Birth. It was a long time ago, back in 1968."

"Ah." A slow, happy smile spread over Simon's face. "I remember him so well. So well."

The man behind the sewing machine was indeed the Simon Gingerich that Brad's father had spoken of so often. Brad had never met him before. Twenty years of life experience had not diminished the man's perception and spiritual insight. With many words of thanks, Brad went back to the car where his wife and children waited patiently.

As Brad told the story, Tom's heart swelled with happiness at the memory of his old friend.

"I think I've told you before, Brad," Tom said. "But I'll tell you again. I've met a lot of people in my life. But I've never met one so memorable as Simon Gingerich."

chapter forty-two

Reading, Writing, and Hallucinating

When it was finished, Tom moved into the log building he had built by himself.

In the moving process, in a cluttered corner of his bedroom, Tom found a card. Mom had written it on July 26, 1955, shortly after Tom and Sharon's marriage.

"Dear Sharon and Tom,"

His eyes unaccountably filled with tears.

"Well, how is everything going with you folks?"

Mom's penciled words ran across the face of the notecard like the melody of music that symbolized her entire life.

"I hope fine. We are all okay. It has been so hot here. Joan & I washed today. It looked like rain yesterday so we didn't wash until this morning. Dad told

The log house Tom built

me not to this morning as the weather was so hot. But Joan hung them out. And we are done once more."

A pang of pain and fondness shot through Tom's heart. What care Dad had lavished on Mom!

"Joe is playing ball for Needmore Baptist Church. He, Keith Davis, Ross Kirkman & Jerry Rollins are boys from Avoca on the team. They won again last night. Joe's girl got back from Clearwater, Florida, on her vacation yesterday, so she came to Bedford & stayed all night. Joe went & got her for the ballgame. She sat with Joan. Joan said, 'She was awful nice.' "

Just like Mom, bringing out the good in everyone. She had complimented Joe, his girlfriend, and Joan all in several short sentences.

"I guess you were happy for Ike to get home? Ha! Ha!"

Tom couldn't help but smile as he thought of that time, long ago in 1955. Ah, yes, Dwight and Mamie had flown to Geneva, Switzerland, hoping to convince Khrushchev to embrace Eisenhower's idea about Open Skies. Tom wondered what he had told Mom that made her write that humorous statement. Probably he had gushed about how much more relaxing it was when the chief executive was out of town.

"Have you decided about coming home? Just suit yourselves. Dad thinks he will have to go get work before too long. He sure hates to go. He even said he might go back to Bloomington so he can be home each night. But I sure hate for him to go to Bloomington to work. Sharon, are you going to wait until it gets cooler to go to work? It is too hot now to go to work. Are you feeling pretty good now? I sure hope so. Last night it was so hot when I fixed supper. Joan & I were the only ones that ate. I fried potatoes, sliced a dish of tomatoes, & a bowl of

cucumbers & onions and some roasting ears. Dad ate half of a roasting ear—that was all, said it was too hot. I sure hate to cook & no one eats."

Tom finished the letter with tears shining in his eyes. For two reasons. It made him sad, yes. But it also made him praise God, the one who had healed him. The one who had enabled him to read this letter without bitterness. The one who had taken away his anger at the untimely death of his greatest confidante on earth.

After settling into the log building, Tom picked up his pen and paper and began to write. He wrote a book about one of his ancestors, a man from North Carolina who had married a Native American woman in Indiana. He titled it *Once Upon a Hide*.

He wrote a poem too, thinking of the old days.

> I'd like for Mom to warm my blanket,
> Help me say my prayers and tuck me in.
> And by the stove in the morn have Dad
> To fit my socks just right before putting on my shoes again.
> I'd like to have my old desk at school with all my classmates there,
> And have my sister scrub my ears and comb and part my hair.
> I'd like to win a marble game and hit a home run or two.
> Teenage years, my first old car and wouldn't I look good if it was new!
> Years went by—oh where did they go?
> I don't move too fast—in fact I'm rather slow.
> My memories are precious—I love them so,
> Of family and friends, things and places—my highs and lows.
> Of all the things in life I miss most—or might have been—
> I'd like to sit down and rest and rock my kids again.

Tom had long had a dream of hand-lettering the Bible on parchment paper. As he grew older, he began to realize he might never get this done.

In 2009, Tom began to notice that he grew short of breath when he climbed the stairs. He noticed a tightness in his chest when he exerted himself.

Finally, after the insistence of his family, Tom made an appointment with a

Tom at a church function

doctor. He failed a cardiac stress test, so the family doctor referred him to a cardiologist.

"I'll have to refer you to a heart surgeon, I'm afraid," the cardiologist said.

Tom looked squarely back at the doctor. It was not the same cardiologist his mother had seen. That man had retired long before. This cardiologist was a talkative man with a surprisingly large stomach. His bookcases and walls were stocked with photographs of children and dogs and sandy beaches instead of portraits of former presidents. He had spent thirty minutes with Tom and Brad, showing him the results of his heart catheterization. A number of blockages hindered blood flow in the critical arteries feeding his heart muscle.

"What about those stents you talked about?" Tom growled. He had never liked cardiologists, and he assumed he would like a heart surgeon even less.

"Ah, yes, we could give stents a try," the cardiologist said affably, undeterred by Tom's dog-like response. "But research has shown that once you have more than one or two blockages, patients are better served with standard heart surgery."

"Standard?!" Tom exploded, then broke into a laugh, as if he were opening a valve and letting off steam. "Mr. Cardiologist, do you know the story of the heart doctor who took his car to the mechanic to have the engine repaired?"

"Tell me," the cardiologist said easily. Tom had the impression that he probably did know the story and was just trying to humor a cantankerous old patient. That was okay. Tom wanted to be humored at this doleful moment.

"The mechanic says to the heart doctor, 'Since we both fix engines, why do you get paid ten times as much as I do?' The heart doctor turns the ignition on the car and the engine roars to life. The heart doctor looks at the mechanic and says—" Tom paused and glanced at the round man behind the desk, to see if he was listening.

The cardiologist didn't miss a beat as he replied, "Try fixing *your* engines without turning them off."

"Exactly!" Tom said, pleased. They both laughed.

Around the same time as his visit with the cardiologist, the local *Washington Times* paper posted an article about Tom. The reporter found Tom's life fascinating. He told Tom that he had heard him described as talented and eccentric.

"Is it true that you worked in the White House? Is it true that you joined the Amish church?"

Tom told as much of the story as he felt was appropriate. He did not mention the sketches for Eisenhower. He did not mention the CIA. He recounted with fondness his time in the Amish church and confessed that even now he preferred not to think of the circumstances that took him away from that community. He tried not to think of the long, lonely road that had been the story of his marriage to Sharon. When the marriage had finally dissolved, Tom could not bear going to the Amish church as a divorced man. He simply could not set that precedent in the quiet, family-based community.

But Tom spoke nothing of this. Tom told the reporter about Simon Gingerich, the Amish man who had led him to saving faith in Christ.

"I have never met a more brilliant man," Tom said. "I would chuck all this stuff and go back to the Amish church in a heartbeat."[1]

One thing Tom would not have needed to chuck was a smooth-shaven face. He had kept his long beard.

The heart surgeon informed Tom that the beard, while it was most likely clean, still posed an infection risk to his incision.

"I have to cut your breastbone open, right down the center of your chest," he explained. "I'll put it back together with wire and it will heal in a few months and be as good as new. But what we can't have is an infection in that incision. You need to shave the beard."

This was the last straw for Tom. He told the heart surgeon that he was not about to have his beard shaved and that he would just go back home and take his chances on the blockages. The heart surgeon responded with stories of people whose breastbones had gotten infected. He painted a dire picture of these ignorant people languishing for the rest of their lives on a wound VAC, a type of therapy to help wounds heal.

"Dad, your beard will grow back," Brad said.

Tom finally relented.

"Don't worry," the surgeon said. "You'll get over it in a few months and feel much better and your beard will grow back. You just need to protect that breastbone in the meantime. You won't be able to drive or lift anything heavier than ten pounds for a few months, and then you'll be back to normal."

"Will I be able to play the banjo after surgery?" Tom asked.

"Not if you can't now!" the surgeon replied with a dry laugh.

Tom stared at him for a second.

"I play all the time!"

"Oh, really!" the surgeon said. "I thought you were joking. I get people all the time who ask me if they will be able to play the piano after surgery. If I assure them that they will, they say, 'Oh good, because I can't play the piano now!'"

"I never got around to learning the saxophone," Tom said. "Why don't you wire that skill into me while you're sewing bypass grafts?"

After the heart surgery, the saxophone was the last thing on Tom's mind. His breastbone, which had been sawed apart, burned like fire. He could not get comfortable in the hospital bed. When he grabbed the rails at the side of the bed, the nurses leaped to his side and held his arms.

"Mr. Kirkman, don't use your arms! You'll tear your breastbone back open!"

Tom sighed. He saw the nurse fasten a syringe to his IV port, and a sudden fear came over him. Maybe she was trying to kill him. Maybe he was being given mind-altering drugs. Maybe he was being used in a psychological experiment. He fought to take the syringe from her hand, but she anticipated him. Quickly she emptied the syringe into his veins and backed away.

"Tom, you're doing just fine. The doctor is pleased. I just had to give you a little medicine to help you relax and get some rest."

When Tom awoke, Brad was sitting beside his bed. When Tom tried to sit up, pain shot through his chest. He grabbed for the side of the bed, and an alarm went off. Tom looked out the hospital window beside his bed. He saw a shape on the roof of a lower building.

"It's the helicopter! I've got to evacuate!" he said to Brad as two nurses rushed in. "I've got to get this intel to Jack!"

Brad helped the nurses settle Tom back in bed.

"Dad," he said firmly, "Jack is just going to have to wait."

chapter forty-three

Last Days

About a year after the first heart surgery, Tom needed to have another procedure done. As Brad rolled him down the hall of the hospital in a wheelchair, Tom had a question.

"Are they going to cut my beard again?"

"I don't know, Dad."

"Well, if they are, take me home. I'm not doing it this time."

In the pre-operative area, the nurse listened to Tom's terms.

"For this procedure, I think we can braid it and tape it to your shoulder in a hair net," she said.

"Braid it?" Tom exclaimed.

"Yes, braid it," the nurse said. "But I'll have to check with the doctor to see if that's an option."

It was, and Tom's beard escaped with no more harm than a few extra wrinkles from the braids.

Finally, as his health faltered, Tom moved into a building on his son Brad's property. Brad had been ordained as a minister in the Mennonite church. He had children of his own, and now grandchildren. In past years, two of Brad's daughters had run a daycare from an outbuilding on their property. This building was refitted for Tom's use. His bed was placed under a window so he could easily see out.

Brad's choices in life pleased Tom, but he was not inclined to praise him. In fact, he got snippy with Brad at times, especially now that he had moved onto his property. He tried to be nice, but it seemed the words often came out wrong. Tom concluded that he was turning into a grouchy old man. He was glad Brad didn't kick him out.

Playing with children was a favorite pastime of Tom's. Here his beard came to his aid. He convinced numerous children that he had swallowed a pencil, when actually the pencil had slipped into his beard and down the front of his shirt.

"Now, Dad," Brad said one day. "When I get home from work tonight I'm cutting your hair. Your haircut is long overdue. If you are sleeping, I'm going to wake you up."

"Oh, you don't have to give me a haircut," Tom said.

"I know I don't have to, but I want to," Brad said.

When he could evade Brad's barbering no longer, Tom tried to give his son instructions on the best methods for cutting hair.

"Now, Dad," Brad said, "I'm sixty years old, and I've been cutting hair for a long time. If you're as good-looking as you think, it doesn't really matter what I do to your hair, it's not going to hurt your looks. Just let me cut your hair."

"Brad," Tom said one evening, "I'd like to have a computer."

"Sure, I can get you a computer," Brad said. "But are you sure you really need one?"

"How else will I find out about my friend David Eisenhower?" Tom asked.

One day Brad brought Tom a photograph of a Black Angus bull.

"Dad, look at this."

Tom looked at it and recognition dawned immediately.

"That's Eisenhower's bull!" he said. "Where did you get this picture?"

Brad explained that he and his wife had stopped at the Gettysburg farm, now a national monument, on a trip East. He had taken a picture of a picture.

As Tom's body weakened, Brad provided more care. Every morning Brad came to Tom's apartment to make his coffee and toast. Tom sat on the edge of his bed, hunching over just a little. *I'm slowly withering away,* he thought.

"I'll have an egg with that too," Tom added some mornings when Brad brought him the toast. So Brad returned to the little kitchen and fried an egg.

Sometimes Tom made Brad run to the refrigerator to get cream to put in his coffee. Sometimes he did not.

Then Brad would sit down with the Bible.

"What do you want me to read this morning?" he would ask.

Tom announced the chapter he wanted, peering at Brad over the top of his glasses. Brad began to read.

"Stop!" Tom said, pointing his finger at Brad when a Scripture was particularly meaningful. He expounded on the verse, and when he was finished, Brad continued reading.

One summer evening, Tom sat outside in a lawn chair watching the sunset. Brad sat with him.

"What a beautiful sunset!" Brad said.

"Brad," Tom said, "you have no idea how beautiful Moscow is after dark, the way they shine the lights on the Kremlin."

Tom saw Brad blink in surprise.

"I never knew you were in Moscow, Dad."

Perhaps I shouldn't talk about my time in the CIA, even now, Tom thought. But he concluded it didn't matter anymore.

"Well, I was there. I was hired because I could keep a secret."

Inside his apartment one day, Tom pulled a twenty-dollar bill out of his pocket.

"Let me show you something, Brad," he said. He turned the bill to the side that showed the White House. He circled one of the windows above the North Portico.

"Right here, in this room," Tom said, "is where I sketched on canvas for President Eisenhower. He liked color and he liked to paint, but he didn't like drawing. Sometimes I did that at Gettysburg too, although I also did a lot of work on the library there. Eisenhower had a lot of books!"

"Interesting," Brad said.

Tom grew weaker and weaker. Soon he was unable to get out of bed. But often he had something he wanted to say, and he would say it with all the sincerity of his younger and stronger days.

"You will always remember someone who leaves an impact on your life, Brad. Always," Tom said one day. "And you will remember them in great detail. You'll remember their face, you'll remember their name, and you'll remember the sound of their voice."

Brad nodded.

"For example," Tom went on, "I had supper with Queen Elizabeth's mother one evening, and the next morning we had breakfast together. At noon we had a light lunch, and then I held her hand as she walked up to the plane to go home."

Tom was becoming so weak he could barely move. But he could still point his finger at people, and he pointed it now, as best he could, at Brad. He wanted Brad to get his message and remember it.

"You will always remember someone who leaves an impact on your life," he repeated. "I don't remember the name of the Queen Mother. I remember she was a small lady and that she seemed nice. I don't remember her voice, and I don't remember any facial features. She did not leave a deep impact on my life. But Simon Gingerich, he not only left an impact, he changed my life."

Tom mentioned various others. He mentioned his Amish friend Nick, another named Alva, and another man named Ora.

"Ora's smile is amazing," Tom said.

"Hmmm," Brad said. "Where would the Kirkman family be today if Simon Gingerich hadn't shared Christ with you?"

"Can you still say the Lord's Prayer in German?" Tom asked Brad.

"Yes," Brad said.

Together, father and son recited the prayer in German.

"Dad, can you tell me your wish?" Brad asked, referring to the statement that new believers made at their baptism in the Amish church.

"Yes," Tom said, and recited the entire statement in German that he had recited at the time of his baptism in the Amish church.

Tom told Brad who he wanted to officiate at his funeral. He wanted Floyd to speak, the man who had once been a young friend of Brad's at the Beachy church. He then chose another Mennonite friend and an Amish friend to speak at his graveside service.

Soon, Tom knew, his life was reaching the end. To ease his journey, Tom was transported to the hospital.

"Brad, I've gotta go," he told his son. "But some people still have their feet in the fire. They need to be pulled out." Brad wondered whether he should attribute his father's cryptic remark to the medicine he was taking or to his end-of-life reflections.

All of Brad's children were there to see their grandfather off. They sat on the bed with him to pray.

Tom knew they were waiting for him to slip away. He didn't mind. He was ready to go, and he only hoped it would be smooth. Brad sat beside the bed.

"I think I'll let someone else take care of the message Sunday morning," Brad told his dad.

"Is it your turn?" Tom snapped from his position on the pillow. His voice was weak, but his tone was unmistakable.

"It is," Brad said.

Tom understood perfectly. He realized that the doctors had given him no more than a day to live, and that was why Brad wanted someone else to fill in for him.

"You absolutely will not," Tom said. "I trained you to make your calling and election sure. Now don't go at it halfway. It's your turn. You take it."

Epilogue: The Last Word

Tom Kirkman died within an hour after instructing his son to take his turn preaching. Brad took his father's fingers and shut his eyes. "Dad, I'll see you later!"

"Would you like some time?" the doctor asked after confirming the death.

"He isn't here," Brad said. "We've had our time. The best is yet to come."

After Tom died, Brad tried to get a message ready for his sermon on Sunday. He struggled and struggled. He tried to get it together, but it just wasn't coming. Finally he went to sleep Saturday night praying about it.

That night was the only time of Brad's life that he could remember having such a vivid dream. In his dream, Brad walked in the back door of Tom's apartment. He prepared his father's coffee and toast. Then he sat down beside his father with the Bible as he always did.

"What do you want me to read this morning, Dad?"

"1 John 3," his father said.

Brad began reading in 1 John 3.

"Stop!" Tom exclaimed, pointing a finger at his son.

Brad stopped.

"Struggling with that, ain't you, boy?"

"Oh, Dad, I am. I am struggling. I just can't get it," Brad said in his dream.

"You're in the way," Tom said. "Get out of His way!"

At that point Brad woke up. Dazed, he considered the dream.

"Lord," he prayed, "if I'm in your way, move me."

A few hours later, the Lord gave Brad a message on 1 John 3.

Author's Notes

Is this a true story? I call it a work of biographical fiction. It is biographical because it concerns an actual person. It is fiction because I filled in many of the blanks in Tom Kirkman's life. I also added some characters. When I could find evidence, I tried to abide by the facts. Following is an explanation of some of the facts I had to write this story:

Part I, Chapters 1-9

- *Did Tom's family really live in a chicken house?* Yes, for a short time. His father did receive help to buy land from a man by the name of Ernest Davis. On this land, he built a log cabin.

- *Did God really give the Kirkmans a broom?* Yes. There also was a Fuller Brush peddler by the name of Jimmy, according to *A Stone Porch on*

"P" Street (see Bibliography), although I do not know that this was the one who visited the Kirkmans.

- *Is the Kirkman family portrayed factually?* I did my best to base descriptions of the family off available photos and Brad's memories. The Kirkmans loved to sing and play musical instruments and drink coffee. With characteristic humor, they described coffee as the "Kirkman curse" and would drink it hot or cold, freshly brewed or hours old. The Kirkman family also loved jokes, word plays, and puns. Tom's mother did crochet. Tom's niece Polly kindly supplied me with photos of glass holders made by Tom's mother. Tom's father worked in construction and on the trains. Bob joined the Navy and was in the Pacific during the Battle of Midway. His grandparents woke up with a dream about him during that time. He took up drinking and did not change his life until the meeting with Opal in the woods. Bill independently took a stand of nonresistance and worked in the construction branch of the Navy. Tom did investigate his older brother's visits to the beech tree in the woods.

- *Did Tom's mother really get sick from high blood pressure?* Yes. She, like Franklin Roosevelt, suffered from untreatable high blood pressure. Diuril was not released for use until the late 1950s. The specific cardiologist is from my imagination. The Kirkmans traveled from place to place to seek help for Mrs. Kirkman's condition.

- *Is Jim Diehl real?* Yes, indeed. I spoke to him on the phone and he told me he was in Joe's class in school. For that reason, I introduced him early in the book as a visitor doing homework with Joe. I made up this scene to introduce him to the story. However, he did come to Tom for sketching help at IU. Tom did not share about sketching for Eisenhower. Jim did come to Tom's farm after he joined the Amish church, and he helped with engineering the rotary engine. "Did you ever have reason to doubt anything Tom Kirkman said?" I asked Jim Diehl. He replied: "If Tom Kirkman said it, that's the way it was."

Part II, Chapters 10-20

- *Did you make up information about public figures?* I used extreme caution in writing about public figures. I did write dialogue for them that I cannot verify as historical. I did my best to keep their comments true to what I was able to research about them. All the letters quoted are actual. Mamie Eisenhower did not like footprints on the carpet and, according to the White House seamstress, she did object to the word *okay*. President Eisenhower loved to make stew and to paint. His words often rambled as he painted. Robert Schulz and Sergeant Moaney were both close companions of Eisenhower before, during, and after his presidency. I based my characterization of Schulz off his photo as well as interviews by and about him.

- *Are the calligraphers real?* Yes, Adrian Tolley and Sandford Fox both served as calligraphers in the White House. It is not entirely clear to me when Sandford Fox began his time in the Calligraphy Office.

- *Did Tom really have to look up the word "calligraphy" after agreeing to take the job?* Yes!

- *Did Adrian Tolley really scold Tom for being late?* Yes!

- *Did Tom have dinner with the Queen Mother?* Yes! The Queen Mother, also known as Queen Elizabeth, visited the White House in the fall of 1954. The Queen Mother's husband, George, had been King of England. When he died in 1952, the heir to the throne was their daughter Elizabeth. To avoid confusion, the new queen became known as Queen Elizabeth II and the earlier Queen Elizabeth became the Queen Mother.

Part III, Chapters 21-33

- *Did Tom really hitchhike home when his mother was dying?* Tom did hitchhike a lot, but I do not know for sure that he did this time. Whatever he did, I am confident that he was in despair. I fit the scene to reflect the despair.

- *Are the Moscow chapters real?* The Russia chapters are probably the most fictionalized of the book. I have corresponded with the CIA extensively, but have yet to have them release any information to me. We only know from Tom's brief, off-hand comments to Brad that he was in Moscow, in a cold tunnel in Russia, and in a fast photography plane over Cuba. And we know that he left his supervisor with the same words I have recorded.

- *Did God speak to Tom in the car?* I have tried to relay the story as closely as possible to the way Tom told it to Brad.

Part IV, Chapters 34-43

- *Is Simon Gingerich real?* Absolutely. There are many newspaper articles about him from that period.

- *Is Ed Cole real?* Yes, and according to newspapers he did want a fleet of jets twice the size of 747s to send cars to Moscow. The story of his death in a plane crash is fascinating. Many newspaper articles attest to his interest in new ideas, the rotary engine in particular. Tom told Brad about meeting with Ed Cole and the offer of millions of dollars. No parties involved are living now. I searched through boxes of dusty records collected off the street by the Gilmore Car Museum when Checker Motor Corporation disbanded. Most of these records contain parts lists and designs, and I found nothing relevant. Certainly, Tom's story fits well with the persona of Ed Cole and his interest in the rotary engine. The fascinating 1972 *Popular Mechanics* article mentioned contains most of the information I quoted, and should be referenced by those who have further interest.

- I have only brushed over Tom's later life. He continually designed and built. He built a log building by himself, which can be seen in Avoca, Indiana, today near the post office. He lived with Brad toward the end of his life.

My biggest question, one that would confirm or else undermine Tom

Kirkman's credibility still lingered: *Did Tom really help President Eisenhower make his sketches?*

Even though I added many fictional details to this story, this point bothered me for a long time. I had no reason to doubt Tom because his reputation for honesty was well established by a variety of people from Amish men to engineers. But I did wish for some small piece of evidence that proved Eisenhower got other people to sketch for him.

With the help of my friend Sherilyn Yoder of Kansas, I contacted an expert from the Dwight D. Eisenhower Presidential Library and Museum in Abilene, Kansas. Mr. Snyder was helpful and courteous, but he did not shed much favorable light on Tom's claims. He said, "I have never heard that anyone ever helped Ike with his paintings, beyond advice from Winston Churchill and Thomas Stephens. Not that this couldn't have happened, mind you, but painting for Ike was a very personal and private thing."

This was disheartening, but I still felt convinced about Tom's integrity. Finally, the day after New Year's Day, 2020, my husband and I visited the Eisenhower Presidential Library in Abilene, Kansas. I spent two days combing through dozens of archive boxes from the Eisenhower years. I found little about Tom, which did not surprise me. However, I did find what to me was even more important: a handwritten note from President Eisenhower to Robert Schulz. It says, "Here is a picture I'd like to have sketched . . . When you can, get the sergeant to do it." If you wish to see this yourself, it is in the Robert Schulz Papers, subseries "Personal Correspondence" 1961-1962, Box 31.

I also found a story about a man who, like Tom Kirkman, had been a soldier in the White House under Robert Schulz and later became a professional illustrator. This man went to the newspapers after his time in the White House and claimed that he had sketched for Eisenhower. When the newspapers called Robert Schulz to ask about this, they were not given much information. Robert Schulz did not deny the claims but merely said, "I have checked my records and find that a soldier by that name was assigned by the Department of Army to duty in my office. He was not under my immediate supervision. His complete record would be in the Department of Army files. I do not feel it proper to comment further." This you can find in Box 32 of the same collection I mentioned above.

These two pieces of information told me all I needed to know. Almost without question, President Eisenhower did ask military assistants to prepare sketches for him. Tom Kirkman, despite the doubt of an authority in the field, had been proven trustworthy.

One other thing bothered me. Brad Kirkman told me his father worked as a calligrapher in the basement of the White House. Yet, in all my research, I could only find confirmation that the calligraphers worked in the East Wing of the White House. During my research, I emailed former White House calligrapher Rick Paulus with a different question. I did not mention the basement. In the course of his reply, he said the following: "The calligraphers have long been situated on the second floor of the East Wing. In fact, I thought they had been there since this version of the East Wing was built, in 1942. However, I have heard a quote that Mrs. Kennedy said when she and John Kennedy toured the White House before moving in. She said, 'Jack, there's a nest of calligraphers down there!' referring to a few calligraphers in the basement."

Many thanks to Rick Paulus for once again proving Tom Kirkman trustworthy.

These pieces of research give me the same confidence that Jim Diehl had for his friend. "If Tom Kirkman said it, that's the way it was."

Endnotes

CHAPTER THREE

[1] There are many sites online where the Pearl Harbor broadcast of December 7, 1941, can be heard. Here is one example: <http://www.otr.com/r-a-i-new_pearl.shtml>.

CHAPTER SIX

[1] D-Day: First Radio Bulletin on NBC. <https://www.youtube.com/watch?v=K9xk9GaV0NE>. Although this broadcast was shared in the early morning hours while the Kirkmans were likely asleep, I chose to retain it as the best record of the initial D-Day announcement.

CHAPTER SEVEN

[1] Radio Reports on the Death of Franklin D. Roosevelt, April 12, 1945. <https://www.youtube.com/watch?v=djcuhhg6prq>.

[2] Audio file can be accessed here: <http://jeff560.tripod.com/sounds.html>.

CHAPTER FIFTEEN

[1] Parks, Lillian Rogers. *My Thirty Years Backstairs at the White House.* Ishi Press International, New York, 2008.

CHAPTER SIXTEEN

[1] Robert Schulz Oral History Transcript from Columbia University, 1968, 293 pp. I don't believe this is available anywhere online. Robert Schulz requested that only three copies be made of the transcript: one for him, one for Columbia University, and one for the Eisenhower Library in Abilene, Kansas, where I found it.

CHAPTER EIGHTEEN

[1] Smith, Jean Edward. *Eisenhower in War and Peace.* Random House, New York, 2013, p. 638.

CHAPTER NINETEEN

[1] Ann C. Whitman to General Nevins, September 16, 1955. DDE Papers as President, Gettysburg farm series, Boxes 1-6. Dwight D. Eisenhower Library, Abilene, Kansas.

CHAPTER TWENTY-SIX

[1] Rasenberger, Jim. *The Brilliant Disaster,* audiobook. Simon & Schuster, 2011. Paperback published April 10, 2012.

CHAPTER THIRTY

[1] Central Intelligence Agency Office of Research and Reports. Photographic Intelligence Memorandum, "Omsk Aircraft Plant Stalin 166," November 26, 1957. Retrieved February 20, 2020, from <https://www.cia.gov/library/read-ingroom/docs/cia-rdp78t04753a000400010019-9.pdf>.

CHAPTER THIRTY-ONE

[1] Brugioni, Dino A. *Eyeball to Eyeball: The Inside Story of the Cuban Missile Crisis.* Random House, New York, 1991.

[2] National Security Archive Book Briefing, by Thompson, Jenny, and Sherry. *The Kremlinologist.* Retrieved February 21, 2020, from <https://nsarchive.gwu.edu/briefing-book/russia-programs/2018-11-19/tommy-thompson-kremlinologist>.

CHAPTER THIRTY-TWO

[1] There are a number of articles on this topic. Here is one from newpapers.com: *The Courier-Journal,* Louisville, Kentucky, February 15, 1962, p. 1. Downloaded on January 17, 2020.

CHAPTER THIRTY-FOUR

[1] This is an example of one of the articles: *Muncie Evening Press,* Muncie, Indiana. "Buggy Reflectors Opposed by Amish," August 21, 1968, p. 8. <https://www.newspapers.com/image/249616064>. Downloaded on September 13, 2019.

CHAPTER THIRTY-SEVEN

[1] I.U. Museum 7th Annual report, 1969-1970. Retrieved September 15, 2019, from <http://fedora.dlib.indiana.edu/fedora/get/iudl:1129978/overview>.

CHAPTER THIRTY-EIGHT

[1] *Popular Science.* "Gm Rotary Engine for the '74 Vega," May 1972, p. 108.

[2] *Washington Times Herald.* "The Man Who Would Be Amish" by Dan Emmons, March 13, 2009. Retrieved September 15, 2019, from <https://www.washtimesherald.com/news/local_news/the-man-who-would-be-amish/article_ea1873b7-d3c5-59bf-b3d7-26734b2516c7.html>.

[3] *The Indianapolis News,* Indianapolis, Indiana. "Ex-Curator Designs Engine," March 26, 1976, p. 7. <https://www.newspapers.com/image/312205816>. Downloaded on September 19, 2019.

CHAPTER THIRTY-NINE

[1] *Detroit Free Press,* Detroit, Michigan, May 1977. Downloaded on January 8, 2020, from newspapers.com.

CHAPTER FORTY

[1] *Detroit Free Press,* Detroit, Michigan. "Air Crash Kills Ex-GM Chief Cole," May 3, 1977. Downloaded on January 8, 2020, from newspapers.com.

CHAPTER FORTY-TWO

[1] *Washington Times Herald.* "The Man Who Would Be Amish" by Dan Emmons, March 13, 2009. Retrieved September 15, 2019, from <https://www.wash-timesherald.com/news/local_news/the-man-who-would-be-amish/article_ea1873b7-d3c5-59bf-b3d7-26734b2516c7.html>.

Bibliography

Brower, Kate Andersen. *The Residence: Inside the Private World of the White House.* HarperCollins, New York, 2015.

Brugioni, Dino A. *Eyeball to Eyeball: The Inside Story of the Cuban Missile Crisis.* Random House, New York, 1990.

Dwight D. Eisenhower Presidential Library, Museum, and Boyhood Home in Abilene, Kansas. <https://www.eisenhowerlibrary.gov/>.

Eisenhower, David. *Going Home to Glory.* Simon & Schuster, New York, 2010.

Leahy, Jim. *A Stone Porch on "P" Street.* This is a wonderful local history of Bedford, Indiana, that I picked up at the historical society in Bedford.

National Geographic, January 1961. "Mrs. Dwight D. Eisenhower Introduces Inside the White House," by Lonnelle Aikman, B. Anthony Stewart, and Thomas Nebbia.

Newton, Jim. *Eisenhower: The White House Years.* Anchor Books, a division of Random House, New York, 2012.

Parks, Lillian Rogers. *My Thirty Years Backstairs at the White House.* Ishi Press International, New York, 2008.

Popular Science Magazine. "GM Rotary Engine for the '74 Vega," May 1972.

Rasenberger, Jim. *The Brilliant Disaster,* audiobook. Simon & Schuster, 2011. Paperback published April 10, 2012.

Smith, Jean Edward. *Eisenhower in War and Peace.* Random House, New York, 2013.

West, J. B. *Upstairs at the White House: My Life With the First Ladies.* Open Road Integrated Media, New York, 2016. First published in 1973.

The White House Museum at <http://www.whitehousemuseum.org/>. This site had wonderful interactive floor plans of the White House, with historical photos tied to each room.

About the Author

A lifelong writer, Katrina is the author of seven previous books including *Captain Garrison, Blue Christmas,* and *Shatterproof.* She grew up in Stratford, Wisconsin, with two brothers and three sisters, all of whom developed a love for words through the coaching and example of their parents.

Katrina loves reading, especially inspirational books and historical fiction. She enjoys visiting Lake Michigan at Promontory Point, Chicago, where her husband Marnell proposed in 2017. Katrina and Marnell live in Elkhart, Indiana, where they seek to join God's work with their small urban Anabaptist church.

Find more at katrinahooverlee.com. For extra content about Tom Kirkman that didn't make it into this book, join Katrina's mailing list by writing to Katrina: Katrina@500-words.com OR Katrina Hoover Lee, 410 Brady Street, Elkhart, IN 46516.

About Christian Aid Ministries

Christian Aid Ministries was founded in 1981 as a nonprofit, tax-exempt 501(c)(3) organization. Its primary purpose is to provide a trustworthy and efficient channel for Amish, Mennonite, and other conservative Anabaptist groups and individuals to minister to physical and spiritual needs around the world. This is in response to the command to ". . . do good unto all men, especially unto them who are of the household of faith" (Galatians 6:10).

Each year, CAM supporters provide 15–20 million pounds of food, clothing, medicines, seeds, Bibles, Bible story books, and other Christian literature for needy people. Most of the aid goes to orphans and Christian families. Supporters' funds also help to clean up and rebuild for natural disaster victims, put up Gospel billboards in the U.S., support several church-planting efforts, operate two medical clinics, and provide resources for needy families to make their own living. CAM's main purposes for providing aid are to help and encourage God's people and bring the Gospel to a lost and dying world.

CAM has staff, warehouses, and distribution networks in Romania, Moldova, Ukraine, Haiti, Nicaragua, Liberia, Israel, and Kenya. Aside from management, supervisory personnel, and bookkeeping operations, volunteers do most of the work at CAM locations. Each year, volunteers at our warehouses, field bases, Disaster Response Services projects, and other locations donate over 200,000 hours of work.

CAM's ultimate purpose is to glorify God and help enlarge His kingdom. ". . . whatsoever ye do, do all to the glory of God" (1 Corinthians 10:31).

The Way to God and Peace

We live in a world contaminated by sin. Sin is anything that goes against God's holy standards. When we do not follow the guidelines that God our Creator gave us, we are guilty of sin. Sin separates us from God, the source of life.

Since the time when the first man and woman, Adam and Eve, sinned in the Garden of Eden, sin has been universal. The Bible says that we all have "sinned and come short of the glory of God" (Romans 3:23). It also says that the natural consequence for that sin is eternal death, or punishment in an eternal hell: "Then when lust hath conceived, it bringeth forth sin: and sin, when it is finished, bringeth forth death" (James 1:15).

But we do not have to suffer eternal death in hell. God provided forgiveness for our sins through the death of His only Son, Jesus Christ. Because

Jesus was perfect and without sin, He could die in our place. "For God so loved the world that he gave his only begotten Son, that whosoever believeth in him should not perish, but have everlasting life" (John 3:16).

A sacrifice is something given to benefit someone else. It costs the giver greatly. Jesus was God's sacrifice. Jesus' death takes away the penalty of sin for all those who accept this sacrifice and truly repent of their sins. To repent of sins means to be truly sorry for and turn away from the things we have done that have violated God's standards (Acts 2:38; 3:19).

Jesus died, but He did not remain dead. After three days, God's Spirit miraculously raised Him to life again. God's Spirit does something similar in us. When we receive Jesus as our sacrifice and repent of our sins, our hearts are changed. We become spiritually alive! We develop new desires and attitudes (2 Corinthians 5:17). We begin to make choices that please God (1 John 3:9). If we do fail and commit sins, we can ask God for forgiveness. "If we confess our sins, he is faithful and just to forgive us our sins, and to cleanse us from all unrighteousness" (1 John 1:9).

Once our hearts have been changed, we want to continue growing spiritually. We will be happy to let Jesus be the Master of our lives and will want to become more like Him. To do this, we must meditate on God's Word and commune with God in prayer. We will testify to others of this change by being baptized and sharing the good news of God's victory over sin and death. Fellowship with a faithful group of believers will strengthen our walk with God (1 John 1:7).